AF522258

Modern Methods of Teaching Home Science

Sangeeta Rani
and
Madhulika Parmaar

Modern Methods of Teaching Home Science

ISBN 978-93-5111-845-9

Published in 2016 in India by

RANDOM PUBLICATIONS

4376-A/4B, Gali Murari Lal, Ansari Road
New Delhi-110 002
Phone : +9111-43580356, 011-23289044, 011-43142548
e-mail: sales@randompublications.com,
info@randompublications.com, randomexports@gmail.com

Reprinted 2025

Type Setting by : Friends Media, Delhi-110089
Digitally Printed at : Replika Press Pvt. Ltd.

Preface

Home Science as a field in education has come a long way since its humble beginnings as a domestic skill oriented course offering inputs in housekeeping, home deco ration, cookery, child rearing, stitching etc. Such an education was appropriate in the past since it helped to draw women out of their homes to improve the skills that had been handed down to them by the elderly women in the family. A plan of teaching Home Science must begin with an understanding of the discipline of home science. What is needed is a simple, direct explanation of the relevance and significance of home science in the modern context. People often ask ho w home science is associated with the home. This question brings out the basic premises upon which the discipline of home science is built.

The science of the home is concerned with the maintenance and enrichment of human relationships through the development and judicious use of all available human and material resources to achieve a maximal satisfying life for all members of the family. Home science education prepares youth for the greatest of all vocation - Home Making. It orients young girls and boys towards preparation for several professions- teaching , nursing, dietetics, research, welfare, management, art application, extension work and communication. There are several ways of managing homes. Men as well as women have played the roles of breadwinners and homemakers. It has become necessary for men to share housework, to enable women as professional persons to contribute to the nation.

– Author

Contents

1

Home Science and Teaching Skills

The essence of being an effective teacher lies in knowing what to do to foster pupils' learning and being able to do it. Effective teaching is primarily concerned with setting up a learning activity for each pupil which is successful in bringing about the type of learning the teacher intends. The difference between knowing what to do and being able to do it can be well illustrated by making an analogy with playing tennis. A player may know that in a particular situation a lob over the opponent's head is required, but whether that shot can be played successfully may be an entirely different matter! The player's skills involve three elements. First, the knowledge about possible types of shots; second, the decision-making involved in deciding that a lob is in fact the most appropriate shot required; and third, the action involved in executing that shot.

THE NATURE OF TEACHING SKILLS

Successful teaching skills thus crucially involve knowledge, decision-making and action. This distinction between these three elements underpinning skills is extremely important, because skilful teaching is as much a thinking activity as it is observable actions. Developing your skills as a teacher therefore is as much about developing and extending your knowledge about the decision you may take in a particular situation as it is about the successful execution of the observable action. Almost all teachers during their initial training will spend some time observing experienced teachers, and increasing numbers of experienced teachers now spend some time observing colleagues as part of their own or their colleagues' programme of professional development. Such observation can be immensely valuable; seeing how another teacher performs can stimulate your own ideas about your teaching. It may do this simply by acting as a model, either good or bad. Equally well, and more frequently, observation is stimulating because of the creative tension caused by trying to match your own decision-making about teaching with the decisions you infer your colleague has made. For example, you may normally go over some key points regarding why an experimental design used might be suspect, with the class as a whole, only to see a colleague using small group discussion instead.

As a result, you may be stimulated to think about the reasons for this. Indeed, the benefits of classroom observation are greatly enhanced by having some time available before and after the lesson for discussion about the teaching.

THE FEATURES OF TEACHING SKILLS

Over the years, much has been written about classroom teaching skills. The impetus for this has included those concerned with the initial training and the in-service training of teachers, those concerned to monitor the standard and quality of teaching performance, those involved in schemes of teacher appraisal, and those concerned with understanding, as a research endeavour, what constitutes successful teaching. As such, there is now a massive literature available for study. Overall, it appears that teaching skills can usefully be considered in terms of three key features:

- They involve purposeful and goal-directed behaviour.
- Their level of expertise is evidenced by the display of precision, smoothness and sensitivity to context.
- They can be improved by training and practice.

STUDIES OF TEACHING SKILLS

Studies of teaching skills have typically focused on how such skills are developed and displayed by beginning teachers and how beginning teachers differ from experienced teachers. Wragg sees teaching skills as strategies that teachers use which facilitate pupils' learning and which are acknowledged by those competent to judge as being skills. Wragg also argues that the skill should be capable of being repeated. He further points out that focusing on particular skills in isolation can be unhelpful because they can become less meaningful out of context. Wragg believes that it is better to analyse particular skills in relation to broad areas of activity, such as class management, questioning and explaining.

TEACHERS' THINKING

As well as studies focusing on developing skills amongst student teachers, a number of writers have focused on studying what experienced teachers think about the skills they use in teaching. Such studies have viewed teaching as a complex cognitive skill, based on knowledge about how to construct and conduct a lesson, and knowledge about the content to be taught. This skill enables the teacher to construct lesson plans and make rapid decisions in the light of changing circumstances. The difference between novice teachers and experienced teachers is that the latter have developed sets of well-organised actions that they can apply flexibly and adapt with little mental effort to suit the situation. A useful analogy here is that of going to a restaurant. Once you have been to several types of restaurant, you develop knowledge about the procedure that generally operates: whether you find a table or are shown to one; how to order from a menu; and when and how you pay. Such experience enables you to go to a new restaurant and cope with getting what you want reasonably skilfully. For someone who has never been to a restaurant, few sets of organised actions have been built up. For all the person may know, you may have to go to the kitchen, select some meat, and cook it yourself! Similarly, experienced teachers have built up a repertoire of many sets of behaviours from which to select that behaviour most appropriate to the immediate demands of the situation, whether it is dealing with a pupil who is unable to answer a question, or noticing a pupil looking out of a window. Indeed, the reason why teaching is so demanding in the early years is because new teachers have to build up their expertise of knowing what to do and being able to do it. A number of writers have pointed out that a particular feature of teaching skills is their interactive nature. A teacher's actions during a lesson continuously need to take account of changing circumstances, many of which may be unexpected. Indeed, a teacher's effectiveness in the classroom is very dependent on how well they can modify and adapt their actions in the light of how well the lesson is going. In this sense, teaching is more like driving which involves negotiating a series of busy roundabouts than it is like driving along a quiet motorway. With experience, much of this interactive decisionmaking gradually becomes routine so that the teacher is hardly aware at a conscious level of the many decisions they are making during a lesson. In contrast, for a novice teacher, each new demand seems to require careful attention and thought.

TEACHERS' KNOWLEDGE ABOUT TEACHING

Another important feature of teaching skills is that they clearly draw upon the teachers' knowledge about effective teaching. Shulman famously argued that at the very least this knowledge base includes:

- knowledge about content
- knowledge about broad principles and strategies of classroom management and organisation
- knowledge about curriculum materials and programmes
- knowledge about the teaching of particular content topics
- knowledge about pupils
- knowledge about educational contexts, ranging from the classroom group to aspectsof the community
- knowledge about educational aims and values.

For Shulman, teaching skills are bound up with teachers' thinking which draws upon their knowledge base as a basis for judgement and action. This notion that as much emphasis in considering teaching skills must be given to the knowledge base as to the decision-making process, may seem odd, since clearly all decision-making must draw on teachers' knowledge about teaching.

The basic point here is that such knowledge is largely implicit and taken for granted. However, if one is concerned with how teachers develop their teaching skills, this knowledge base needs to be made more explicit. A very effective way of doing this is to show teachers a video of their teaching and probe their thinking about what they did and why through this 'stimulated recall' method. This approach essentially tries to re-create the teacher's thinking in progress while they were actually teaching. A number of researchers have argued that in order to explore the teacher's knowledge base it is important to use a range of methods, such as in-depth interview, classroom observation, stimulated recall, and task analysis, in order to probe as clearly as possible the teacher's thinking that underpins their classroom decision-making.

MENTORING

Writings and studies looking at school mentors and their role in the professional development of student teachers and newly qualified teachers have also served to highlight the key skills that need to be developed in the early years of teaching. Indeed, the increasingly important role played by mentors in schools during initial teacher training has indicated how turning effective teachers into effective trainers of new teachers is not unproblematic. A teacher may know how to teach well, but that may not translate easily into the role of how best to guide and help student teachers develop their own expertise. Writings and studies looking at effective mentoring have thus attempted to highlight the key skills involved in teaching and to explore how mentors can best foster such skills amongst beginning teachers.

DEFINING ESSENTIAL TEACHING SKILLS

Teaching skills can be defined as discrete and coherent activities by teachers which foster pupil learning. In the light of our consideration of teaching skills so far in this chapter, three important elements of skills are discernible:

- *Knowledge,* comprising the teacher's knowledge about the subject, pupils, curriculum, teaching methods, the influence on teaching and learning of other factors, and knowledge about one's own teaching skills.
- *Decision-making,* comprising the thinking and decision-making that occurs before, during and after a lesson, concerning how best to achieve the educational outcomes intended.
- *Action,* comprising the overt behaviour by teachers undertaken to foster pupil learning.

An over-riding feature of teaching skills is that they are purposeful and goal-directed activities which are essentially problem-solving. At its broadest, the problem is how best to deliver effectively the educational outcomes, in terms of pupil learning, required. More specifically, teaching skills are concerned with all the short-term and immediate problems faced before, during and after the lesson, such as 'How can I lay out the key points of this topic in a PowerPoint presentation?', 'How can I signal to a pupil to stop talking without interrupting what I am explaining to the whole class?', 'What can I write when assessing a piece of work by a pupil to highlight a flaw in the pupil's argument?'. Teaching skills are also concerned with the long-term problems of effective teaching, such as 'Which textbook series best meets the needs of my pupils?', 'How best can I update my subject knowledge?', 'How do I best prepare pupils for the work they will be doing in future years?'.

IDENTIFYING ESSENTIAL TEACHING SKILLS

One of the major problems in trying to identify a list of essential teaching skills is that teaching skills vary from very broad and general skills, such as the planning of lessons, to very specific skills, such as the appropriate length of time to wait for a pupil to answer a question in a particular type of situation. Overall, in considering teaching skills, it seems to be most useful to focus on fairly broad and general skills which are meaningful to teachers and relate to how they think about their teaching. More specific skills can then be discussed as and when they help illustrate and illuminate how these general skills operate. Nevertheless, given the nature of teaching, it is clear that whatever set of general skills is chosen to focus on, the overlap and interplay between them will be marked, and a good case can always be made by others for focusing on a different set. For example, Hay McBer identified the following list of teaching skills:

- high expectations
- planning
- methods and strategies
- pupil management/discipline
- time and resource management
- assessment
- homework.

Over the years there has been a wealth of writing about and use of lists of teaching skills, both by those involved in teacher education and by educational researchers. There is no definitively agreed list. A consideration of the various writings, however, indicates that a fairly typical list of teaching skills can be identified. Such lists of teaching skills have proved to be very useful in helping both beginning and experienced teachers to think about and develop their classroom practice.

THE EFFECTIVE TEACHER

Writings on the notion of the effective teacher have also yielded a mass of material on the skills displayed by teachers considered to be effective.

Teachers judged to be effective appear to display the following skills in their teaching:

- establishing an orderly and attractive learning environment
- concentrating on teaching and learning by maximising learning time and maintaining an academic emphasis
- purposeful teaching through the use of well-organised and well-structured lessons

coupled with clarity of purpose

- conveying high expectations and providing intellectual challenge
- monitoring progress and providing quick corrective feedback
- establishing clear and fair discipline.

TEACHER APPRAISAL AND PERFORMANCE REVIEW

Another important source of information about teaching skills can be found in the wealth of material dealing with the appraisal and performance review of established teachers. These include a whole host of lesson observation schedules and rating scales used to identify and comment on the extent to which teaching skills are displayed in the lessons observed. Such writings and schedules typically focus on areas such as:

- *Preparation and planning:* e.g. selects short-term objectives related to the school's curriculum guidelines, and is aware of and uses, as and when appropriate, a variety of equipment and resources.
- *Classroom organisation and management:* e.g. uses time and space to maximum advantage and ensures smooth transitions from one activity to another.
- *Communication skills:* e.g. uses questioning and explaining effectively.
- *The setting of work for pupils:* e.g. work is appropriate for age and ability, is of sound quality, and displays fitness for purpose.
- *Assessment of pupils' work and record keeping:* e.g. provides feedback to pupils that helps them improve their work in future.
- *Knowledge of relevant subject matter:* e.g. uses a knowledge of the topic to develop and guide pupils towards a secure base of understanding.
- *Relationships with pupils:* e.g. shows a genuine interest in and respect for children's words and thoughts and focuses on children's behaviour rather than personality.

SKILLS IDENTIFIED BY THE DFES

The Department for Education and Skills (DfES) has increasingly been involved in drawing attention to the teaching skills underpinning good classroom practice in both primary and secondary schools, and these have featured heavily in support materials and training to help teachers to adopt the type of classroom practice advocated by the DfES in delivering various national strategies in its consideration of teaching in secondary schools produced a training pack dealing with teaching skills in the following areas:

- Designing lessons
  - — structured learning
  - — teaching models
  - — lesson design for lower attainers
  - — lesson design for inclusion
  - — starters and plenaries
- Teaching repertoire
  - — modelling
  - — questioning
  - — explaining
  - — guided learning
  - — group work
  - — active engagement techniques
- Creating effective learners
  - — assessment for learning
  - — developing reading
  - — developing writing
  - — using ICT to enhance learning
  - — leading in learning
  - — developing effective learning
- Creating conditions for learning
  - — improving the climate for learning
  - — learning styles.

Packs dealing with teaching skills.

QUALITIES LOOKED FOR BY OFSTED

For many years Her Majesty's Inspectorate (HMI) and the Office for Standards in Education (Ofsted) have published reports dealing with the quality of teaching observed during their inspections of schools. This includes an annual report on standards in education, the publication of handbooks and other support materials used by inspectors in their inspection of schools, and also the findings of reports focusing on specific subjects, levels and topics, and on specific aspects of teaching, such as the quality of teaching displayed by newly qualified teachers and the quality of teaching experienced by particular groups of pupils. From these reports one is able to build up a clear picture of the types of skills school inspectors expect to see displayed when good teaching is taking place. These can be inferred from the following descriptions commonly used by Ofsted:

- Lessons should be purposeful with high expectations conveyed.
- Pupils should be given some opportunities to organise their own work (over-direction by teachers needs to be guarded against).

- Lessons should elicit and sustain pupils' interest and be perceived by pupils as relevant and challenging.
- The work should be well matched to pupils' abilities and learning needs.
- Pupils' language should be developed and extended.
- A variety of learning activities should be employed.
- Good order and control should be largely based on skilful management of pupils' involvement in the lesson, and mutual respect.

The teaching skills looked for by Ofsted are modified from time to time to take account of new DfES policies. For example, the introduction by the DfES of the Every Child Matters agenda led to a revision of Ofsted's lesson observation schedule so that it was 'aligned' with those teaching skills which related to this agenda. This agenda views pupil performance and pupil well-being as going hand in hand, and identifies five outcomes for children:

- *Being healthy:* helping pupils to adopt healthy lifestyles, build their self-esteem, eat and drink well and lead active lives.
- *Staying safe:* keeping pupils safe from bullying, harassment and other dangers.
- *Enjoying and achieving:* enabling pupils to make good progress in their work and personal development and to enjoy their education.
- *Making a positive contribution:* ensuring that pupils understand their rights and responsibilities, are listened to, and participate in the life of the community.
- *Achieving social and economic well-being:* helping pupils to gain the skills and knowledge needed for future employment.

In the revised form, a lesson graded as outstanding included the following characteristics:

- Excellent relationships are most conducive to pupils' personal development.
- All pupils are challenged and stretched whatever standard they are working at.
- Assessment of pupils' work successfully underpins the teaching and pupils have a clear idea of how to improve.

SKILLS TO BE DEVELOPED DURING INITIAL TRAINING AND BEYOND

A further source of information relating to teaching skills comes from writings and materials concerned with the teaching skills that student teachers are expected to develop during their initial teacher training. These include a variety of profiling documents developed by teacher training institutions to help foster and record student teachers' progress in developing teaching skills over the course of their training. A study by Hobson *et al.* asked student teachers to rate the importance of eight different types of knowledge and skills that beginning teachers needed to develop. The student teachers' ratings of these in order of importance were:

- ability to bring about pupil learning
- ability to maintain discipline in the classroom
- ability to use a range of teaching methods
- knowledge about their teaching subject(s)
- ability to deal with pastoral issues
- staff supervision/management skills
- knowledge/understanding of education policy
- awareness of research findings about effective teaching methods.

Of particular significance in this respect is the attempt by government agencies to specify the list of skills to be developed. For example, the TDA published a list of professional standards that primary and secondary school student teachers in England and Wales need to have acquired in order to be awarded Qualified Teacher Status (QTS) from September 2007. The QTS standards are grouped into three areas:

- Professional attributes
  - — relationships with children and young people
  - — frameworks
  - — communicating and working with others
  - — personal professional development
- Professional knowledge and understanding
  - — teaching and learning
  - — assessment and monitoring
  - — subjects and curriculum
  - — literacy, numeracy and ICT
  - — achievement and diversity
  - — health and well-being
- Professional skills
  - — planning
  - — teaching
  - — assessing, monitoring and giving feedback
  - — reviewing teaching and learning
  - — learning environment
- – team working and collaboration.

The QTS standards are used by the TDA and Ofsted to monitor the quality and effectiveness of initial teacher training courses. This list will undoubtedly be modified from time to time. Indeed, the above list superseded lists drawn up earlier. Parts of the specific criteria within each area are worded the same for both primary and secondary teachers, whilst some parts are worded differently. Overall, however, an attempt has been made to use, as far as possible, the same form of words to describe the standards expected of both primary and secondary school teachers. A similar list of standards has also been drawn up to set out the teaching skills that newly qualified teachers are expected to display during their first year (the induction year). Newly qualified teachers are required to achieve these induction standards in order to have their QTS ratified. The induction standards require newly qualified teachers to continue to meet the QTS standards, but to add to these some areas of enhancement. Three further lists of standards have been drawn up by the DfES to cover the teaching skills (and other work) expected of more experienced teachers. These are:

- the threshold standards
- the advanced skills teacher standards
- the excellent teacher standards.

Looking at the description of the teaching skills associated with these three sets of standards (compared with the QTS standards and the induction standards) there is much greater emphasis here on evidence that their teaching produces higher pupil attainment, on their awareness of what constitutes best classroom practice, and on their ability to develop the practice of colleagues.

EVIDENCE-BASED CLASSROOM PRACTICE

Another set of increasing literature on teaching skills comes from the attempts to provide an evidence base to inform developments in policy and practice in education. This approach includes both original research studies and systematic reviews which look at the existing research literature on a particular topic; they also synthesise the research evidence in order to assess what impact different types of teaching approaches and intervention strategies have on pupils' learning. Such research often highlights particular aspects of teaching skills that are crucial in determining the extent to which a particular approach has had a positive impact on pupils' learning. For example, a systematic review looking at the impact of daily mathematics lessons, introduced as part of the National Numeracy Strategy in primary schools, highlighted the need for many teachers to develop the skills necessary to sustain the 'interactive' aspect of whole-class 'interactive' teaching that was advocated in the National Numeracy Strategy. In the USA, a number of authors have a used synthesis of the evidence-base for 'what works' to identify the key sets of teaching skills. For example, an analysis by Stronge identified five sets of key teaching skills:

- the teacher as a person
- the teacher as classroom manager and organiser
- organising for instruction
- implementing instruction
- the teacher teaching: monitoring pupil progress and potential.

In contrast, another analysis in the USA, by Marzano, identified three sets of key skills:

- instructional strategies
- classroom management
- classroom curriculum design.

Both Stronge and Marzano, however, illustrate how the expert teacher differs from the beginning teacher in the extent to which they display a high level of these skills.

A LIST OF ESSENTIAL TEACHING SKILLS

Overall, the essential teaching skills involved in contributing to successful classroom practice can be identified and described as follows:

- *Planning and preparation:* the skills involved in selecting the educational aims and learning outcomes intended for a lesson and how best to achieve these.
- *Lesson presentation:* the skills involved in successfully engaging pupils in the learning experience, particularly in relation to the quality of instruction.
- *Lesson management:* the skills involved in managing and organising the learning activities taking place during the lesson to maintain pupils' attention, interest and involvement.
- *Classroom climate:* the skills involved in establishing and maintaining positive attitudes and motivation by pupils towards the lesson.
- *Discipline:* the skills involved in maintaining good order and dealing with any pupil misbehaviour that occurs.
- *Assessing pupils' progress:* the skills involved in assessing pupils' progress, covering both formative (i.e. intended to aid pupils' further development) and summative (i.e. providing a record of attainment) purposes of assessment.
- *Reflection and evaluation:* the skills involved in evaluating one's own current teaching practice in order to improve future practice. Two important points, however, need to be borne in mind when considering these skills. First, there is clearly an interplay between these seven areas, so that the skills exercised in one area may simultaneously contribute to another area. For example, smooth transition between activities is included within lesson management, but at the same time will also contribute to maintaining discipline. Second, all the skills involved in lesson presentation, lesson management, classroom climate and discipline, are interactive skills. In other words, exercising these skills involves monitoring, adjusting and responding to what pupils are doing. Unlike acting on a stage, where one can perform without an audience, these skills cannot be displayed in isolation from their interaction with pupils' behaviour. Even when giving an explanation, for example, a teacher would, at the very least, be

attentive to the faces of pupils to judge whether it was being pitched appropriately for their needs, and might elaborate, alter the pace of delivery, tone of voice, content, or even stop and ask a question, in the light of what the facial expressions indicated.

THE DEVELOPMENT OF TEACHING SKILLS

In defining teaching skills earlier, three elements were highlighted: knowledge, decision-making and action. Almost all beginning teachers will have had much experience of being taught as pupils themselves in a school. Without doubt, this will be the single most important influence on their knowledge about teaching and the models they have of how to conduct a lesson.

Numerous studies, however, have indicated just how inadequate a base this is for attempting to teach one's first few lessons. Long experience of being taught certainly provides a broad framework for thinking about how to teach, but once the teacher's role is taken on, it becomes very evident that a whole range of teaching skills needs to be developed.

For example, common problems experienced by beginning teachers include not knowing what to do when, having given an explanation, the pupil does not understand, other than repeating the same explanation; not knowing how to cope with pupils working at different rates, ranging from those who finish early to those making little progress; not knowing which curriculum elements require more attention and emphasis in teaching; and not knowing what to do with pupils they cannot control.

Some studies have explicitly compared beginning teachers (either student teachers or newly qualified teachers) with experienced teachers to highlight the development of teaching skills.

These indicate that beginning teachers more often became engrossed in private exchanges with pupils so as to lose overall perception of what was going on elsewhere.

Experienced teachers, on the other hand, are more able to split their attention between the pupil and the rest of the class, and can break off and comment on what is happening elsewhere, as and when appropriate. When it comes to planning lessons, experienced teachers are more selective in using the information provided by others, and prefer to rely on their knowledge of what they could typically expect from pupils of the age and class size given. In effect, the experienced teachers are able to use their repertoire of how to set up and deliver learning activities, which is largely denied or non-existent for beginning teachers.

ESSENTIAL TEACHING SKILLS

- Planning and preparation
- The lesson plan has clear and suitable aims and objectives.

- The content, methods and structure of the lesson selected are appropriate for the pupil learning intended.
- The lesson is planned to link up appropriately with past and future lessons.
- Materials, resources and aids are well prepared and checked in good time.
- All planning decisions take account of the pupils and the context.
- The lesson is designed to elicit and sustain pupils' attention, interest and involvement.
- Lesson presentation
- The teacher's manner is confident, relaxed, self-assured and purposeful, and generates interest in the lesson.
- The teacher's instructions and explanations are clear and matched to pupils' needs.
- The teacher's questions include a variety of types and range and are distributed widely.
- A variety of appropriate learning activities are used to foster pupil learning.
- Pupils are actively involved in the lesson and are given opportunities to organise their own work.
- The teacher shows respect and encouragement for pupils' ideas and contributions, and fosters their development.
- The work undertaken by pupils is well matched to their needs.
- Materials, resources and aids are used to good effect.
- Lesson management
- The beginning of the lesson is smooth and prompt, and sets up a positive mental set for what is to follow.
- Pupils' attention, interest and involvement in the lesson are maintained.
- Pupils' progress during the lesson is carefully monitored.
- Constructive and helpful feedback is given to pupils to encourage further progress.
- Transitions between activities are smooth.
- The time spent on different activities is well managed.
- The pace and flow of the lesson is adjusted and maintained at an appropriate level throughout the lesson.
- Adjustments to the lesson plan are made whenever appropriate.
- The ending of the lesson is used to good effect.
- Classroom climate
- The climate is purposeful, task-oriented, relaxed, and with an established sense of order.
- Pupils are supported and encouraged to learn, with high expectations conveyed by the teacher.

- Teacher–pupil relationships are largely based on mutual respect and rapport.
- Feedback from the teacher contributes to fostering pupil self-confidence and self-esteem.
- The appearance and layout of the class are conducive to positive pupil attitudes towards the lesson and facilitate the activities taking place.
- Discipline
- Good order is largely based on the positive classroom climate established and on good lesson presentation and management.
- The teacher's authority is established and accepted by pupils.
- Clear rules and expectations regarding pupil behaviour are conveyed by the teacher at appropriate times.
- Pupil behaviour is carefully monitored and appropriate actions by the teacher are taken to pre-empt misbehaviour.
- Pupil misbehaviour is dealt with by an appropriate use of investigation, counselling, academic help, reprimands and punishments.
- Confrontations are avoided, and skilfully defused.
- Assessing pupils' progress
- The marking of pupils' work during and after lessons is thorough and constructive, and work is returned in good time.
- Feedback on assessments aims not only to be diagnostic and corrective, but also to encourage further effort and maintain self-confidence, which involves follow-up comments, help or work with particular pupils as appropriate.
- A variety of assessment tasks are used, covering both formative and summative purposes.
- A variety of records of progress are kept.
- Some opportunities are given to foster pupils' own assessments of their work and progress.
- Assessment of pupils' work is used to identify areas of common difficulties, the effectiveness of the teaching, and whether a firm basis for further progress has been established.
- Assessment is made of the study skills and learning strategies employed by pupils in order to foster their further development.
- Reflection and evaluation
- Lessons are evaluated to inform future planning and practice.
- Current practice is regularly considered with a view to identifying aspects for useful development.
- Use is made of a variety of ways to reflect upon and evaluate current practice.
- The teacher regularly reviews whether his or her time and effort can be organised to better effect.

- The teacher regularly reviews the strategies and techniques he or she uses to deal with sources of stress.

MONITORING YOUR OWN TEACHING

Another source of information about how teaching skills develop concerns the efforts of experienced teachers to monitor and develop their own skills or to assist with developing those of colleagues. Such work has taken place either as part of formal schemes of teacher appraisal and staff development or simply as part of the teacher's own concern to monitor and develop their own practice. Of particular interest as an example of the latter, has been the growth of teacher action research.

This involves a systematic procedure in which teachers look at some aspect of their own or the school's practice that is giving rise to some concern, identify the precise nature of the problem, collect some data on the problem, and then devise, implement and evaluate a solution.

Many teachers have used this approach to develop some aspect of their teaching skills, ranging from dealing with new approaches to teaching and learning to simply improving skills that are already well developed (such as the quality of giving individual help). Studies reporting the efforts of experienced teachers to develop their teaching skills well illustrate that all teachers, not just beginning teachers, are continually involved in such development. Indeed, it is the sense that teaching skills continually need development to improve one's own practice and to meet new demands that makes teaching such a challenging profession.

STAGES OF DEVELOPMENT

Perrott, in her analysis of how teaching skills are acquired and developed, focuses on three stages. The first stage is cognitive and involves developing an awareness, by study and observation, of what the skill is, identifying the various elements of the skill and their sequencing, knowing the purpose of using the skill, and knowing how it will benefit your teaching.

She identifies the second stage as practice, normally in the classroom but occasionally in a controlled setting as part of a training course in which there is a short practice of a specific skill. The third stage is feedback, which enables the teacher to improve the performance of the skill by evaluating the relative success of its performance.

Such feedback can range from simply an impressionistic sense of its successful performance to detailed feedback given by an observer, the use of audio-visual recording, or systematic data collected from pupils about their work, behaviour or opinions. Perrott sees this three-stage process as a cycle, in which the third stage feeds back into the first stage as part of an on-going development of the skill.

HAVING THE ABILITY TO DEVELOP YOUR SKILLS

While it is clear that teachers are continually reflecting upon and developing their skills, it is also evident that this does not automatically lead to skilled performance. There are many teachers who, after years of experience, still have evident shortcomings in some teaching skills. In part, this reflects the fact that skilled performance also depends on ability and motivation. The teacher needs the ability to profit from reflection and practice, and the motivation to do so. If we consider questioning skills as an example, clearly all teachers need to develop such skills. However, while some teachers have built up great skills in the variety and range of question types they use and the skill with which they target pupils and elicit and elaborate pupils' responses, other experienced teachers may still show shortcomings in these respects.

Why should this be so? Earlier, I argued that skills involve knowledge, decision-making and action. All three of these elements are subject to the various general abilities of teachers. The teacher may simply not have built up the knowledge about the effective use of questioning skills, or have difficulty in making the appropriate decisions which use that knowledge, or have difficulties in carrying out the actions required in a skilled manner. If we extend the example of questioning skills further, an example where the fault lies with inadequate knowledge would be a teacher who is simply unaware of the educational importance and benefits of using 'open' questions (questions where a number of correct answers are possible) as well as 'closed' questions (questions where only one correct answer is acceptable). An example where the fault lies with decisionmaking would be an inappropriate decision to simply repeat the same question to a pupil having a difficulty answering, rather than to phrase the question in a different way or perhaps provide a hint. An example where the fault lies in action would be a teacher who is unable to ask a question in a clear and unambiguous way. The relevant general abilities of the teacher involved here may not simply be intellectual ones, since much skilled performance depends on aspects of the teacher's personality or even acting ability. Some teachers find it easier than others to continually ask questions sounding as though they are genuinely curious and interested in the replies, and comfortable with the longer pauses of silence required to give pupils time to think when being asked a more complex question.

BEING MOTIVATED TO DEVELOP YOUR SKILLS

Developing teaching skills also depends on the teacher's motivation. Teachers vary immensely in the extent to which they are prepared to invest time, energy and effort to reflect upon, evaluate and improve their teaching skills. This is particularly a problem once a teacher has developed a sufficiently adequate range of teaching skills to give satisfactory lessons. Teaching often then becomes a matter of routine. This can become even more confirmed once various materials, examples and strategies have been prepared and practised. In addition, to some extent teachers' approaches to lessons tend to play to their own strengths. Thus, for example, a teacher who finds lessons generally work well if based on worksheets, close monitoring of progress, and one-to-one help, but in contrast finds lessons involving group work and class discussion tend to become noisy and chaotic, is more likely to design lessons based on the former than to develop and extend the skills involved in making the latter type of lessons successful. Indeed, one of the main reasons underlying the hostility against a particular curriculum innovation that may be felt by some teachers relates to the changes in their general approach and teaching skills required by the innovation. It says much for the professional commitment and sense of vocation of teachers, that the vast majority do spend much time and effort in continuing to develop their teaching skills and to develop new approaches to their teaching in the educational interests of their pupils.

YOUR PROFESSIONAL DEVELOPMENT

It is also important to note that the responsibility to develop and extend your teaching skills is not simply your personal responsibility. Rather, it is also the responsibility of those within the school and agencies outside the school to ensure that such development is facilitated as part of your professional development, and as part of staff development at the school as a whole. Mention has already been made of teacher appraisal and of the impetus that comes from curriculum innovation. Equally important, however, is the climate that exists within the school to facilitate the development of teaching skills as an ongoing process. An important part of school improvement and the capacity of the school for self-renewal is the ability of the school to create a positive climate which facilitates staff developing their teaching skills. The characteristics of schools that are particularly good at creating this type of positive climate tend to include the following:

- a sense of common ownership amongst staff for the educational aims to be achieved
- a constant generation of ideas
- sharing problems
- mutual support
- respect for each other's opinions
- an open and co-operative approach to dealing with conflicts and crises
- allowing styles to vary according to situations and needs
- encouraging anyone, not just leaders, to propose improvements
- an 'organic' rather than 'bureaucratic' management style (the former being more informal and flexible, with decision-making shared rather than directed from the top through a hierarchy, and with less emphasis on reports and record keeping).

Finally, it is worth bearing in mind that, despite the immense importance of developing sound teaching skills and seeing this as on ongoing process throughout your teaching career, teaching also involves a whole host of other important demands, both inside and outside the classroom.

The reality of life as a teacher requires a prioritising and monitoring of the whole range of skills in doing your job effectively, and it will be both normal and sensible to find that skills other than those considered here will occasionally need attention. Perhaps it is best to view the development of your teaching skills as a process that is always in operation, but which varies in intensity depending on the situation and context you find yourself in. If your teaching is to retain the sharpness, freshness and cutting edge that characterises the most effective teaching, it is crucial that your skills are never allowed to rest for too long on the back burner.

2

Planning and Preparation

The key task facing teachers is to set up a learning activity which effectively achieves the learning outcomes intended for each pupil. At the start of a lesson, all teachers need to have some idea of what learning they wish to take place and how the lesson will facilitate that learning. While student teachers on teaching practice are usually required to make explicit lesson plans, experienced teachers more often rely on their extensive experience to form a mental framework of how they want the lesson to proceed. This does not necessarily mean that the lesson plans of established teachers are any less detailed than those of beginning teachers, simply that the lesson plans have become internalised through repetition.

THE ELEMENTS OF PLANNING AND PREPARATION

Much has been written over the years about the planning and preparation of lessons. This has identified four major elements involved in planning a lesson:

- *A decision about the educational objectives* that the lesson will be designed to foster.
- *A selection and scripting of a lesson*, which involves deciding on the type and nature of the activities to be used, the order and timing of each of these activities, and the content and materials to be used.
- *A preparation of all the props to be used*, including materials, worked examples, checking that apparatus is ordered, delivered and in working order, arranging the layout of the classroom and, on occasion, even a rehearsal.
- *A decision regarding how you will monitor and assess pupils' progress and attainment* during and after the lesson to evaluate whether the intended learning has taken place.

MEETING THE NEEDS OF LEARNERS

Ofsted in their evaluation of lessons, typically focus on two crucial aspects in relation to planning and preparation. First, is it clear what the purpose of the lesson is? Second, has the lesson taken adequate account of the learners' needs?

The former question addresses the question of how clearly specified the educational objectives of the lesson were. The latter question addresses the extent to which the educational objectives take adequate account of the range and type of pupils' abilities, their previous learning, and their progress towards future educational attainment. It is perhaps the teacher's sensitivity to pupils' needs that is the most important of all the skills involved in effective teaching. This refers to the ability of the teacher to plan lessons and adapt and modify their delivery by taking account of how the lesson will be experienced by different pupils and foster their learning. It is impossible and meaningless to attempt to evaluate the quality of a lesson plan without taking into account how well it meets the needs of the pupils in the context in which it will take place.

SKILLS IN PLANNING

As noted in the previous chapter, an additional source of information concerning essential teaching skills comes from an examination of the attempt to list the skills that should be developed during a course of initial teaching training. For example, the TDA QTS standards include a number of elements on planning. These focus on:

- planning for progression across the age and ability range
- designing effective learning sequences within lessons and across a series of lessons
- designing opportunities for pupils to develop literacy, numeracy and ICT skills
- planning homework and other out-of-class work to sustain pupils' progress
- incorporating a range a teaching strategies and resources, including e-learning
- taking practical account of diversity and promoting equality and inclusion
- building upon pupils' prior knowledge.

EDUCATIONAL OBJECTIVES

Selecting the educational objectives for a lesson is no mean task. At the very least, they must contribute to broad educationally worthwhile aims. However, fashions change, and what is regarded as worthwhile at one time may now be considered inappropriate. Many schools list a number of educational aims in their prospectuses. The aims of the school's curriculum, as specified in the 1988 Education Reform Act, lay down an important framework. This states that the school's curriculum should:

- promote the spiritual, moral, cultural, mental and physical development of pupils at the school and of society

- prepare such pupils for the opportunities, responsibilities and experiences of adult life.

The Education Reform Act established a National Curriculum which specified the subjects that should be offered in the school curriculum, together with particular Attainment Targets that should be addressed during the pupils' school careers. Despite the great detail specified by the National Curriculum, this only provided a broad framework within which teachers still needed to plan individual lessons.

In selecting educational objectives, the teacher is obliged to specify clear learning outcomes which can usefully be analysed in terms of the development of pupils' knowledge, understanding, skills and attitudes. This planning is extremely complex, because a teacher inevitably has a range of outcomes in mind for a particular lesson, and indeed, the outcomes intended may differ markedly between the pupils in the class. In addition, all lessons involve an interplay between intellectual development and social development. A teacher may thus have the development of an understanding of the concept of area as a major educational objective for a particular lesson. At the same time, there may be an overlay of other objectives in operation, such as the intention to give a particular able pupil the opportunity to do some extended work on this topic, the intention to help and encourage a pupil who has been showing a lack of interest, and the intention to use this topic to show that doing mathematics is fun and relates to important real-life applications. Only by being aware of such differing intentions can an observer make sense of the teacher's behaviour in the lesson.

TEACHERS' USE OF OBJECTIVES IN PLANNING

While the notion of setting educational objectives is widely agreed to be an essential aspect of planning, some research on teachers' planning appears to indicate that many teachers do not start their planning of lessons by identifying educational objectives and then designing a lesson to deliver these objectives. Rather, they approach the task of planning in a more problem-solving manner by addressing the problem of how best to structure the time and experience of pupils during the lesson.

This would suggest that many teachers may plan lessons without having clear learning outcomes in mind. I think, however, this is a misinterpretation based on the fact that if you ask a teacher to talk about their planning of a lesson, the educational objectives for the lesson are often left implicit, and greater attention is devoted to their description of the activities to be employed. Indeed, there is clear research evidence that teachers do think about educational objectives in planning their lessons, and that this is often made explicit by teachers when they talk about the thinking that occurs during and after the lesson. Overall, it appears that part of the problem in identifying how and when teachers specify the educational objectives for a lesson simply concerns how they articulate their thoughts to others.

THE PURPOSES AND FUNCTIONS OF PLANNING

There are a number of important purposes and functions to the planning of lessons which are worth noting. First and foremost, it enables you to think clearly and specifically about the type of learning you wish to occur in a particular lesson, and to relate the educational objectives to what you know about the pupils and the place of the lesson in the general programme of study. Second, it enables you to think about the structure and content of the lesson. This includes, most importantly, thinking about how long to devote to each activity. Indeed, one of the most important skills in teaching is that of judging how much time should be spent on each activity in a lesson and the best pace of progress through the activities.

Third, planning quite considerably reduces how much thinking you will have to do during the lesson. Once the lesson is in progress, there will be much to think about in order to maintain its effectiveness. The fact that the lesson as a whole has been well planned means that you can normally focus your attention on the fine-tuning of the lesson, rather than trying to make critical decisions on the hop. Indeed, many decisions about a lesson can only adequately be taken in advance.

For example, if it becomes evident that a map is needed during a lesson, there may be little you can do about it if you had not realised this during your planning and had one available in case the need arose. A related point to this is that being under pressure is not a good state to be in when trying to make sensible decisions about teaching.

You can all too easily find that trying to direct or alter the course of a lesson while teaching can lead to difficulties, until you have developed with experience a good sense of what will work and how, in the circumstances you face. Fourth, planning leads on to the preparation of all the materials and resources in general that will be needed. For example, having some work already prepared for any pupils who might finish the intended work for the lesson well ahead of the majority, or a summary of some key points you wish to review between two activities, all enable the lesson to progress more smoothly and effectively.

A fifth important purpose of planning is that keeping your notes will provide a useful record for your future planning, particularly in relation to giving a similar lesson to another group of pupils and in your planning of future work with the pupils which will extend what they have done in that particular lesson. Indeed, it is very useful, particularly in the early years of teaching, to make a brief note at the end of each lesson of any point you want to draw to your attention at some future time when you need to refer to the lesson notes again.

TIME SPENT PLANNING

The amount of time spent planning also varies immensely between teachers and for the same teacher between lessons. While beginning teachers will certainly need to spend more time planning, some of the differences between teachers at the same level of experience seem to relate to their general style or approach to planning. In essence, some teachers feel more secure and relaxed about the tasks of teaching if a lesson has been well planned. Others, to some extent, need the pressure generated by the close onset of a lesson to concentrate their minds to the task at hand. Certainly, the ideal approach will be one in which the teacher is able to devote some time, well in advance, to the planning of each lesson. The reality of life as a teacher, however, is that there are many competing demands on your time. The amount of time for planning is thus somewhat constrained. As a result, more extensive and formal planning is likely to focus on those lessons where something new or more demanding will take place.

FLEXIBILITY

Another very important aspect of planning is the need to be flexible about the implementation of your plans. Effective teaching depends on the ability to monitor, adapt and develop what goes on in the classroom in the light of how pupils behave during the lesson. No matter how careful and well thought out the planning of the lesson was, once it starts, the immediate demands of how things are going, take complete precedence. It may become apparent that some of the ideas you intended to introduce and discuss at length appear to be well understood by pupils already or are much more difficult to understand than you envisaged; or you may notice that a large number of pupils are having difficulties in carrying out a task you had set and which you had planned to allow them to undertake largely uninterrupted for most of the lesson. In such circumstances, a change in your original plan would be appropriate to ensure that the pupils' needs were being met.

Unfortunately, beginning teachers are occasionally in the position of reaping the worst of both worlds. They invest a great deal of time and energy in preparing their plan for a lesson and at the same time have a greater need to be flexible and adapt their plan in the light of ongoing feedback. Thus, for example, a worksheet may have been carefully prepared only to find the tasks set are too difficult, and a swift change to whole class teaching may be required. For experienced teachers, such a situation is less likely to occur, but if it did, changing to another activity would pose little problem. For the beginning teacher, this situation is more likely, and the difficulty of switching to an unprepared activity is more demanding. Indeed, because of this, student teachers are particularly likely to persist with their original plan unless the problems arising are much more acute and, until they build up experience, are more often than not wise to do so. In contrast, changing horses in mid-stream, to switch from one activity to a more appropriate one, is almost a skill of delight for the experienced teacher, in the extent to which it calls upon their professional knowledge and experience to be able to do so successfully.

DEVELOPING LESSON PLANNING SKILLS

A major difference between beginning teachers and experienced teachers is the latter's ability to take a longer view of how a whole sequence of lessons will fit together. Indeed, experienced teachers tend to be much more aware of the end point of learning that they want pupils to have reached after dealing with a topic over several weeks, whereas beginning teachers tend to focus much more on the short-term learning outcomes for a particular lesson.

This is well illustrated in a detailed case study of a secondary school English teacher reported by McCutcheon and Milner; it shows the way the teacher was able to draw upon his rich content knowledge in planning lessons, and the way he viewed the planning of individual lessons and his thinking about interconnected themes, and which curriculum materials and activities to employ, as being very much subordinate to his overall long-term perspective on planning. Another major difference is the degree of pedagogical content knowledge that experienced teachers are able to draw upon when planning lessons. Having taught a particular topic several times, experienced teachers are very much aware of the difficulties involved in teaching that topic, and the areas where the pupils' understanding may need to be developed and strengthened. They are also more aware of what aspects of the topic are the key elements that need to be grasped, and how much time needs to be devoted to doing this. It is sometimes claimed that an experienced teacher should be able 'at the drop of a hat' to teach an acceptable lesson on any topic in their area. They would probably first of all want to know something about the pupils' age, general ability and motivation; they would then want information on what the pupils already knew about the topic.

After that, the teacher's experience of having taught this topic before with different groups of pupils would be enough to provide the teacher with a clear idea of how to organise the lesson. Beginning teachers lack this wealth of pedagogical content knowledge. A study by Van Der Valk and Broekman explored student teachers' pedagogical content knowledge by asking student teachers to prepare a lesson plan about a topic as if they had to teach it, and then interviewed the student teachers about their lesson plans. These interviews provided a very useful way of exploring their pedagogical content knowledge. Indeed, feedback from tutors and mentors on lesson plans provides a very important learning experience for beginning teachers in developing their lesson planning skills.

LESSON PLANNING

As noted earlier, there are four major elements involved in lesson planning:

- deciding on educational objectives
- selecting and scripting a lesson
- preparing the materials and resources to be used
- deciding how to monitor and assess pupils' progress.

The preparation of materials and resources will be considered in the final section of this chapter. The other three elements will be the focus of our attention in this section.

DECIDING ON EDUCATIONAL OBJECTIVES

The most important aspect of an educational objective is that it is a description of an aspect of pupil learning. To gain knowledge about prime numbers, to understand the nature of causality in History, to acquire the skill of drawing a river's path to the sea through contour lines, or to feel empathy for the victims of the slave trade, would all be examples of educational objectives for a lesson contributing to pupils' intellectual development. To develop the skills involved in co-operating with other pupils, to become more able to listen attentively to other pupils' statements during class discussion, and to feel more confident about one's own capabilities in the subject, would be examples of educational objectives for a lesson contributing to pupils' social development. Educational objectives cannot be stated in terms of what pupils will be doing, such as working through an exercise, drawing a map or small group discussion. These are activities used to *promote* learning.

The educational objectives must describe what is to *constitute* the learning. One of the major pitfalls in teaching is to neglect thinking precisely about educational objectives and to see planning as simply organising activities. While the two go hand in hand, it is all too easy to think that a lesson that went well logistically was effective, until you ask yourself what the pupils actually learned. In selecting your objectives, a great deal of thought needs to be given to how these objectives relate to previous and future work the pupils are involved in, and how appropriate they are to extending their current abilities, attitudes and interests. For example, in deciding to introduce the notion of prime numbers, do the pupils already have an adequate grasp of what it means for numbers to have factors? Indeed, linking new learning to previous learning is immensely important, and particularly effective if the new learning can be seen to grow out of the previous learning. Thus a lesson on prime numbers may first of all utilise an activity in which pupils can apply their previous knowledge and understanding of factors. They may then identify numbers only divisible by one and itself, which are then given a special name. This would combine a linking of previous learning with a sense of discovery and growth, and also extend the previous learning.

SELECTING CONTENT

Selecting the content for a lesson involves a number of considerations. Even working within the framework of the National Curriculum still leaves a great deal of choice to teachers. The selection of content will clearly need to relate to the overall programme of study for pupils, but the decision on how much emphasis to give to particular topics will depend on the teacher's view of its importance and difficulty. Indeed, a very important teaching skill is that of separating a topic into distinct elements or aspects, and designing a sequence or progression through these elements that makes coherent and intellectual sense and effectively facilitates learning. One of the most demanding aspects for beginning teachers is trying to decide how best to do this in a way that satisfactorily meets the pupils' needs.

This demands good subject knowledge by the teacher, an awareness of how to separate and sequence the elements of the topic, and an awareness of pupils' needs. Beginning teachers tend to rely somewhat on established practice in the school, particularly if a scheme of work is in use. With experience, however, teachers become much more confident and authoritative in deciding on the nature and structure of the content they wish to use, and also better able to judge the pace of progress to expect through the content elements and the likely areas of difficulty or misunderstanding that may arise. The problem for experienced teachers becomes that of keeping abreast of developments in the teaching of their subject and topics in line with changes in required educational attainment.

SELECTING LEARNING ACTIVITIES

The selection of learning activities offers much scope and choice for teachers. The decision about which activity or combination of activities to use within a lesson depends on the teacher's beliefs about the relative effectiveness of the different activities for the type of learning intended. This decision, however, also needs to take account of a range of factors relating to the context of the lesson.

First, will the activities selected meet the needs of this particular group of pupils, taking account of their abilities, interests and motivation, and the way they are likely to respond to these activities? You may feel that because a particular class seems to work well when group work tasks are used, you will incorporate group work into their lesson. Equally well, you may decide to incorporate group work into the lesson because the class has not worked well with this activity, and you feel more practice and experience with this activity will be of value to them in developing associated skills and benefits. Indeed, the fact that an activity has not worked well may suggest a need to use it more often rather than to avoid using it. A second important factor concerns when the lesson occurs. The type of activities that might be effective on a Friday afternoon, or following morning assembly, or extending work done in a previous lesson when a number of learning difficulties were encountered, may be influenced by this context. Third, such planning decisions are also influenced by logistics, other demands and time pressures facing the teacher. A lesson that requires a lot of planning effort and preparation is perhaps best avoided in the middle of a week in which you have to mark a heavy load of examination scripts, or when you know that the particular equipment needed is in great demand for other activities.

THE VARIETY AND APPROPRIATENESS OF ACTIVITIES

When thinking about the learning activities to be used, you also need to think of the lesson as a coherent whole, such that the total package of experience provided for pupils achieves your intended learning outcomes. As such, not only must the activities deliver the appropriate intellectual experience for this learning to occur, but also facilitate the ease with which pupils can engage and remain engaged in this experience.

The activities must thus elicit and sustain pupils' attention, interest and motivation. Even when interest and motivation are high, pupils will find it difficult to listen to a teacher's exposition for a long period; doubly so if they are young or the exposition is difficult or unclear, or if it is a hot day. As such, most lessons will involve some variety of activities. The initial phase of the lesson may be designed to set the scene and elicit interest, the major part of the lesson may involve the main learning experiences, and the ending may involve some review or general comments about the importance, relevance or quality of the learning that took place. While a variety of activities is important, each activity must be appropriate to the learning at hand. Thus, for example, developing pupils' ability to articulate and communicate their ideas orally is much more likely to be achieved through practice, feedback and critiquing others, rather than by extensive reading about how to do it. A variety of activities also provides pupils with an opportunity to learn in different ways, and thereby to build up and develop the skills to do so effectively. At the same time, however, this does not mean that every lesson must involve a variety of activities. It is just as important to provide extended periods of work based on one type of task in order to allow pupils to develop the skills of organising and sustaining their concentration and effort, particularly in relation to a task where the quality of what is produced depends on the marshalling and development of the work undertaken.

USING ICT

When using information and communication technology (ICT), you need to take extra care to check the educational purpose for its use. Is it to help develop pupils' ICT skills? Is it to illustrate to pupils how ICT can be used to explore the topic in hand? Is it to motivate the pupils? Is it to encourage pupils to work in a particular way, e.g. individualised work, small group work? Is it to develop a deeper understanding of the topic? All these different purposes are valid, but you need to be sure what you intend for the use of ICT in this particular lesson. The type of ICT and the way you use it might need to be quite different if you are primarily using it to motivate pupils compared with when you are trying to foster a higher quality of understanding of the topic. Research on the impact of ICT on pupils and their learning indicates that teachers need to develop two sets of skills when using ICT:

- being able to use the ICT with adequate technical competence; and
- being able to use the ICT in a way that promotes higher-quality pupil learning.

Teachers need to master the first set of skills before they can develop expertise in the second set of skills. Recognising the purpose you have for using ICT will enable you to check that you have developed the necessary skills which go hand in hand with the particular purpose you have in mind for its use. Of particular importance when planning to use ICT, is being able to move beyond the stage of using ICT simply as a means of engaging pupils in the work to being able to use ICT to enhance pupils' deeper understanding of the subject matter. Whilst using ICT can act as a powerful motivator for pupils in the short term, it is only when pupils use ICT in a way that promotes their learning more effectively that a sustained impact on their self-confidence and attainment can be realised.

This, of course, places demands on you to develop your ICT skills to support your teaching. This is recognised by the inclusion of ICT skills development for student teachers in the TDA QTS standards to support their teaching and wider professional activities.

MONITORING AND ASSESSING PUPILS' PROGRESS

Once the lesson has begun, you will need to monitor and assess pupils' progress and attainment to ensure that the lesson is being effective and is likely to deliver the pupil learning intended. At the same time, this will also give you feedback on what aspects of the lesson, as originally planned, need ongoing modification and adaptation to maintain effectiveness. This requires more than just being responsive and reactive to feedback, such as waiting for a pupil to say they do not understand how to approach the task set. Rather, it requires you to be active, and to probe, question, check and test whether the progress and attainment intended is occurring.

While there is much feedback available to the teacher simply by looking at pupils' facial expressions or responding to those who confess to having difficulties, all too often most pupils will adopt strategies and techniques which indicate superficially that they understand and can do the work set. Only when exercise books are collected in, or questions asked at the end of the lesson, or subsequent tests are given, might it become evident that much less learning was going on than appeared to be the case. Unfortunately, it is all too easy to avoid active probing of progress and attainment; if the lesson appears to be going well, you naturally feel that to do so will be making problems for yourself that will need to be dealt with. It requires a great deal of integrity on the teacher's part to, in essence, look for trouble.

However, that is in fact the very cutting edge of the skill involved here. Simply approaching a pupil who appears to be working well and asking the question 'How are things going?' and probing with a few telling questions, can often reveal difficulties that either the pupil was not aware of, or was even deliberately trying to avoid you noticing.

It is important to be aware of just how well some pupils manage to avoid being noticed by teachers, by avoiding eye contact and appearing to be working well whenever the teacher is nearby.

The 'ripple effect' refers to the way pupils appear to be working hard at the task in hand when the teacher walks around the room, with those pupils the teacher is approaching having their eyes glued to their work, whilst those pupils whom the teacher has just passed start to relax, and in some cases resume talking to their neighbour. Such active monitoring and assessment of pupils requires some forethought and planning.

At what stages during the lesson, and how, are you going to get the necessary feedback? For example, one may usefully use a transition period between one activity and another for some quick whole class questioning and discussion about what was covered and whether any problems have arisen. This does not mean that every lesson must have some in-built testing of attainment; rather, a more subtle form of ongoing probing and reviewing should be employed that will be sufficient to enable the teacher to feel confident that the intended learning is occurring.

Nevertheless, there is a role here for formal tests from time to time, and also the use of homework to explicitly probe the learning covered as well as to generate new learning.

LESSON PREPARATION

Preparation primarily refers to the preparation of all the resources and materials to be used in the lesson, including the writing and running off of copies of worksheets, the ordering, delivery and checking of equipment, arranging desks and chairs in the required layout, and making notes about the content of the lesson to be presented.

Clearly, planning and preparation go hand in hand, and many planning decisions are taken while preparation is going on. Nevertheless, there are a number of important skills involved in preparation that are worthy of attention and may be crucial to the effectiveness of the lesson.

SHOWING YOU CARE

The care and effort that teachers take over preparation can have a major positive impact on pupils' sense that the teacher cares about their learning and that the activities to be undertaken are worthwhile and important. In contrast, a lack of preparation, such as may be evident if the teacher has to leave the room at a crucial point to find some statistical tables that need to be handed out, does not simply disrupt the flow of the lesson, but may be perceived by pupils as insulting to their sense of worth as learners.

While such problems will arise from time to time even in the best prepared circumstances, and pupils will tolerate these, the regular occurrence of poor preparation must be avoided. To be able to say in the middle of a lesson, 'I have already prepared for you . . .', and then reveal some materials, equipment, or using PowerPoint to display a diagram or set of key questions, can have a marked rousing effect on pupils' selfesteem, enthusiasm and sense of purpose for the next part of the lesson.

REHEARSAL, CHECKING AND BACK-UP

The use of any sort of equipment always poses potential problems for the teacher. Three key words are relevant here: rehearsal, checking and back-up. If you are going to use equipment or materials for any sort of experiment or practical work, you will often find it useful and worthwhile to have a rehearsal of some sort before you deliver that lesson for the first time. Practicals that appear to be virtually problem-proof can have surprises in store for you. For example, you may find that the length of time it takes for a particular effect to be visible takes much longer than you had planned for; or that connecting to the internet is particularly slow. Another problem can arise if the equipment available is different in some form from that you have used in the past. Some lessons will also require testing the equipment for its purpose. For example, if you are going to take a group of pupils pond-dipping, you may want to check on the type of creatures currently in the pond and whether the jars, nets or whatever is needed are available. Another aspect of rehearsal involves trying to experience the use of the equipment and materials from the pupils' perspective.

In preparing an overhead transparency, for example, is what is projected onto the screen clear and readable from the back of the classroom? In using an audio-tape, is the sound clear at the back of the room? In making a construction from card, is the card too flimsy or too thick for its purpose? Is the visual display of material on a laptop sufficiently clear for the task in hand? Checking simply refers to the need to ensure, shortly before the lesson is due to start, that the resources needed are to hand and in good working order. For anything electrical, this is almost mandatory. Such checking is made easier if you have marked on your lesson notes those items that need a check in this way. Nevertheless, even with adequate rehearsal and checking, things will happen that require a change in your lesson plan. It is here that some thought to back-up can be extremely helpful. While you cannot have a back-up for every piece of equipment, as a matter of regular practice, it is always worth having, for example, a spare light bulb for an overhead projector. More appropriately, you do need to think of what you will do if a particular piece of equipment fails, or if the lesson grinds to halt for some other reason. In planning a lesson, some thought, even if only limited, can be usefully devoted to how another part of the lesson or some alternative activity can be used to good effect if problems arise.

TEACHING MATERIALS

Worksheets, overhead transparencies, task cards and ICT software packages are commonly employed in schools, and their design and use involve a number of preparation skills. Often it is important to regard such preparation as a team activity, shared with colleagues, rather than something you do in isolation. Resources of this sort can be used many times over and, as such, if they can be designed to fit well into the programmes of study, are also used by colleagues, and can be linked carefully to assessment tasks, then the time spent in producing high-quality items will be well worthwhile. However, before embarking on such preparation, it is a good idea to explore whether such resources are already available and can be purchased, borrowed or copied. Some textbook schemes provide a set of parallel worksheets that can be used. Websites often contain a whole host of well-prepared resources of a high quality that can be adapted and used for your purposes. Some schools have gone to great lengths to develop and catalogue materials into a resource centre, either school-wide or subject-specific, and some teachers have similarly indexed materials which they have in their personal possession or have easy access to. There are many excellent resources and activity packs now published, including mathematical games, facsimile documents for historical analysis, and ICT simulations, all of a quality well beyond that which teachers can normally producc.

However, there is a danger in using such materials, particularly ones that have been commercially produced and look very attractive. The danger is that one can be misled into thinking that because such materials have been produced at a high level of quality in appearance, then effective learning is likely to follow from their use. In fact, it is extremely important for the teacher to carefully consider what learning will actually follow from their use, in order to ensure that the educational outcomes intended are realised. In preparing worksheets, task cards or similar types of materials, quality of presentation is of the highest importance. They need to be well laid out, not contain too much information, and should attempt to elicit pupils' interest. Particular attention needs to be paid to the language used; you need to be sure it is neither too simple nor too difficult for the range of pupil ability for whom it is intended. You also need to give careful thought as to whether such materials are going to be introduced by you and supplemented with various instructions, or whether they are to be self-explanatory.

Worksheets and task cards can range from simple exercises and tasks aimed at extracting facts from what is given to answer the questions posed, to quite sophisticated materials aimed to give pupils an opportunity for creative analysis. An example of the former is a worksheet on percentages containing cut-out adverts from a newspaper concerning the prices of various items with percentage reductions; questions here involve calculating which items are the best buys. An example of the latter is a series of line-drawn pictures about which pupils have to write a story. As well as examples designed to be used by individual pupils, other materials can be designed for small group work, such as using a facsimile of a letter written by a king as a source of evidence to interpret a historical event; here the use of small group discussion may highlight the extent to which the interpretation and validity of evidence involve personal judgements.

ASSESSMENT MATERIALS

Preparation skills also include the need to prepare assessment materials. Indeed, the monitoring of pupils' progress and attainment throughout their school careers requires a formal and regular record to be kept. While some of this will involve formal tests given at the end of periods of study, much assessment is also based on observing performance during normal classroom activity. This is particularly so in relation to monitoring the development of various pupil skills defined in the National Curriculum. This requires that appropriate assessments are prepared and built into the planning of lessons, and a formal note made of pupils' performance. This means that some activities in the lesson will be deliberately planned with a view to an assessment being made. As such, the activity must offer a fair opportunity to monitor the performance being examined. Two important planning decisions are involved here. First, how many pupils will you attempt to assess in a particular lesson? Second, what procedures will you adopt? In designing assessment materials to be used during normal classroom activity, particular care needs to be taken to ensure that they validly explore the learning you intend to examine. This involves not only assessing what it purports to assess, but assessing it in the way and to the degree required. Consider, for example, the following two framework planning objectives for design and technology, which can be linked to the DfES Key Stage 3 National Strategy for developing thinking skills:

- Pupils should be taught to predict and manage the time needed to complete a short task.

- Pupils should be taught to prepare an ordered sequence for managing the task.

The DfES illustrate how these can then be developed into the following two objectives for year 7 pupils in a design and technology lesson:

- Pupils should evaluate group and individual processes used in recreating the instructions for using a construction kit.
- Pupils should analyse how the components of a LEGO construction kit fit together to make a complete model.

Before being able to even begin to prepare for the assessment of these pupils' performance in this lesson, the teacher will need to be clear about what exactly is being assessed and how, and how the assessment will be recorded. In addition, for such assessments to be fair, the assessment materials and procedures adopted will need to be standardised so that each pupil is assessed in the same way. For example, in this lesson, the teacher might prepare a set of levels of success criteria, and then identify the extent to which each pupil's performance matched a particular level of success criteria.

RECORD KEEPING

Advanced thought and planning about how records are to be made and kept is also required. These will almost certainly need to be developed and agreed with other colleagues, so that the school's records will be consistent and coherent as the pupils progress through their school careers. A variety of assessment materials need to be used and types of responses given. This includes ICT designed to track pupils' progress against national attainment targets and programmes of study.

PREPARING YOURSELF AND PUPILS

Another aspect of preparation is the need to prepare yourself. While most teachers can teach most topics most of the time with little need to stimulate their subject knowledge, there will be some topics where you will need to learn about the topic in advance of teaching about it. In that sense, you need to stay one jump ahead of the pupils. Indeed, in areas of rapid curriculum development, you may be hard pressed to do this.

This means that private study of particular topics will be needed, ranging from making use of appropriate teacher guides that are available, to attending formal courses or workshop activities for teachers. At its best, the need to do this can add a sense of freshness and curiosity for these topics that you can share and delight in with your pupils. The TDA QTS standards include the need for student teachers to have a secure knowledge and understanding of their subjects / curriculum areas and how these relate to the age and ability range they are teaching and to the relevant aspects of the National Strategies. In addition, you must consider whether pupils need to be prepared in any way.

You may need to give them advance warning of certain topics, particularly if they will have to do some preparatory reading, revise some previous work, or bring certain equipment or articles with them. In such circumstances, you also need to check that they are prepared as required, and you may need to have spares of the equipment available. Indeed, in some schools, having spare pens to hand is almost essential for the smooth running of lessons. Preparing pupils to use ICT, such as interactive whiteboards, laptops and graphic calculators, is particularly important, in order to ensure that pupils do not feel threatened or marginalised by lacking the required ICT skills when using such equipment during the lesson. Indeed, a whole class interactive style of teaching using ICT will generate a lot of pupil frustration if the necessary ICT skills have not been developed and practised first.

3

Lesson Presentation

Lesson presentation refers to the learning experiences you set up to achieve the intended learning outcomes by pupils. As a result of the many different types of teaching methods that have been developed, there is now a staggering range of learning activities available that can be deployed to good effect. These include, by way of example, exposition, practicals, worksheets, ICT, role play and small group discussion. Moreover, teachers are actively encouraged and expected to make use of a variety of teaching methods in their programme of lessons.

In considering learning activities that a teacher can use, a useful distinction can be made between those activities largely dependent on teacher talk and those that can proceed with little or no direct teacher participation. The former includes teacher exposition, teacher questioning and, to a greater or lesser extent, classroom discussion channelled through the teacher. I shall call the former *teacher talk activities*. The latter includes, for example, practicals, investigation and problem-solving activities, worksheets, ICT, role play and small group discussion. I shall call these *academic tasks*. These two classes of activities will be discussed later in this chapter. Before doing so, however, it is important to consider first of all another aspect of lesson presentation: the teacher's manner.

THE TEACHER'S MANNER

When it comes to lesson presentation, the way that you do it is just as important as what you do. Asking a question with interest conveyed in your tone of voice and facial expression, as opposed to sounding tired and bored, makes a world of difference to the type of response you will get, no matter how appropriate the actual question was. Similarly, circulating around the room to monitor progress and help anyone having difficulties, rather than sitting at your desk at the front marking work from another lesson, also conveys an attitude to pupils about the importance of the lesson. All such cues together create a general impression regarding how much effort you feel it is worthwhile to put into the lesson to ensure pupil learning takes place. To elicit and sustain effective learning by pupils, in general, your manner needs to be confident, relaxed, self-assured and purposeful, and should generate an interest in the lesson. In addition, you need to exude positive expectations concerning the progress you expect to be achieved during the lesson.

POSITIVE CUES ABOUT YOUR MANNER

There are a number of skills involved in conveying to pupils that you are confident, relaxed, self-assured and purposeful. However, the most crucial aspect of doing this is that you *are* in fact confident, relaxed, self-assured and purposeful! The starting point is not one of being nervous and anxious, and then thinking how you can convey that you are relaxed and confident. Rather, the starting point should be that by sound planning and preparation, and with developing experience, you will quite naturally and unconsciously convey these positive cues. Nevertheless, there are times, particularly when beginning a career in teaching, or occasionally when things are going wrong, that you will feel anxious. In such circumstances, it is helpful to try to consciously induce a sense of relaxation as far as possible, and also to be aware of the aspects of your behaviour involved in conveying this. The positive cues are largely conveyed by your facial expression, tone of voice, speech, use of eye contact, gestures and positioning. When you feel nervous, you will naturally tend to look and sound nervous, avoid eye contact, and make awkward or repetitive gestures. As such, when feeling nervous, consciously make an effort to ensure that your speech is fluid, clear and audible, that you maintain regular eye contact with pupils and scan around the classroom, and that you spend time standing centre-stage at the front and erect when appropriate. For the vast majority of beginning teachers, such skills develop fairly quickly; for others, it takes somewhat longer. Some student teachers appear to feel at home in the classroom from the very first lesson; others only start to feel really relaxed and confident during their first year or two of teaching. It must be recognised, however, that there are some for whom the act of teaching will always be anxiety provoking. For those who are unable to feel at home in the classroom, most will not pursue a career in teaching for long. This largely reflects the fact that although much of the teacher's manner can develop through training and experience, it is in part also bound up with the teacher's personality. This is why it is so important for beginning teachers to capitalise on their strengths and mitigate their shortcomings, rather than attempt to model themselves on any particular style of teaching they have witnessed or that is being advocated to them.

OTHER IMPORTANT ASPECTS OF YOUR MANNER

Over the years there has been much discussion and research on other aspects of the teacher's manner which contribute to effective teaching, and it must be said that no clear and consistent picture has emerged. Undoubtedly this is because it is possible to be effective through different means. For one teacher, the key to success may largely stem from being firm; for another teacher, it may stem from a warm and caring attitude. Nevertheless, in general it does appear that the quality of conveying enthusiasm and interest for the subject matter at hand is important. Less consistently supported by research evidence, although widely advocated, are the qualities of patience and a sense of humour.

TEACHER TALK ACTIVITIES

Teachers spend a great deal of their time talking, whether it be lecturing, explaining, giving instructions, asking questions, or directing whole class discussion. As such, it is not surprising that the quality of teacher talk is one of the most important aspects of effective teaching. Indeed, many would claim that it is the most important quality of effective teaching. Communicating effectively with pupils and, in particular, the teacher's effective use of language when using explanations, questions, discussions and plenaries, feature as an important element of the TDA QTS standards.

EXPOSITION

There is a wealth of research evidence to support the claim that clarity of explanation makes a major contribution to greater educational attainment. Teacher clarity certainly enhances teacher talk activities, and also makes a contribution to the effectiveness of a variety of academic tasks, for example in briefing and debriefing role-play activities, or in the content and layout of a worksheet. Periods of teacher exposition typically occur throughout a lesson. In schools, it rarely takes the form of a lecture for any great length of time, nor should it, as pupils will find it difficult to pay attention to a lecture, except for a short length of time.

Indeed, for this reason, many teachers use a series of questions and the development of pupils' replies to trace out what they want to say, rather than an uninterrupted exposition. This not only involves the pupils more, but also enables you to check on pupils' understanding.

STARTING THE LESSON

What you say at the start of the lesson can be particularly important as it serves a number of functions. First, it must elicit and sustain pupils' attention and interest in the lesson. Establishing a positive attitude at the start of the lesson provides a good springboard for what follows. To create a positive mental set amongst pupils, it is important to ensure that pupils are paying attention when the lesson begins. Second, it is useful to indicate what the purpose or topic for the lesson is, and its importance or relevance. You will also need to outline the main structure for the lesson. A short warm-up or starter activity can usefully function as a quick recap of a previous lesson or be linked to the topic for the current lesson. In introducing the main part of the lesson, a question to the class, rather than a statement, can usefully arouse their curiosity and induce a problem-solving thrust towards what follows. A fairly quiet but audible voice level is best as it encourages listening, discourages background noise, and makes varying the tone and volume of your delivery easier. Having elicited attention and indicated the purpose of the lesson, the third function of your introduction may usefully be to alert pupils to any links with previous lessons they need to be aware of, or any particular problems or aspects of this lesson they should be alert to, in order to best prepare them for what is to follow. Such preparation may include practical matters concerning the equipment they will need to use or the pace at which they will be expected to work. Finally, you can discuss and share with pupils how the main learning intentions will be linked to success criteria and targets for learning, and whether the lesson will be linked to subsequent lessons and to a homework activity.

EFFECTIVE EXPLAINING

Explaining often goes hand in hand with questioning, with the teacher switching from one to the other as and when appropriate. Often this switch is influenced by whether the teacher feels it is appropriate to pull ideas together swiftly to facilitate a move to the next phase of the lesson, using a synthesising statement, or whether the teacher feels more involvement and probing of pupils' ideas is needed. For both explaining and questioning, it is particularly important to ensure that the nature and complexity of the language used by the teacher is at an appropriate level for pupils to understand. Indeed, the skill of the teacher to pitch language use appropriately by taking account of pupils' current level of understanding is one of the most important skills the beginning teacher needs to master. Writings and research on explaining have highlighted seven key aspects involved in enhancing the effectiveness of an explanation:

- *Clarity:* it is clear and pitched at the appropriate level.
- *Structure:* the major ideas are broken down into meaningful segments and linked together in a logical order.
- *Length:* it is fairly brief and may be interspersed with questions and other activities.
- *Attention:* the delivery makes good use of voice and body language to sustain attention and interest.
- *Language:* it avoids use of over-complex language and explains new terms.
- *Exemplars:* it uses examples, particularly ones relating to pupils' experiences and interests.
- *Understanding:* the teacher monitors and checks pupils' understanding.

Perhaps the most important aspect of explaining, however, is the skill in deciding the size of step that pupils can take in going from what they know at the start of the lesson to the learning you intend will take place by the end of the lesson. This decision about the size of step has crucial implications for the type and sophistication of the explanations offered. In summary, explanations should, by and large, be grammatically simple, make good use of examples, define any technical terms and, most importantly, not go on for too long!

QUESTIONING

Questioning skills are also central to the repertoire of effective teaching. There can be few professions to compare with teaching where you spend so much time every day asking questions to which you already know the answer. Research studies looking at teachers' use of questioning has identified the various reasons given by teachers for asking questions as follows:

- to encourage thought, understanding of ideas, phenomena, procedures and values
- to check understanding, knowledge and skills
- to gain attention to task, enable teacher to move towards teaching points, as a 'warmup' activity for pupils
- to review, revise, recall, reinforce recently learned points, remind about earlier Procedures
- for management, settling down, to stop calling out by pupils, to direct attention to teacher or text, to warn of precautions
- specifically to teach whole class through pupil answers
- to give everyone a chance to answer
- to prompt bright pupils to encourage others
- to draw in shyer pupils
- to probe pupils' knowledge after critical answers, re-direct questions to pupil who asked or to other pupils
- to allow expressions of feelings, views and empathy.

TYPES OF QUESTIONS

A useful distinction can be made between 'open' and 'closed' questions. Open questions can have a number of right answers, whereas closed questions will only have one right answer. Another useful distinction can be made between 'higher order' questions and 'lower order' questions. Higher order questions involve reasoning, analysis and evaluation, whereas lower order questions are concerned with simple recall or comprehension. Much research indicates that teachers overwhelmingly ask more closed and lower order questions than open and higher order questions. While, in general, open and higher order questions are more intellectually demanding and stimulating, and research does indicate that more of these types should be used, one does need to bear in mind the range of purposes behind asking questions, as indicated earlier. Given that open and higher order questions are more time consuming, it would be difficult to use these very frequently without constraining other intentions, such as the need to maintain an appropriate pace to the lesson, or to involve most of the pupils. As with all aspects of teaching skills, a balance is required in meeting a range of different intentions at the same time.

EFFECTIVE QUESTIONING

Kerry has highlighted seven questioning skills:

- pitching the language and content level of questions appropriately for the class
- distributing questions around the class
- prompting and giving clues when necessary
- using pupils' responses in a positive way
- timing questions and pauses between questions
- learning to make progressively greater cognitive demands through sequences of higher order questions
- using written questions effectively.

When asking questions there are two extremely important points to bear in mind. First, answering a question, particularly in front of classmates, is an emotionally high-risk activity. As such, it is essential that the classroom climate during questioning is one of support and respect for the pupil's answer. Second, do not allow some pupils to opt out of questioning. It is evident that some pupils are adept at avoiding being noticed and will do whatever they can to terminate quickly any interaction with the teacher. Such pupils need to be involved and helped to contribute to the lesson.

A number of features characterise skilful questioning. It is a useful technique not to name the pupil whom you want to answer the question until you have finished the question. This helps to ensure that all pupils are attentive. When asking the question, try to ensure that it is as clear and unambiguous as possible. If the pupil is in difficulties, it can be useful to rephrase the question in a different way or guide the pupil towards an answer through the use of scaffolding.

Allowing pupils some time to talk to partners and to share answers can be useful in promoting higher-quality thinking. Most importantly, ask the question in a manner that conveys you are interested in the reply, maintain eye contact with the pupil and ensure that other pupils have the courtesy to listen in silence. When prompting or helping a pupil, remember that the object of this is to assist the pupil's thinking, not to enable the correct answer to be guessed from the clues given. Finally, it is often worthwhile to check how a pupil arrived at the answer given, as this can give you some useful insight into the thinking involved.

DIRECTING CLASSROOM DISCUSSION

The third area of teacher talk activities to be considered here is that of classroom discussion channelled through the teacher: a mixture of teacher and pupil explanations, views and questions. Classroom discussion begins at the point when pupils ask questions and when one pupil responds to what another pupil has said. When classroom discussion takes place, there are two key decisions you need to take. First, you need to consider how best to lay the room out. Second, you need to consider the extent to which you are going to direct the discussion and make a leading contribution to shaping the flow and development of what is said. In using classroom discussion to good effect, it is useful to indicate the purpose of having such a discussion, to indicate how long the discussion is intended to last, and to summarise at the end what conclusions can be drawn. It is particularly important to remember that one of the prime reasons for having classroom discussion is to give pupils the opportunity to develop and express their ideas. This will need encouragement, and a tolerance to allow badly formed and incorrect notions to be expressed.

WHOLE-CLASS INTERACTIVE TEACHING

In recent years a style of teaching referred to as whole-class interactive teaching has been widely advocated. This style of teaching involves the skilful use of exposition and questioning to engage pupils in higher level thinking about the topic in hand. This is often characterised as being done with pace, in order to sustain a lively and buoyant feel to the lesson, but the teacher also needs to give pupils adequate thinking time when appropriate in order to allow higher-quality responses to questions. A teacher will typically also give pupils short tasks to do or ask them to talk in pairs for a few minutes before asking for answers. Unfortunately, in unskilled hands, this style of teaching can regress back into a more conventional whole-class teaching. Indeed, a study by Smith *et al.* looking at the quality of interactive whole class teaching in the National Literacy and Numeracy Strategies reported that traditional patterns of whole class interaction have not been dramatically transformed by the Strategies. The skills needed lie in being able to sustain pupils' engagement and contributions, and in particular to ensure that less able pupils and more socially reserved pupils in the class do not feel intimidated by this style of teaching. At its best, pupils will be encouraged to argue with and comment on both what the teacher says and on what other pupils have said. Generating high-quality pupil talk in this way is perhaps one of the most challenging and important tasks facing being teachers.

ACADEMIC TASKS

Academic tasks refer to activities set up by teachers to facilitate pupil learning, which can proceed with little or no direct teacher participation once they are up and running. Examples include doing experiments or other practical tasks, investigation and problemsolving activities, worksheets, ICT, role play and small group discussion. Almost all such activities tend to involve the teacher circulating around and monitoring progress, giving individual help as and when necessary. Nevertheless, some teachers prefer to maintain a high level of direction during such activities, while others see important educational benefits deriving from being less directive.

SETTING UP ACADEMIC TASKS

For academic tasks to be successfully employed, it is absolutely crucial that it is clear to pupils what they have to do, and to indicate the relationship between the task and the learning intended. It is easy to fall into the trap of thinking that the most important aspect is to get the pupils under way quickly with the task and then to deal with any problems as they arise. Doing so can lead to your having to dash from one desk to another throughout the lesson, or else having to interrupt the class as a whole on several occasions. In fact, the most important aspect for success is the careful preparation of the tasks and materials to be used coupled with a clear briefing of what is required before the task is started.

Some pupils may not pay attention during this briefing session if they know that you will simply give an individual briefing to anyone who wants one once the work has begun. If several pupils have this attitude, there will be many demands made on you at the start. As such, it is well worthwhile to ensure that as many pupils as possible are clear about the task in hand before the class is allowed to start the work.

Another aspect of academic tasks that is of great importance is to ensure that pupils possess the skills required to undertake the task successfully, or, if not, that the skills are helped to develop. All tasks, whether it be extracting information from a set text, using a worksheet, extracting data from the internet, loading a CD, carrying out an experiment, or participating in small group discussion, involve a number of skills. It is all too easy to assume that pupils already have appropriate skills or can develop these by trial and error. In fact, many pupils get into difficulties simply because they are unsure about how to proceed and what is expected of them.

A nice example of this is that of a teacher asking pupils to spend a lesson writing a poem about winter. Now, for some pupils the processes involved in writing a poem are rather mysterious, and little headway may be made. However, if the teacher was first to spend a lesson composing a poem from scratch on the blackboard in front of the pupils, and demonstrate, by thinking aloud, how one can start from some ideas or phrases and rework these and change words, the whole process for pupils could then be demystified. This demystification is essential for almost all academic tasks. How do you extract information from a set text? How do you make successful use of small group discussion? What steps are involved in conducting an investigation? Paying explicit attention to pupils' learning skills before, during and after academic tasks can have a major impact on the quality of learning which takes place. One of the advantages of setting work for individuals is that it allows pupils to work at their own pace, it helps them to organise and take responsibility for their own effort, and it enables the work to be structured and tailored to their own level of difficulty. Where pupils are working individually on an extended piece of work or a project, or through a work scheme, careful and regular monitoring of progress is essential.

CO-OPERATIVE ACTIVITIES

Co-operative activities, such as small group discussion or collaborative problem-solving, enable pupils to share ideas, to develop the skills involved in co-operative interaction, to communicate clearly and to work as a team. Generally speaking, a group size ranging from two to six seems to be best for most co-operative tasks. Pairs are most commonly used, in part for logistical reasons and in part because both partners will get more contribution time than when in a larger group. However, it is important to make use of larger groups, which will enable pupils to develop wider communication and organisational skills. Some teachers, however, are reluctant to make use of co-operative tasks because they fear that by relinquishing tight control over the learning activities, it will be harder to sustain good order. There is little doubt that such activities do depend on good teaching skills, but fortunately with the increasing use of such activities, pupils are more familiar and more skilled at using such activities to good effect than when such activities were relatively novel in schools. It is important to note that pupils require help and support to use small group cooperative activities effectively. Research indicates that the way the activity is structured can have a positive impact on the quality of learning that takes place. A study by Gillies identified three key elements of a structured activity:

- The pupils understand what they are expected to do and how they are expected to work together.
- The task is established so that all group members realise they are required to contribute to completing it and to assist others to do likewise.
- Pupils are taught the interpersonal and small group skills needed to promote a sharing and respectful attitude towards others.

Gillies found that pupils in structured groups worked together much better and more effectively than pupils working together in unstructured groups.

ACTIVE LEARNING

Active learning refers to any activities where pupils are given a marked degree of autonomy and control over the organisation, conduct and direction of the learning activity. Most usually, such activities involve problem-solving and investigational work, and may be individualised or involve small group collaboration. In essence, active learning may usefully be contrasted with expository teaching, in which pupils are largely passive receivers of information which is tightly under the teacher's control. A number of educational benefits have been claimed for active learning activities:

- They are intellectually more stimulating and thereby more effective in eliciting and sustaining pupil motivation and interest.
- They are effective in fostering a number of important learning skills involved in the process of organising the activities, such as when organising their own work during individualised activities, and interaction and communication skills during co-operative activities.
- They are likely to be enjoyed, offer opportunity for progress, are less threatening than teacher talk activities and thereby foster pupil attitudes towards themselves as learners and more positive attitudes towards the subject.
- Co-operative activities in particular enable greater insights into the conduct of the learning activities through observing the performance of peers and sharing and discussing procedures and strategies.

In considering active learning, however, you need to be aware that this term has not been used by teachers with any consistency. As well as referring to teaching methods or learning activities, it is sometimes used to refer to the mental experience of learning by discovery. Nevertheless, in the sense of activities such as small group work, teachers are generally expected to make use of such activities as well as teacher talk activities. The message, in effect, is that how pupils learn is as important as the content of what they learn. In addition, active learning can sometimes offer a much more powerful experience or insight into what is to be learned than expository teaching.

ACADEMIC TASKS VERSUS TEACHER TALK ACTIVITIES

Much discussion has taken place over the years concerning the relative merits of teachers using whole-class teaching methods based on teacher talk activities compared with the use of academic tasks, particularly those characterised by active learning. Comparisons of educational attainment in different countries coupled with a whole host of research studies of effective teaching suggest that an approach described as 'direct teaching' is probably the most effective approach to promoting higher levels of pupil attainment. Direct teaching essentially consists of lessons that follow five main stages:

- The teacher sets clear goals for the lesson.
- The teacher teaches through exposition of what is to be learned.
- The teacher asks questions to check pupil understanding.
- There is a period of supervised practice.

- The teacher assesses pupils' work to check that the goals have been achieved.

Nevertheless, one should not use such findings to call for teaching to become predominantly based on whole-class teaching methods employing teacher talk activities. It is widely accepted that teachers need to make use of a variety of teaching methods. Doing so helps pupils to develop the skills of learning in different ways and also provides for a greater variety of learning outcomes. What is needed is the right mix of activities.

TEACHING STYLES AND LEARNING STYLES

Discussion of the skills involved in lesson presentation has sometimes made reference to the way in which some teachers seem to adopt a typical approach to their teaching, and also the way in which some pupils seem to have strong preferences about how they prefer to learn. This has given rise to consideration of whether certain teaching approaches may be particularly effective, and whether an attempt should be made by teachers to take account of differences between pupils in their preferences for certain learning activities.

TEACHING STYLES

Studies of classroom practice have attempted to categorise teachers in terms of their *teaching styles,* which refers to their tendency to make frequent use of certain types of learning activities in their teaching. For example, some teachers tend to make much greater use of teacher-centred, exposition-dominated activities, together with teacher-directed seatwork tasks. At its most traditional, this approach may be coupled with the organisation of desks into rows and a great deal of guided practice. This approach has often been described as a 'formal teaching style'. In contrast, some teachers make much greater use of student-centred activities, involving small group work and giving pupils' more control over the direction of their work. This may be coupled with arranging desks together to form groups of pupils seated together, and the use of more open-ended tasks negotiated with pupils. This approach has often been described as an 'informal teaching style'. Attempts to identify and describe teaching styles, however, have been problematic, because there are a wider variety of styles than can be described and most teachers use a mix of styles and also vary their mix of styles from lesson to lesson and from class to class. Nevertheless, some consistent differences between teachers in terms of their general approach to teaching do seem to be discernible.

LEARNING STYLES

Similarly, attempts have also been made to describe pupils in terms of their *learning styles*. This term refers to the types of learning activities and tasks pupils prefer to experience and which they feel are more effective in promoting their own learning. It also includes their preferences about the types of strategies for learning they prefer to adopt when given a choice, and their preferences regarding the physical and social characteristics of the learning situation. For example, some pupils prefer to read, work alone, find things out for themselves, and have tasks tightly prescribed. The point is sometimes made that if pupils are taught more often in their preferred learning style, more learning will take place. As such, teachers should try to match learning activities to pupils' preferences.

Whilst I agree that it is important for teachers to be aware that pupils differ in their learning styles, I think the idea of matching of work to pupils' preferred learning styles involves a number of problems. First of all, it is important to help pupils to develop the skills to learn effectively in their non-preferred learning styles, as pupils who are taught overwhelmingly in their preferred learning style may not be able to develop a full range of learning skills. Second, pupils' learning styles are not easy to determine and also vary from lesson to lesson and from subject to subject. Third, the logistics of classroom life would make it extremely difficult to cater differentially for the variety of pupils' learning preferences in the same class.

PERSONALISED LEARNING

The debate about the relative effectiveness of different teaching methods and learning activities is a complex one, and what works best will vary from situation to situation, depending on the type of class taught and the particular type of learning outcomes being fostered. However, one important implication of research on teaching styles and learning styles is that teachers do need to make use of a variety of learning activities in their teaching. In addition, teachers can use their awareness of the differences between pupils in their learning preferences to help sustain each pupil's motivation by making use of their preferred activities when appropriate, and also by providing additional support and encouragement when making use of their non-preferred activities. The consideration of how teachers can best meet the learning needs of pupils by taking careful account of each pupil's circumstances, ability and motivation, and preferred learning styles, has given rise to the notion of 'personalised learning', which refers to how a school can tailor the curriculum and teaching methods to the specific learning needs of each pupil, and offer each pupil the type of personalised support that will enable them to develop the skills needed to access learning activities to better effect.

The genesis of personalised learning was initially seen as a way of combating disaffection amongst lower-attaining pupils, but it gradually began to be conceived in terms of being good practice to better meet the needs all pupils. Personalised learning has featured heavily in a range of DfES policy statements which have been produced in its drive to improve the quality of education and to raise the levels of pupil attainments. The DfES also notes that personalised learning needs to be based on the regular assessment of pupil progress to identify each pupil's learning needs in order to teach them accordingly. The essence of personalised learning is for the pupil to experience learning as something that is relevant to their needs and which they can readily engage in with success. Some attempts have also been made to indicate how the development of personalised learning in schools can be informed by research evidence. The importance of personalised learning is reflected in its inclusion as an element of the TDA QTS standards. Student teachers need to have knowledge and understanding of a range of teaching, learning and behaviour management strategies and to know how to use and adapt them, including how to personalise learning and provide opportunities for all pupils to achieve their potential. In recent years a number of research reports have highlighted the ways in which the skilful use of ICT can support personalised learning. A number of these reports can be found at the British Educational Communications and Technology Agency website. Becta argue that ICT can personalise learning by:

- personalising content sources and resources
- providing pathways through content that are personalised to individual pupils' needs
- presenting a range of interfaces appropriate to an individual pupil's level and ability
- facilitating effective assessment and reporting tools
- providing flexibility regarding when, where and with whom pupils learn.

MATCHING WORK TO PUPIL ABILITY AND NEEDS

Matching the learning experience to the ability level and needs of each pupil in the class is one of the most skilful aspects of teaching. The difficulty of doing this successfully is in part a reflection of the complexity of the teacher's task: namely, that the class may well have about 30 pupils in it, comprising a wide range of ability and needs. One of the problems facing teachers is that there is a tendency to pitch the lesson towards meeting the needs of the broad middle range of ability within the class, and then to provide additional material, demands or help for those at the extremes. Part of the problem with this approach is that the more able pupils need more enriching and more stimulating demands, not simply more of the same or more difficult work. Similarly, less able pupils also need more enriching and stimulating demands, not simply less of the same or easier work.

A number of work schemes based on individualised programmes of work have been particularly successful in enabling this match to occur across a broad range of ability. The notion of matching work to pupils does not mean setting work at a level that pupils can already do fairly successfully. Rather, it deals with the idea of what pupils of a certain level of ability are able to achieve in the way of new learning. 'Matching the work' thus refers to deciding how much progress pupils can make in a given lesson or over a course of lessons and then pitching the work to achieve the optimal progress the pupils appear to be capable of. Studies looking at the school factors influencing pupil progress have indicated that a key factor contributing to greater progress was intellectually challenging teaching. However, many studies have noted that the match of task demands to pupils indicated that a majority of tasks were not well matched to pupils, in the sense of promoting the optimal progress pupils were capable of. In some cases the tasks were too easy, whilst in other cases they were too difficult.

SETTING AND STREAMING

Another approach used to help match work to pupils is that of grouping pupils into narrower ability bands. This can be done by streaming, where pupils in a particular ability band stay together as a group for all lessons and topics; or setting, where pupils are put into a separate ability group for each subject or topic. Reviews of research on the advantages and disadvantages of grouping pupils by ability indicate that such grouping can be very help in terms of:

- allowing pupils to make progress in line with their ability
- making it easier for the teacher to set work that meets the needs of the whole group
- more able pupils not being held back by the less able
- less able pupils not being discouraged by the more able.

At the same time, research has indicated that there are dangers here, most particularly that pupils grouped together into a low-ability band or set may get caught up in a vicious circle of lowered teacher and pupil expectations concerning what they are capable of.

MIXED-ABILITY GROUPS AND DIFFERENTIATION

In some schools mixed-ability groups are used. This may be because the small size of the age group or the small number of pupils doing a particular subject or topic does not allow setting. Additionally, some schools wish to make use of the advantages of having mixed-ability groups in allowing pupils from different backgrounds to mix socially and academically, and to avoid having to teach low sets. It is also important to note that all classes of pupils, even those where some selection by attainment has been made, will involve a range of ability. Differentiation involves adapting the way the work is set and assessed in order to meet the needs of a range of abilities within the same class. Seven types of differentiation have been highlighted:

- *differentiation by task,* where pupils cover the same content but at different levels

- *differentiation by outcome,* where the same general task is set, but it is flexible enough for pupils to work at their own level
- *differentiation by learning activity,* where pupils are required to address the same task at the same level, but in a different way
- *differentiation by pace,* where pupils can cover the same content at the same level but at a different rate
- *differentiation by dialogue,* where the teacher discusses the work with individual pupils in order to tailor the work to their needs
- *differentiation by support,* where the degree of support is tailored to the needs of individual pupils, with less support offering more challenge and opportunity for initiative
- *differentiation by resource,* where the type of resource used is tailored to the pupil's ability and skills.

These seven types of differentiation are not mutually exclusive, but rather a matter of emphasis.

INCLUSION

Inclusion refers to the way in which teaching and learning in a school is organised in a way that enables the school to cater for pupils with a broad range of ability and needs. Some pupils with moderate or severe special educational needs, including those whose behaviour can be regarded as challenging to deal with, are now being taught in mainstream schools when in the past they would have had their special educational needs catered for in special schools. Teachers need to be skilled at handling a wide range of pupils' needs in the classroom, and this may often involve being able to plan and teach with the help of a support teacher. The importance of the skills involved in doing this are recognised in the TDA QTS standards in which student teachers need to:

- know and understand the role of colleagues with specific responsibility for pupils with special educational needs and disabilities and other individual learning needs
- know how to make effective personalised provision for those they teach, including those for whom English is an additional language or who have special educational needs or disabilities, and how to take practical account of diversity and promote equality and inclusion in their teaching.

SKILFUL MATCHING

One of the useful ways in which teachers can help ensure that a match is achieved is through careful monitoring of pupils' progress and questioning to check understanding. Unfortunately, many pupils are reluctant to confess to difficulties and are likely instead either to do little work in silence, or else to use various strategies to get the work demanded done with little or even incorrect understanding. As such it is of crucial importance that you take the initiative in monitoring progress, rather than wait for difficulties to be drawn to your attention. Expectations also play a role in sometimes obscuring what pupils are capable of. Most pupils will do slightly less than is typically demanded of them. This can easily result in a downward spiral of teacher demands, if what the teacher demands of each lesson is the level of work that was produced in previous lessons.

Hence you need to be consistently conveying expectations of a higher quality of work and progress in each lesson than is typically achieved. This will create an impression of encouraging and expecting a standard just higher than the norm previously produced, but not so much higher that pupils feel discouraged or that you are dissatisfied with genuine effort on their part. Matching work to pupils also involves the need to take account of pupils' interests and needs. This includes taking advantage of examples and topics and their applications that are likely to be of interest or relevance to the pupils in your class. In addition, as noted earlier in this chapter, it includes providing a variety of ways of working, using both teacher talk activities and a range of academic tasks, so that pupils can build up the skills involved in working successfully in these different ways.

Some pupils will also have particular needs that must be met. These may range from a pupil who is rather shy and needs encouragement to participate, to a pupil who has difficulty producing legible handwriting. Some pupils will require individual attention for their needs to be met. Some pupils may well have a marked learning difficulty and be identified as having a special educational need. In such cases, the teacher may be able to meet these needs, or there may be additional help or resources available. Indeed, all teachers need to be alert to the possibility that a pupil may have a special educational need and to ensure that such needs are identified and met. Learning difficulties may stem from a physical handicap of some sort, a long period of absence from school, very low general ability, or social and emotional problems.

TUTORING

Another aspect of matching work to pupils is the use of one-to-one teaching, sometimes referred to as tutoring. As well as whole-class teaching and the monitoring of progress on academic tasks, teachers also spend much of their time helping individual pupils on a one-to-one basis. This type of help is a crucial part of effective teaching, not only because of the academic support offered, but also because it is a personal and private encounter between you and the pupil. As such, it offers an important opportunity to emphasise your care, support and encouragement for the pupil's progress. It also provides an important opportunity to assess the pupil's general ability and motivation, and to identify any particular needs. One of the most important aspects involved in skilful tutoring is that of *scaffolding*. The notion of scaffolding deals with how skilful tutoring can involve helping the pupil with a task by directing their attention to the key elements necessary for applying and developing their current understanding, and thereby enabling them to carry out the task successfully. A number of studies of classroom practice have shown that the teacher's ability to do this effectively requires a sensitive awareness of both the pupil's current level of understanding and the subject matter in hand. The effectiveness of tutoring has long been recognised, and some schools now make use of parents as helpers in the classroom or use other pupils, either the same age or older pupils, to provide additional opportunities for one-to-one help in the classroom. The use of pupils as tutors, often referred to as 'peer tutoring', is fairly widespread and a number of studies have indicated that where pupils are asked to help other pupils in this way both pupils seem to benefit. Of particular importance in using other adults or pupils as tutors in this way, is that they are carefully briefed about their role and the need to offer encouragement to pupils during the interactions.

USING RESOURCES AND MATERIALS

There is a vast range of resources and materials available for use in the classroom, including interactive whiteboards, laptops, PowerPoint, overhead projector transparencies, CDs, worksheets and simulation materials. Perhaps the golden rule concerning their use is always to check their quality and appropriateness for the lesson. It is all too easy to think that because such resources are going to be used, that is an excuse for accepting a somewhat lower quality or something not quite appropriate for the intended learning. As a result, pupils all too often have to watch videos with poor sound quality or work through a software package that is unclear or even inappropriate to the topic being investigated.

While the desire for pupils to acquire a familiarity with such materials may be important enough to warrant this on the odd occasion, you must be rigorous in your appraisal of the suitability of such materials for the learning outcomes you intend. It is also important to familiarise yourself with the content of such materials if you have not used them before or for some time, since it could prove difficult to deal with any problems that may arise unexpectedly. In addition, since many resources may be used by pupils with little or no help from the teacher, difficulties could arise which you may not be aware of until after the lesson or not at all, unless you carefully monitor progress.

USING THE BOARD AND PROJECTOR

The board is still the most widely used teaching aid and the quality of your board use will be a major indicator of your teaching. Well-prepared and clear use of the board is not only effective as a teaching aid, but is also an example to the class of the standard or quality of work and presentation you expect. The board can also usefully be a reminder or record of important points: for example, the spelling of new or difficult words, a note of the task pupils are to undertake when the present task has been completed, or a list of pupils' ideas to be used for later analysis.

One pitfall for beginning teachers to note is talking while facing the board. When you are writing on the board and have something important to say, you must turn your head to face the class as you speak. Similar points can be made about the use of interactive whiteboards and data projectors, although here it is possible to produce materials in advance to good effect. Always ensure that the projection onto the screen is clearly visible from all parts of the classroom, and that you are not obscuring the view yourself.

INDIVIDUALISED SCHEMES OF WORK

One marked area of development in the use of resources and materials has been the widespread use of individualised schemes of work based on software packages. One of the skills involved in their effective use concerns the organisation of how and when pupils use these, and how and when they receive feedback on their progress. Many studies have indicated that one of the key factors in promoting greater pupil attainment is the ability of the teacher to maximise the time that pupils spend educationally benefiting from the learning activity in hand.

The more time they spend waiting to use resources or waiting for help when they are in difficulties, the less time they are making progress in their attainment. The procedures used by teachers to ensure good organisation in using such resources is thus of great importance. One advantage of some software packages is that they are designed to be self-explanatory and often provide feedback about correct answers and help for pupils in difficulties. Nevertheless, most such resources do still require teacher assistance from time to time, and for teachers to be involved in assessing progress. As such, you need to ensure that the arrangements you make allow such time to be given. One particularly useful strategy, more commonly employed in primary schools, is to organise a lesson such that different groups are working on different tasks, ranging from tasks involving minimal teacher contact, to those involving a great deal of contact.

By dividing the class up in this way, you will be able to spend more time with those pupils needing your help without this being to the detriment of other pupils. Another useful strategy is to establish routines or procedures that pupils are required to follow, so that they do not waste time wondering what to do next in a particular situation. A simple rule stating what pupils are expected to do if they get into difficulties or have finished a piece of work, can help to ensure smooth running of classroom activities, and enables you to check whether the activities set are causing problems, are too easy, too difficult, or are unclear in any respect.

TREATING RESOURCES AND MATERIALS WITH CARE

Finally, when pupils use resources and materials that are to be used again by others, it is worth emphasising that the resources must be handled with care and respect. This is important not only because loss or damage may be costly and also inconvenience other pupils, but also because it highlights that in life everyone will be sharing resources and that such common ownership and use imposes responsibilities and obligations on each user. What is true in this respect within the community of the school is also true for society in general.

4

Lesson Management

Teaching a class of 30 pupils requires a whole range of management and organisational skills if sufficient order necessary for pupil learning is to be maintained. In many ways, I think the task of teaching is rather like the act one sometimes sees on a stage where a person has to spin plates on top of several canes simultaneously.

To do this successfully requires the performer to set new plates spinning while occasionally returning to those plates that have slowed down and are near to falling off, for a booster spin. In the same way, successful lesson management requires you to keep switching attention and action between several activities to ensure that pupils' learning proceeds smoothly. The key task facing you as a teacher is to elicit and sustain pupils' involvement in the learning experience throughout a lesson which will lead to the learning outcomes you intend.

At any one time you are likely to have several demands pressing on you for action. For example, you may be dealing with a pupil having problems with the task in hand, then become aware that another pupil needs an item of equipment, also notice another pupil is staring out of the window apparently day-dreaming, and be approached by another pupil who wants some work checked.

Lesson management essentially refers to those skills involved in managing and organising the learning activities such that you maximise pupils' productive involvement in the lesson as much as possible. Given the large size and range of ability of most classes, this is no mean task! Research based on classroom observation and interviews with beginning and experienced teachers has identified how a successful lesson hinges on certain key lesson management skills. Paradoxically, watching successful experienced teachers in action tends to provide student teachers with little explicit guidance on successful lesson management skills, since such teachers make everything look too easy. It is only when such teaching is contrasted with that of teachers where problems arise, that the differences in what they do become evident, and the skills used by successful lesson managers can be described.

BEGINNINGS, TRANSITIONS AND ENDINGS

One of the key areas of lesson management concerns the skills used in beginning a lesson, handling the transitions within the lesson between activities and bringing a lesson to a successful ending.

BEGINNING PUNCTUALLY

The two most important aspects concerning the beginning of the lesson are punctuality and mental set. It is important for the lesson to start punctually, i.e. fairly soon after the time formally timetabled for its start. This requires that both you and your pupils have arrived for the lesson in good time. Ideally, it is a great help if you can be in the classroom first, to greet pupils as they arrive and to ensure that pupils enter the classroom in an orderly fashion and settle down quickly. Certainly you should convey to pupils that lateness is not acceptable without good excuse.

The first few minutes of a lesson is usually a period of dead time during which pupils settle down, books may be distributed, or you may check material or notes. If possible, you can use this time to good effect by having a social exchange with one or two pupils, or deal with some matters outstanding from a previous lesson, such as a pupil's overdue homework. Once you are happy that everyone has arrived, you need to signal that the lesson itself is ready to begin.

This is probably the most important moment in the lesson. It signals the moment that pupils are to pay attention and begin their involvement in the lesson. A clear explicit signal, perhaps saying 'Okay everyone' or 'Pay attention now', is required. It is immensely important for pupils to start paying attention immediately. If you are not happy that all pupils are paying attention, you should indicate this. Trying to continue with the start of a lesson when a few pupils are not paying attention often acts as a signal for others to do likewise in future.

ESTABLISHING A POSITIVE MENTAL SET

Most lessons begin with the topic in hand or with some short activity that needs to be dealt with first, such as comments on homework, or some comment about equipment or materials that everyone should have ready. Whether you start with the topic itself or some other activity, it is important to stand centre-stage, at the front of the room, and to use a clear voice, eye contact and scanning, to ensure everyone is paying attention. A pause followed by a stare at someone not paying attention is often sufficient to signal this. Once you begin to introduce the topic in hand for the lesson, you need to think about how to elicit and sustain pupils' interest.

The best way to do this is to convey in your tone of voice and general manner, a sense of curiosity and excitement, and a sense of purposefulness about what is to follow. Two useful techniques are to establish a link with previous work or to pose some questions. Such techniques help to establish a positive mental set towards the lesson, i.e. an attitude of mind in which the pupil prepares to devote attention and mental effort towards the activities you set up. A successful introduction to a lesson, which establishes a positive mental set, makes it far easier to sustain learning as the lesson unfolds. Another aspect of establishing this mental set is to check that every pupil is ready and prepared for the start of the lesson. Are there still pupils with bags on the desk, or standing up talking to each other, or looking for an exercise book that was not handed back? One of the skills involved here is deciding whether to hold up the start of the lesson and chivvy pupils to settle down quickly or whether, if you simply start, pupils will quickly pay attention. Once a routine for a quick and smooth start to lessons has been well established, you can normally relax the formality of the start, as pupils will quickly respond. However, it is useful from time to time to re-emphasise the procedure and expectations to ensure that they continue to operate well.

At the same time, you need to check that you are ready and prepared for the start of the lesson. Are the materials you intend to use readily to hand, has the diagram you wish pupils to talk about been drawn on the board, are the copies of the worksheets to be used ready for distribution? A state of readiness on your part will contribute to your own mental set and this will in turn influence the mental set of pupils. It is well established that giving pupils 'advanced organisers' at the start of a lesson can be helpful. Advanced organisers refers to ways in which the teacher alerts pupils to how the content and activities of the lesson can be organised and related to their previous knowledge and understanding. However, it appears that explicitly sharing with pupils the learning objectives for the lesson at the start can also have a positive impact on the quality of their work. A study by Seidel *et al.* indicated that in lessons where the pupils were given a clear idea of the lesson goals, the pupils characterised the lesson as providing a more supportive classroom climate for their learning and they made greater progress in their learning as indicated by their subsequent attainment test scores.

SMOOTH TRANSITIONS

The notion of 'smoothness' is helpful when considering whether a lesson has started smoothly and whether there has been a smooth transition between activities. This can best be described by contrasting it with the notion of 'jerkiness'. Jerkiness would be evident if the teacher had to repeat instructions because pupils had not heard or were confused by what was said, or if, having begun a new activity, the teacher kept referring back to the previous activity. The worst form of jerkiness is attempting to start an activity only to find that some prior activity needed to be undertaken first, and as a result of this needing to stop the activity and change to the prior activity. An example of this would be having to tell pupils who had started working through a worksheet, that they should have been told to read a passage in their textbook first. This not only interrupts the pupils, but makes them feel that their efforts have been wasted through the teacher's poor planning and lesson management. Effective beginnings and transitions are smooth in the sense of lacking jerkiness. Clearly, from time to time, such jerkiness is inevitable and occurs for good educational reasons, such as if it becomes evident that an unforeseeable learning difficulty has arisen.

Nevertheless, skilful teaching tends to be characterised by a minimum of unnecessary and avoidable instances of jerkiness. Two other aspects of transitions contribute to smoothness. First, the teacher needs to be sensitive to how a lesson is progressing in deciding when to initiate a transition. For example, if pupils seem to be working fairly well at a task but somewhat slower than anticipated, the teacher may well decide that it is better to allow more time for the task to be continued, rather than interrupt the activity before it is completed to move them on to another activity. In some cases this may be crucial. A transition to discussion following group work may be harder to set up effectively if the group work has not continued long enough for the issues or ideas to develop that were to form the basis for the discussion. The second aspect of transitions worthy of note is deciding when to give instructions to the class as a whole, rather than to individuals. All too often a teacher interrupts a class embarking on a new activity simply to issue a further or elaborated instruction which is only of use to two or three particular pupils. It may well have been better and less disruptive for the teacher to talk to each of those pupils privately.

The same pitfall can be associated with issuing a reprimand, which again may disrupt the working of a whole class when simple and silent eye contact might have been more effective and less disruptive. The key point to bear in mind about transitions is that care and attention in setting up a sequence of activities in which pupils are working steadily are just as important as the effort you put into dealing with the content of the learning activities.

ENDING THE LESSON

The ending of lessons can usefully include a few words of praise about the work covered and some conclusions or summary about what was achieved. There are three important issues of management relating to endings. First, a lesson should end on time, neither early, nor, except for special reasons, late. Good time management is one of the skills that pupils will reasonably expect you to have. Ending early can imply a lack of concern about the worthwhileness of using all the time available. Should some time be available at the end of the lesson, this can usefully be spent reviewing or probing the topic covered. Ending late can imply that you lack the organisational skills to marshal the activities, and will deprive you of the opportunity to finish the lesson in a well-ordered and unhurried fashion. Most pupils will naturally resent lessons running over time on a regular basis. A second management issue is the procedure for getting pupils ready for the end of the lesson. This may involve collecting books and equipment, giving feedback on the work done, and setting homework or other action needed before the next lesson. While this should be done in good time, you also need to ensure that some pupils do not start to pack away too early or before you have signalled that they may do so. Third, the exit from the classroom should be well ordered. If necessary, it should be controlled, with you dismissing groups of pupils at a time, rather than allowing a rushed exit, until such time as pupils are used to making a well-ordered exit from the classroom without your explicit control.

MAINTAINING PUPILS' INVOLVEMENT

Once the lesson is under way, your main task is to maintain pupils' attention, interest and involvement in the learning activities. The task is *not,* however, one of simply keeping pupils busy. There may be a number of activities that you could set up that would effectively keep pupils busy, but they may not be effectively promoting the learning you intend. What makes lesson management skills so sophisticated is the task of setting up activities that are both educationally effective and maintain pupils' involvement. While the two should go together, it is easy to find some activities erring too far towards only the latter.

Skilful lesson management is primarily a question of getting a good balance between the learning potential of an activity and its degree of sustaining pupils' involvement. Since learning cannot occur without involvement, a danger facing teachers is to be uncritical about the quality of learning that occurs when they have successfully maintained a high level of pupil involvement. Nevertheless, at the same time one needs to bear in mind that the learning outcomes which teachers try to achieve include the development of study skills, organisational skills and sustained concentration by pupils.

These can usefully be fostered by lengthy periods of working without interaction with the teacher. Hence a teacher may well choose to use an activity that can sustain high pupil involvement for a long period primarily as a means to foster such skills.

SKILLS IN LESSON MANAGEMENT

An analysis of documents and reports produced by the DfES and Ofsted cover a numbers of skills involved in effective lesson management, although some of these clearly overlap with issues of lesson presentation covered in the previous chapter. In particular these focus on the need to be able to use teaching methods that sustain the momentum of pupils' work and keep all pupils engaged through:

- stimulating their intellectual curiosity, communicating enthusiasm for the subject being taught, fostering pupils' enthusiasm and maintaining their motivation
- structuring information well, including outlining content and aims, signalling transitions and summarising key points as the lesson progresses
- clear instruction and demonstration, and accurate, well-paced explanation
- effective questioning which matches the pace and direction of the lesson and ensures that pupils take part
- listening carefully to pupils, analysing their responses and responding constructively in order to take pupils' learning forward
- providing opportunities for pupils to consolidate their knowledge and maximising opportunities, both in the classroom and through setting well-focused homework, to reinforce and develop what has been learned
- setting high expectations for all pupils notwithstanding individual differences, including gender, and cultural and linguistic backgrounds.

In addition, the TDA QTS standards include a reference to the need for student teachers to be able to manage the learning of individuals, groups and whole classes, modifying their teaching to suit the stage of the lesson.

MONITORING PUPILS' PROGRESS

Overall, the most important skill involved in maintaining pupils' involvement is that of carefully monitoring pupils' progress. This should be done actively, through circulating around the room and asking probing questions, and passively, by having wellestablished routines whereby pupils are encouraged to ask for help. Both active and passive monitoring is important. As a result of such monitoring, key decisions may be made about how best to sustain pupils' involvement. Such decisions may relate to the needs of one or two particular pupils or to the needs of the class as a whole.

PACE AND FLOW OF THE LESSON

If pupils' attention or interest in the lesson seems to be on the wane, a number of possible reasons may account for this. It may be that a particular activity is being employed for too long. Alternatively, it may be that the general pace and flow of the lesson is either too fast or too slow. If the pace of activities is too fast, pupils will simply wilt or find that they are missing important points or ideas. If the pace is too slow, pupils' minds can easily start to wander. Indeed, an important aspect of maintaining the correct pace during exposition involves having a sense of how long to dwell on each particular point for understanding to occur and not spending too long dwelling on minor points or points already well taken. In addition, maintaining a good pace also involves avoiding unnecessary interruptions to the flow of the lesson. For example, if while explaining a task, you stop in order to get a pencil for a pupil, or to find a map you need to refer to, or to reprimand a pupil, the flow of the lesson will be interrupted.

A useful lesson management skill is that of dealing with the demands that arise, or postponing dealing with them, so that they are not allowed to interrupt the flow of the lesson. For example, if while explaining a task you notice two pupils talking, you may continue your explanation while looking at the two pupils concerned, or, if necessary, move towards them. This would enable the flow of the lesson to continue while dealing with the problem. This skill is sometimes referred to as 'overlapping', i.e. dealing with two or more tasks at the same time.

Another example of overlapping is the teacher's ability to monitor pupils' progress and behaviour while giving individual help to a particular pupil. A skilful teacher is able to listen to a pupil reading aloud or give help with some number work, for example, while at the same time periodically scanning the classroom and listening to the background noise to pick out any behaviour giving concern. This involves quickly switching attention between your interaction with the particular pupil and what else is going on in the classroom. Indeed, a particular pitfall for beginning teachers is to become so engrossed in giving individual help and attention that they fail to monitor what else is happening. In contrast, experienced teachers are much more skilful in their attention switching.

WITHITNESS

The general awareness of what is going on in the classroom is commonly referred to as 'withitness'. Experienced teachers are adept at picking up cues and signals which indicate to them what is going on. A quick downward glance by a pupil in the back row, or a furtive look at a neighbour, or simply taking slightly too long to walk to a seat, can all be picked up by a teacher as signalling the onset of possible misbehaviour. Beginning teachers are often so overwhelmed by all the demands of classroom life that they find it difficult to pick up such signals. With increasing experience, which gradually makes the unfamiliar familiar, the teacher becomes better able to pick up and monitor subtle cues of this type.

As such, it is useful for beginning teachers to consciously make an effort to scan the classroom periodically and monitor general behaviour, to see if anything gives concern. It is also useful to bear in mind the times when such monitoring is vulnerable. As well as when giving individual help, times when your back is turned to the classroom while writing on the board or looking in cupboards may interrupt your monitoring. A useful technique when writing on the board is to face sideways or to glance back at the class regularly, and to listen carefully to any background noise. Interestingly, the importance of lesson-managing skills relating to transition, overlapping and withitness, was highlighted in a seminal study by Kounin in which he compared the videotaped classroom behaviour of teachers who were regarded as having few discipline problems with teachers having frequent problems.

What was particularly noticeable was that the former's relative success largely stemmed from them simply being more effective lesson managers, rather than anything to do with how they dealt with pupil misbehaviour itself. Research on teaching skills, including my own, indicates that experienced teachers are generally very skilful in these three important aspects of their classroom practice.

MANAGING PUPILS' TIME

Pupils' involvement in the lesson can also be facilitated if they are given a clear idea of how much time and effort they are expected to devote to particular tasks or activities. For example, if you ask pupils to copy a map into their exercise books and answer three questions relating to the map, some pupils may rush the task, anticipating that ten minutes should be sufficient time, and others may assume the task is intended to last half-an-hour. If you indicate that the task should take about 20 minutes, it will help pupils to tailor their effort to the time available.

There can, of course, sometimes be a danger in encouraging pupils to perhaps take longer than they need. In general, however, it helps to ensure that some pupils do not work slowly only to find they are halfway through a task when you want pupils to move on to another activity. It also helps to maintain attention and interest, since they have a clear sense that another activity is shortly to follow. This also helps to break the lesson up into more attractive chunks of time.

GIVING SUPPORTIVE FEEDBACK

Constructive and helpful feedback also needs to be given to pupils to support and encourage further progress. Such feedback is not only of practical use to pupils in identifying problems or indicating successful work, but also conveys to pupils that their progress is being carefully monitored and that you care about such progress. Such regular feedback thus offers a periodic boost to the motivation and effort.

The skill of offering such feedback is a fairly complex one that needs time and practice to develop. You need to be able to identify the nature of the pupil's problem. Simply indicating a 'correct' method or answer may not be enough to give the pupil the insight necessary. You also need to be able to offer feedback in a way that is unthreatening, since once a pupil feels anxious, it is harder for the pupil to follow what is being said. This requires the use of a sympathetic tone of voice, and locating the problem in the task or activity, rather than in the pupil. In other words, it is better to say 'In this type of question, it is a good idea to start by taking careful note of the information given in the diagram', rather than 'You should have been more careful in your approach'. The former statement is task-focused, whereas the latter locates the fault or blame with the pupil.

This sensitivity to pupils' feelings is now widely appreciated as being an important aspect of the skill involved in providing supportive feedback. Indeed, a number of studies of pupils' views of their teachers have reported that the teacher's capacity to empathise was one of the most valued teacher qualities cited by the pupils. Giving individual feedback privately to each pupil in a fairly large class is clearly going to be demanding, and attempting to do this will almost certainly distract you from other important tasks. Consequently you need to maintain a good balance between giving individual feedback and other strategies, including giving feedback to the whole class, or enabling pupils to correct their own or each other's work.

These other techniques help to ensure that feedback occurs regularly and with sufficient speed to improve the quality of work and learning. However, you do need to ensure that such techniques are used sensitively, given the emotional consequences of identifying failure. It is thus a good idea to circulate around the classroom whilst pupils are engaged in a task, and to give them ongoing feedback on their work in an informal manner. You can take these opportunities to use the technique of 'scaffolding': this is where the teacher helps a pupil who is in difficulty by drawing their attention to the key features of the task and through dialogue with the pupil, gradually guiding the pupil towards the understanding they need in order to complete the task successfully.

ADJUSTING YOUR LESSON PLANS

Careful monitoring of pupils' progress and giving feedback also enables you to consider how best the lesson ought to proceed in the light of its success to date and any problems encountered. While lesson plans are important, all teachers will need to tailor the development of the lesson to the needs of the moment. Part of successful lesson management involves making whatever adjustments to your original plans for the lesson are necessary. In doing so, however, always ensure that you have a good feel as to how the class as a whole is progressing.

Clearly, just because one or two pupils are finding the work too easy or too difficult or lacking interest, this should not be taken as a signal that this is generally true for most of the class. Once you get to know a class fairly well, however, it becomes possible to make useful inferences from the behaviour of just a handful of pupils. If, for example, two or three pupils who normally find the work in hand difficult are suddenly racing through a particular task, you may well be fairly certain that most pupils in the class are going to complete the task quickly without the need for you to check too widely for confirmation.

HANDLING THE LOGISTICS OF CLASSROOM LIFE

Lesson management skills are essential if the learning activities you set up are to take place with sufficient order for learning to occur. Almost any task or activity can lead to chaos unless you give some thought to the organisation of how and when pupils are to do what is required of them. Organised control over the logistics of classroom life, whether it be how pupils answer questions, collect equipment from cupboards, or form themselves into small groups, requires explicit direction from you, at least until the procedures you expect are followed as a matter of routine.

SOCIAL DEMAND TASKS

Research on teachers' management effectiveness indicates that every learning activity involves a 'social demand task'. This social demand task might be, for example, who can talk to whom, about what, where, when, in what ways and for what purpose. Such research highlights the importance of how teachers indicate to pupils what is required of them, and facilitate the smooth and effective running of the activity. Indeed, with the increasing variety of learning activities used, effective lesson management skills need to be applied to a host of very different types of activities to deal with the social demand task involved in each. This has become increasingly evident in looking at the different ways in which ICT use in the classroom has generated new types of social demands which teachers have to manage skilfully.

GROUP WORK

Setting up group-work activities involves a number of decisions about the logistics of their organisation. First, there is the question of the size of the group and how groups are to be formed. If you have a task which, ideally, involves four pupils, you need to think about how the groups of four are to be created, and what to do if there are one or more pupils left over, or, indeed, one or two pupils whom no one wants in their group. A second question concerns the nature of the task.

Is it clear exactly what the task involves, who will undertake which roles, and how and what is to be produced? A clear instruc-tion, such as 'At the end, each group will give a list of the four most important factors involved, in order of importance' is clearer than simply getting each group to discuss the factors involved. Often, it is useful to write the task on the board or on a briefing handout issued to each pupil or group. You may wish to let each group decide who should report back at the end, or name a pupil from each group to do this. A third aspect of group work concerns your monitoring role. While close monitoring is usually desirable, particularly in checking that everyone is clear about the task, your presence may have an inhibiting effect on group discussion and, as such, it is often better to spend only a short while with each group to check that everything is in order, rather than to sit in for any length of time. Fourth, clear time management directions are crucial to most group-work activities. It is useful to say how long each group has for the task as a whole, and also how much time they may spend on any stages that make up the task.

One last aspect concerning group work is the need to help pupils develop the skills involved in successful group work. Pupils need to develop a number of skills to use group work to good effect, and feedback and guidance from you on good practice can help such skills to develop. These points are well reflected in a review of the literature by Kutnick *et al.* which looked at the research evidence on how to use group work effectively. Their report highlighted the importance of ensuring that:

- the task is broken down so that pupils can assess their own progress;
- the group is supported in working independently by providing hints about the task and also about group working; and
- the timing for each component is made explicit.

PRACTICALS

Practicals of any sort present a number of logistical problems, in part because you need to co-ordinate your management of pupils and materials with the sequence and speed of the practical itself. In a science practical, for example, there may be a 20-minute period during which some effect is developing; this period can be actively used to explore with pupils what is going on and to probe their thinking and the care they are taking to observe and record any changes. Another common problem regarding practicals may arise if certain equipment needs to be shared.

Again, a strict rota for the use of such equipment or a procedure to ensure its speedy use and return, can make a large difference to reducing unproductive time. During practicals, there are often times when bottlenecks can occur, such as when everyone wants to collect or return equipment, or perhaps wash apparatus. Simple rules, such as only allowing one pupil from each group to collect apparatus, can help prevent such problems.

USING ICT

Unless you can arrange for all pupils to have ready access to the ICT equipment they need to use at the same time, such as booking an ICT suite, you will need to organise a rota of some sort. One point about pairs or occasionally a small group of three pupils – working together when using ICT is that it is useful in most cases to group together pupils of similar ability, unless you explicitly wish one pupil to act as a tutor. With other types of group work, friendship groupings seem to work well, unless there is a clear educational rationale for forming the groups on the basis of similar ability or in some other way.

MANAGING PUPIL MOVEMENT AND NOISE

Two of the most important aspects of effective management skills are maintaining adequate control over the movement of pupils around the classroom and keeping the degree of noise generated at an appropriate level. In both cases, part of the difficulty lies in there being no fixed acceptable standard; what may be acceptable to one teacher in one context, may not be regarded as acceptable to another teacher in another context. Furthermore, problems over movement and noise can arise simply as a result of pupils being actively engaged in the tasks at hand and not because of any deliberate attempt by pupils to be troublesome.

PUPIL MOVEMENT

We have already touched on some aspects of pupil movement in the classroom earlier in this chapter, such as entering and leaving the room, and collecting equipment. In addition to these, there are some occasions which require particular attention. The first of these involves giving out books at the start of or during the lesson. It is certainly important to issue books rather than allow pupils to collect them from a central point. Often, it is more efficient for you to ask two or three pupils to issue books, rather than do it yourself, unless you feel that distributing books yourself will provide a useful social function or enable you to have a few pertinent words with some pupils. If pupils are issuing the books, ensure that they do so sensibly and with care. The second aspect concerns any mass movement of pupils; this always requires careful control.

Whilst useful routines can be established, there are occasions when you need to organise a somewhat unusual or novel arrangement. For example, you may wish to devise a role-play activity that requires all the classroom furniture, apart from eight chairs, to be moved towards the edge of the classroom. Any complicated manoeuvre of this sort requires prior thought if it is to proceed smoothly. A clear sequence of tasks and who needs to do what is essential. The third aspect involves establishing your expectations concerning when pupils may leave their seat.

Despite new forms of teaching and learning, most pupils will spend the majority of their time in their seats. The management of pupils being out of their seat during periods of work when pupils are expected to work at their desk is important. The normal expectation during such activities is that pupils remain at their desk until given explicit permission to move, unless certain well-established routines allowing movement without explicit permission are followed.

In such circumstances it is useful to ensure that only a handful of pupils at any one time are out of their seats, or away from their work area; it becomes much harder to monitor pupils' progress if several pupils appear to be wandering about, even if their purposes are legitimate. This is one reason why teachers often set an upper limit on how many pupils are allowed to queue up at the teacher's desk. Being out of one's seat for some pupils also acts as a break from their work, and they may feel like extending this break longer than necessary, and may also, as a result, start to disturb others. This needs careful monitoring.

PUPIL NOISE

Managing the general level of noise is also an important management skill. Every teacher develops their own standard of acceptable level of noise. The key thing here is to be reasonably consistent, so that pupils have a clear idea of your expectations.

If the level of background noise during an activity appears to be too high, it is useful to give specific feedback on the work practice you require, rather than make a general complaint that the noise is too high. Thus, for example, it is better to say 'You can talk to your neighbour, but not to other pupils' or 'Try to ensure that only one person in each group is speaking at a time', than simply to say 'The noise level is too high' or 'Less noise please'. It is also worth planning the activities to ensure that noise levels are not disruptive. For example, in a science practical looking at sound as a form of energy, clear instructions on how the apparatus or equipment is to be used can prevent problems occurring through unnecessarily high noise levels.

Indeed, the opportunity to make a lot of noise legitimately is too tempting for many pupils to resist. At the same time, it must be recognised that a certain level of noise is, of course, acceptable and desirable, and that enthusiastic and excited contributions by pupils need to be harnessed to good effect rather than squashed.

Clearly, a balance that ensures sufficient order is what is needed. Some studies, however, have indicated that the teacher's management of noise can sometimes become an end in itself. Given that the noise level of a class is often taken as an indicator of the teacher's level of control, many teachers are very sensitive about their classroom noise level, particularly if they feel it may be heard by colleagues or interfere with colleagues' lessons. Indeed, beginning teachers often feel themselves to be under particular pressure to control the noise level of their classes lest it conveys to colleagues that they lack control. As a result, some teachers may make more frequent use of certain learning activities because they will help sustain periods of quiet work by pupils despite the fact that other learning activities might be more effective for the learning outcomes intended but have more potential to generate noise. Indeed, the reluctance that some teachers have to make greater use of group work is related to the greater level of noise such activity typically generates.

MOVEMENT AND NOISE AS CONSTRAINTS ON YOUR TEACHING

While the management of movement and noise is important, you do need to be on your guard as to whether, as indicated above, you are allowing management considerations to have too great an influence on your choice of effective learning activities. Skilful lesson management involves an interplay between the different constraints within which you operate. Clearly, you need to ensure that a role-play activity involving a lot of movement and noise does not disturb another class, or that one pupil's excitement does not lead to other pupils being constantly interrupted when they are speaking. At the same time, you need to ensure that the learning activity does facilitate and encourage pupils' attention, interest and involvement in the lesson, and that this is not unduly inhibited by management strategies that could be usefully relaxed to good effect. One of the dilemmas facing teachers is that they may feel better able to manage certain types of lessons, and as a result are reluctant to use other types of learning activities.

This reluctance may persist despite the fact that certain curriculum developments have made the need for such change essential. This was evident, for example, in studies of how teachers' classroom practice has been influenced by the introduction of the National Curriculum, with many teachers expressing hostility and resistance towards the need for them to change their established practice.

Indeed, senior managers in some schools welcomed the National Curriculum because it made it easier for them to put pressure on colleagues to change certain aspects of their classroom practice by externalising the source of the need for change: 'Your practice has got to change, not because it's my idea, but because the National Curriculum requires it'. This type of pressure for change was also very evident when the National Numeracy Strategy and the National Literacy Strategy were introduced.

In thinking about your own classroom practice, you should not be wary of setting up activities that may involve more than usual movement or noise, as long as this is well managed and to good purpose. Some years ago a well-known headteacher remarked that effective teaching could sometimes be described as 'organised chaos'. On the one hand, I think that there is some truth in this description in so far as some effective lessons may well appear to have such a quality. On the other hand, there can at times be a danger in thinking that certain activities are so worthwhile in their own right, particularly in terms of the extent to which they may offer pupils a fair measure of control over their work, that the need to maintain sufficient order and control for effective learning can be relaxed. While I am a strong advocate of using a variety of learning activities, particularly active learning methods, there is always a need to ensure that effective learning is going on, and to provide the conditions that will facilitate this. Again, what is required here is an appropriate balance between the management strategies used and the type of learning outcomes you intend, most notably if the learning outcomes are in terms of developing pupils' own skills to organise themselves.

5

The Objectives of Secondary Education

Secondary education serves as a bridge between elementary and higher education and prepares young persons between the age group of 14-18 for entry into higher education. The population of children in the 14-18 age group (the age for secondary and senior secondary level education) has been estimated at 96.6 million, as projected by the National Sample Survey Organisation in 1996-97. However, enrolment figures show that only 27 million children were attending secondary schools, which means that twothirds of the eligible population remains out of the secondary school system. The number of secondary schools in India increased from 7,416 in 1950-51 to 1,16,820 in 1999-2000. However, this number is not adequate to accommodate the out-of-school children and the growing number of upper primary school pass-outs.

The impact of recent initiatives undertaken for the Universalisation of Elementary Education is resulting in an increased demand for the expansion of secondary education. There has been no fundamental change in the structure and organisation of the secondary and higher secondary education system during the Ninth Plan period since the initiation of the National Policy on Education (NPE), 1986. In the wake of the Policy, several centrally-sponsored schemes were launched and national level institutions for school education were established/strengthened. Ten centrally-sponsored schemes are in operation in the secondary education sector.

The experience of the implementation of the programmes as well as various reviews and evaluation studies have highlighted the need to modify and strengthen these schemes. Against a budgetary allocation of Rs. 2,603.49 crore for the sector in the Ninth Plan, the expenditure incurred has been to the tune of Rs. 2,322.68 crore. The focus in the Ninth Plan was on reducing disparities, renewal of curricula with emphasis on vocationalisation and employmentoriented courses, expansion and diversification of the open learning system, reorganisation of teacher training and the greater use of information and communication technology. Hostel facilities for girls, integrated education for the disabled, free education for girls etc. have also received attention. During this period the various Central institutes/organisations like National Council of Educational Research & Training (NCERT), National Open School (NOS), Kendriya Vidyalayas and Navodaya Vidyalayas were further strengthened. Participation of the private sector (including non-governmental organisations or NGOs) in the management of secondary schools with official recognition and, in many cases, with financial assistance, has also increased. Private organisations currently manage around 51 per cent of secondary schools and 58 per of higher secondary schools. In order to meet the educational needs of those who have not been able to enroll themselves in the formal system, opportunities have been provided through the National and State Open Schools, utilising contact centres and multi-media packages.

Distance education in the school sector also got a fillip with the National Open School was started in 1989, identifying new vocational areas and providing on-demand examination. Improvements in the content, process and quality of education, particularly environment education, science, mathematics and computer literacy have been emphasised with central financial support available for schemes related to this. New initiatives taken after the National Policy on Education was revised in 1992 include the revision of the curriculum, setting up of resource centres for value education and a National Centre for Computer-aided Education etc.

Several measures taken to enrich the school curriculum are being continued with added thrust. However, the scheme of vocationalisation of education has not appealed to the stakeholders because lack of industry-institute linkages, manpower demand surveys and various academic constraints. At present, only 10 per cent of the students are opting for the vocational stream, against a target of 25 per cent by 2000. Educational development of children with special needs received an impetus with the enactment of the Persons with Disabilities (Equal Opportunities, Protection of Rights and Full Participation) Act, 1995.

The Act entrusts the appropriate governments and the local authorities to provide children with disabilities access to education, employment, preferential allotment of land for certain purposes, non-discrimination in transport, financial incentives to Universities to enable them to undertake research etc. Programmes for attitudinal changes, capacity building among teachers and training institutions to educate children with special needs have been taken up. Along with providing opportunities for equal access and ensuring a minimum level of learning achievement for all, it is equally important to nurture talented children especially those from the rural areas and those belonging to lower income group.

There are several programmes for the development of talent. Residential Jawahar Navodaya Vidyalayas from Class VI to XII are established in the Seventh Plan as model schools and to provide quality education to talented children from rural areas selected on the basis of a common admission test. Each district is supposed to have one such school. Currently, there are 462 Jawahar Navodaya

Vidyalayas with about 1,25,000 students on their rolls. The National Council of Educational Research & Training (NCERT), New Delhi, conducts a National Talent Search Examination to identify talent.

International Chemistry, Mathematics and Physics Olympiads are held every year to identify talent in these subjects. India has been participating regularly in these Olympiads. Talented students from rural areas are provided scholarships at the secondary stage in order to develop their potential by providing them access to good schools. A total of 38,000 scholarships have been awarded to students. Internal compulsions and international commitments are forcing the secondary education system to gear up to meet the ever-increasing demand for education. Initiatives such as the externally-aided District Primary Education Programme (DPEP), the Sarva Shiksha Abhiyan, increasing number of schools in the private sector and the drive for elimination of the gender gap in line with the Dakar Declaration on Education for All in 2000. Concerted efforts, backed by national consensus, are called for to meet these daunting challenges. The major thrust in the Tenth Plan, thus, is to meet the increased demand for secondary education.

The Government has to play a greater role to the encourage opening of new secondary schools, expansion of capacity of the existing schools including double shifts, upgrading of upper primary schools in backward, unserved and underserved areas, as also expansion and diversification of open schooling and distance education system. One of the many options being considered during the Tenth Plan is for the Kendriya Vidyalaya Sangathan to establish schools in partnership with voluntary agencies. It is proposed to set up 150 Kendriya Vidyalayas (fully funded by the Government) in addition to the present network of 854 schools. Another option is to provide a one-time grant/ seed money to societies, trusts and not-forprofit organisations like the R.K. Mission, the Jesuits, the DAV Trust, which already run reputed schools to encourage them to set up more schools.

It is proposed to establish more Navodaya Vidyalayas to cover the districts which do not have one right now and also to strengthen these existing schools by providing them facilities for cultural activities, computers and sports facilities. It is also proposed to help the Central Tibetan School Administration (CTSA), which runs about 70 schools for children of Tibetan refugees, to set up more schools.

During the Tenth Plan, the National Open School (NOS) would intensify efforts to ensure that the open school system is to the under-privileged groups. A scheme to reimburse to the NOS the fees incurred on scheduled castes/ scheduled tribe (SC/ ST) students, girls and physically challenged students is also on the anvil. The NOS will also be restructured to affiliate regular schools/ centres, which offer NOS curriculum as an alternative to the curricula of other school Boards. The nearly 1,200 study centres are proposed to be increased by around 15 per cent per year. New admissions, which are around 200,000 students a year, is likely to increase at 20 per cent per year. The NOS proposes to implement the schemes of 'On-Demand Admissions' and 'On-Demand Examinations', which give flexibility to the students to take admissions and examinations during mid-session.

The scheme of providing boarding and hostel facilities for girls, initiated in 1993, has already been revised in order to increase the enrolment of girls at the secondary level. The scheme provides for financial assistance to eligible voluntary organisations to improve the enrolment of adolescent girls belonging to the rural areas and weaker sections. In order to make secondary education more relevant in the current context, the NCERT will continue to emphasise modernisation and revision of curriculum, updating of courses and vocationalisation of education.

The Council would operationalise the fifth Regional Institute of Education for the North-Eastern Region at Shillong. The NCERT is starting the nation-wide Seventh All India Educational Survey in order to strengthen the database during the Plan period. The Central Board of Secondary Education (CBSE) and the Council for the Indian School Certificate Examination (CISCE) conduct public examinations at the end of Classes X and XII. Both are self-financing bodies, which do not receive any assistance from the government. A total of 5,850 schools are affiliated to the CBSE as on 15 April 2001 and 1,119 schools to the CISCE as on 31 August 2001. The NOS is the third national-level body conducting equivalent examination at the secondary and senior secondary level. As part of the zero-based budgeting exercise and in order to bring in greater effectiveness in the implementation of the central sector and the centrally sponsored schemes, the schemes of secondary sector have been grouped under following four broad heads.

QUALITY IMPROVEMENT IN SCHOOLS

This comprises the centrally sponsored schemes of Promotion of Sciences Laboratories, Environmental Orientation to School Education, Promotion of Yoga, as well as the central sector schemes of Population Education Project, International Mathematics/ Science Olympiad. The state governments would develop training modules for in-service training of teachers and provide infrastructure and research inputs for quality improvement in schools.

INFORMATION AND COMMUNICATION TECHNOLOGIES (ICT)

This will include the reworked centrally sponsored schemes — Computer Education and Literacy in Schools (CLASS) and Educational Technology (ET) – which seek to familiarise students with IT. Keeping in view the current demand for IT, a major thrust is to be given to this scheme. State governments would prepare Computer Education Plans (CEP) for computer literacy and education. The components of the merged scheme ICT in Schools would include:

- funding support for CEPs;
- strengthening and reorientation of the staff of the State Institutes of Education and Training (SIETs);
- Digitalisation of SIETs' video and audio cassettes in partnership with NGOs;
- web/internet-based education to be managed by the SIETs.

ACCESS AND EQUITY

This scheme will comprise, among other components yet to be designed, the ongoing scheme of Strengthening of Hostel/Boarding Facilities for Girl students.

INTEGRATED EDUCATION FOR DISABLED CHILDREN (IEDC)

In the Tenth Plan, greater efforts will be made to expand inclusive education to cater to the needs of mentally and physically challenged students. The scheme will continue as a separate centrally sponsored scheme and will be redesigned. It will now focus on the following elements: convergence with the Integrated Child Development Services (ICDS) scheme for early interventions; with the DPEP and Sarva Shiksha Abhiyan for education of the mentally and physically challenged up to the elementary level; with the special schools under the Ministry of Social Justice and Empowerment. Other components of the scheme will be inclusive pedagogy and curriculum, training of teachers and preparation of teaching learning material; research and development (R&D), advocacy and evaluation; and funding through the PTAs/VECs/ management committees of the schools.

THE PATH AHEAD

The impact of recent initiatives undertaken for the universalisation of elementary education is resulting in increased demand for expansion of secondary education. Unless steps are taken to expand the secondary education system, it would be difficult to accommodate the increasing number of upper primary pass-outs. While there has been an increase in the number of secondary schools, the spread has been uneven; there are regional disparities and variations in the socio-economic status of various states and Union Territories. The significant gender gap also has to be narrowed down. The key theme in the Tenth Plan is imparting quality education at all stages of education and the pursuit of excellence. The on-going efforts in revision of curricula at the secondary education level, so as to make it more relevant, would continue in the Tenth Plan. The convergence of centrallysponsored schemes will help in imparting science, mathematics and, computer education as well as environmental and value education in a more focused manner. There is a line of thinking which believes that subsidising students through a 'voucher system', as is the practice in some of the Latin American countries, is more effective than 'subsidising' institutions. The students will enroll themselves in reputed schools, letting the market forces weed out the inefficient and poor quality institutions.

UNIVERSALISATION OF SECONDARY EDUCATION IN INDIA – VISION

Secondary education serves as a link between the elementary and higher education, and plays a very important role in this respect. A child's future can depend a lot on the type of education she/he receives at the secondary level. Apart from grounding the roots of education of a child, secondary education can be instrumental in shaping and directing the child to a bright future. This stage of education serves to move on higher secondary stage as well as to provide generic competencies that cut across various domains of knowledge as well as skills. Providing secondary education to all, both boys and girls, with a focus on quality education assumes greater meaning today, when we consider the emerging challenges in our society.

For instance, rising levels of socioeconomic aspirations and also the democratic consciousness particularly among marginalized sections of population such as the dalits, tribals, OBCs, religious and linguistic minorities and girls seek space in the secondary education system for greater access, participation and quality. The recent significant development viz., Universal Elementary Education (UEE) being achieved through Sarva *Shiksha Abhiyan* (SSA) and also the impact of globalisation and rapid growth of new technologies have led to reassessment of India's preparedness to generate required technical manpower, develop new knowledge and skills, and remain competitive at global level. The secondary and higher secondary education system has a key role to play in enabling the nation to move towards these objectives. Given the high transition rate of about 85• from class VIII to IX and the anticipated progress in UEE, which is now widely acknowledged, that the time has arrived for taking proactive measures to plan and provide for universal access to secondary education and senior secondary education in a phased-wise manner. A sub-committee of Central Advisory Board of Education (CABE), which is the highest deliberative and advisory forum on education in the country, was, therefore, constituted in September, 2004. This Committee (2005) was assigned with a responsibility of preparing a blueprint for the universalisation of secondary education consequent upon the attainment of universalisation of elementary education. Deliberating widely on the concerns and challenges of secondary education in India, the Committee submitted its report in June, 2005. Their major recommendations are as follows:

- The guiding principles of Universal Secondary Education should be universal access, equality and social justice, relevance and development, and structural and curricular considerations. There have to be norms for schooling. Such norms should be developed for each state with common national parameters as well as state specific parameters.
- Each state should develop a perspective plan for universal secondary education. Decentralised micro-level planning should be the main approach to planning and implementation of universal secondary education.
- Financial requirements for covering the cost of universal elementary and secondary education will form approximately 5.1 percent of the GDP which is not sufficient. The immediate allocation of 6 percent of the GDP for education and progressive increase in this proportion will be necessary to move towards universalisation of secondary education.

The present vision document reiterates some of the major issues and concerns discussed in the report in the following paragraphs:

- *Guiding Principles*: For achieving the goal to provide quality education to all adolescents both girls and boys, up to the age of 16 by 2015 and senior secondary education up to the age of 18 by 2020, secondary education system needs to strengthen its preparedness for the coming plan periods allowing a paradigm shift in its conceptual design. The four guiding principles for creating the conceptual design of secondary education as visualized by this Committee are reproduced under:
- *Universal Access*: Access is to be envisaged in physical, social, cultural and economic terms – all interwoven in a common concept. This calls for a redefinition of some of the basic features of the Indian school. For instance, it is not sufficient to provide physical access to an orthopedically disabled child. It is equally critical that the disability of such a child is not seen in medical terms alone. The moment a barrier-free physical access is provided, this child's disability disappears and she/he becomes as capable as the rest of her/his peers. In this sense, the disability is a social construct and the matter does not end by solving the problem at the physical level alone but demands a change in the mindsets of her/his classmates, teachers and the curriculum planners or textbook writers. Similarly, in the case of a *dalit* child, access is as much a cultural question as it is one of a school being available in the neighbourhood. There are poignant accounts of how alienating and humiliating school experience can be for children of the deprived sections of society. This kind of alienation is equally visible in gender discrimination as it operates as a 'hidden

curriculum' all the time as an extension of patriarchy embedded in society. In these circumstances, children don't just 'drop out' voluntarily, but either they are 'pushed out' or even 'walk out' in protest. It is only when the school is able to create a new cultural ambience and a child friendly curriculum that universal access would begin to mean more than just concrete, black boards or even computers.

- *Equality and Social Justice:* These two fundamental principles as enshrined in the Constitution imply equality and social justice towards secondary education, inside secondary education and through secondary education. It is only when the school curriculum empowers the child adequately to initially understand, then question and finally deals with that inequality and injustice, the child would be in a position to continue to seek equality and social justice in her life after the school. This is not all. We must draw attention to at least six dimensions of equality and social justice for which the school system will have to strive for viz. (a) gender; (b) economic disparity; (c) social i.e. SCs/STs; (d) Cultural (including the issues of religious and linguistic diversity); (e) disability (both physical and mental), and (f) rural-urban. All these dimensions need to be reflected with sensitivity in the curriculum such that the self-esteem of each child is built up. This is necessary for ensuring that all children are able to complete their secondary education. The issue has a structural dimension too. Almost 25% of the secondary schools today are private unaided schools whose clientele comes only from the privileged sections of society. This means that the children studying in such schools are deprived of the experience of knowing children of different social classes and diverse cultural backgrounds. It is inconceivable that such schools can inculcate a sense of equality or social justice among their students or even build up an appreciation of the composite culture and plural character of India. This anomaly can be taken care of only by including the private unaided schools in a Common School System, as recommended by the Education Commission (1964-66).
- *Relevance and Development*: No education today can be accepted as being relevant unless it (a) helps in unfolding the full potential of the child; and (b) plays the role of linking the development of the child with the society and its political, productive and socio-cultural dimensions. We would like to list five domains in which the developmental role of education can be envisaged: (a) building up citizenship for a country that is striving to become a democratic, egalitarian and secular society; (b) interdisciplinary approach to knowledge, concept formation (not just piling up information) and its

application in daily life and attributes such as critical thought and creativity; (c) evolving values in a plural society that is, at the same time, stratified and hierarchical; (d) generic competencies that cut across various domains of knowledge as well as skills; and (e) skill formation in the context of rapidly changing technology which demands formation of multiple skills, transfer of learning and ability to continue to learn. A substantial proportion of parents send their children to schools with expectation that education will enable their children to face the 'world of work' with confidence and carve out a meaningful livelihood for themselves. For this purpose, it is essential that learning emerges from the child's social ethos and her productive experience, and at the same time ensures that the child will have access to global knowledge and challenges.

- *Structural and Curricular Aspects:* Curricular reforms cannot be delinked from structural reforms. There is a consensus today throughout the country with respect to the 10+2 pattern of school education, as recommended by the Education Commission (1964-66). The Education Commission had also advocated that a minimum of 10 years of common curriculum is required for building citizenship in a democracy and for linking the 'world of knowledge' with the 'world of work'. In this concept, diversified courses will be introduced only at the +2 stage. These recommendations related to curriculum could be implemented by all States/ UTs only because the Central Government enabled a nation-wide switchover to the 10+2 pattern. In contrast, the policy on vocational education of "diverting" at least 25% of the children enrolled at the + 2 stage to the vocational stream by the year 2000 has not found favour with students. According to the Ministry's Annual Reports, less than 5% of the enrolment at the + 2 stage in the year 2003 was in vocational stream. One can infer that the children refused to be "diverted" and preferred the academic stream. The issue has been recently addressed by the National Focus Group on 'Work and Education', as constituted by NCERT, as part of the exercise of reviewing and revising the curriculum framework. The above report (April 2005) recommends a two-pronged strategy with radical structural and curricular implications for the entire school education, including secondary education, viz. (a) Productive work must be introduced in the curriculum as a pedagogic medium for acquisition of knowledge, building values and skill formation from pre-primary stage to the + 2 stage; (b) A nation-vide programme of Vocational Education and Training (VET) must be built up in mission mode and be structurally and administratively placed outside the school system incorporating modular courses with lateral and vertical linkages. As long as the proposed two-pronged strategy of simultaneous structural and curricular reforms is not institutionalised, it is inconceivable that the "world of work" can be meaningfully integrated with the "world of knowledge" and vocational education can become a significant and effective programme. Hence, the four guiding principles, imply a paradigm shift necessary for moving towards the goal of universalisation of secondary education. This shift is expected to simultaneously impact at the level of access, socio-cultural character, developmental objectives and structural-cum-curricular provisions of secondary education - all at the same time and throughout the nation. For speedy change an unambiguous commitment to a policy framework is necessary for translating this vision on the ground.

SECONDARY EDUCATION: NATURE AND SCOPE

Education for the holistic development of the Adolescents

Secondary education spreads over the ages of 15 and 16, and then to 17 and 18 in the senior secondary grades. These are the years of adolescence, and late adolescence. These are the years of transition; indeed, most crucial years of life. There are steady and fast changes in the body structure transforming to adult form and image of life. At this age, the bodily changes take final shape and stabilise. This is also the stage of emotional transformation and maturity that swings between joy and trauma. Secondary education essentially has to be the education of the adolescence. Experiences in schooling have to be designed to be responsive to the needs of transition and stabilisation. Since large number of students is likely to transit from education to the world of work, it is also the stage of transition to work.

Secondary education must foster skills of transition. Though both boys and girls experience transition, there is a special case for girls and it needs special attention. Because of prejudices, taboos and social stigma, phase of transition for girls is more difficult. Also, it will be necessary to develop a gender friendly curriculum. Contemporary secondary education concentrates primarily on learning a few subjects challenging the 'cognitive intelligence', that too largely the lower order cognition.

This very approach to secondary education puts at disadvantage a large number of students because students with differential abilities and potentialities are unable to cope with the demands of the kind of education offered in secondary education; on the other hand, secondary education does not contribute and nurture children native wisdom and imagination that they bring with them to the school. For example, a child who is very good in sports is ridiculed for low scores in mathematics or geography. The future secondary education must be designed to nurture multiple abilities like linguistic or verbal ability, logical-mathematical ability, spatial ability, bodily kinesthetic or sports ability, musical ability, inter-personal ability, intra-personal ability and naturalist or environmental ability.

The primary intention of designing secondary education with a purpose of holistic development of the adolescent is to ensure that a young person with musical ability can emerge as a musician, one with bodily and kinesthetic ability is able to emerge as a sportsperson, as much as the person with linguistic ability can unfold himself or herself as an orator, a writer, etc. Equally important is nurturing the logical-mathematical ability that can produce a scholar in mathematics and science and other such scholastic subjects. In absence of education designed to facilitate holistic development, children with abilities other than scientific and mathematical abilities are treated as weak and not fit for the employment market. This not only makes them underachievers but also demolishes their self-concept and self esteem. In essence, for universalisation, secondary education must offer adequate opportunity for unfolding the full potential in each student.

UNIVERSAL SECONDARY EDUCATION

Universal implies creating universal access and opportunity for all children to receive secondary education. It is evident from the international experiences that secondary education becomes naturally universal once universal elementary education has been achieved.

The transition rate from eighth to the ninth grades in India is almost 85 per cent and this transition rate is further improving. With the universalisation of elementary education through SSA, there will be universal demand for secondary education. What is important is to make good quality education available, accessible and affordable to all young persons in the age group of 14-18 years with special reference to economically weaker sections of the society, the educationally backward, the girls and the disabled children residing in rural areas and other marginalised categories like SC, ST, OBC and Educationally Backward Minorities.

As stated earlier, the CABE committee on Universalisation of Secondary Education (2005) recommends universal secondary education by 2015; As per the report, the projection of enrolment, transition rate indicates full possibility of universal enrolment in secondary education by 2015. By 2020, the target should be universal enrolment, full retention and mastery learning in all kinds of learning tasks by more than 60% learners.

Also, by 2020, there will be provision for universal senior secondary education and universal retention. This will be possible because of high transition rate from 10th to 11th standard and high retention rate in the senior secondary grades even now.

Curricular Structure and Course Offerings

The recommendation of the Education Commission (1964-66) for a common curriculum for until class X within the 10+2+3 framework was accepted in NPE-1968 and a major programme of shift with additional outlays was undertaken throughout the country. NPE- 1986 reiterated this pattern of education as part of the National System of Education. The National Curriculum Framework (1975) proposed a common curriculum for the tenyear school, to be followed by diversification beginning at class XI for the +2 stage. This basic principle is now practiced nation-wide.

The National Curriculum Frameworks prepared successively in 1988, 2000 and 2005 have continued to follow this imperative of NPE- 1986. "However, there are views from many quarters that "the most significant reason for mass scale failure in the tenth board examination is the common curriculum and course offerings ..... nearly 80 per cent of the candidates who fail in the board examination fail in mathematics, English and science . . . besides significant wastage of the educational resources, it affects self-esteem and self-concept of the students." The solution offered by these proponents to the problem of "mass scale failure in the tenth board examination" and its adverse impact on the "self esteem" of students consisted in "diversification of students into several streams of education beyond eighth standard" and offering them a "cafeteria approach" from class IX onwards. But actually the root cause of "mass scale failure" is not the common curriculum offered until class X as per NPE-1986. Instead, the cause of the failure lies in the framework in which subject knowledge is conceived, the manner in which knowledge is transacted and the evaluation parameters and the assessment procedures adopted for examining students.

The right to study and succeed in basic mathematics, science, social science and languages, including English, and other mainstream subjects is as much a fundamental right of a child as to have access to and complete secondary/ senior secondary education." Keeping this in mind, the National Curriculum Framework – 2005 has made several radical proposals to revisit the very character of knowledge, shift to a new pedagogic approach and change the entire examination system. Such changes are urgently required in order to make sure that the nation is freed of this phenomenon of "mass scale failure" and widespread but apparent "under achievement". Without such a paradigm shift, it would not be possible to universalize secondary education either. We need to be especially concerned about the prevailing practice of not offering science or mathematics at Plus Two stage in many rural schools/ urban slums or to SCs, STs, girls or the disabled (or not providing science practical experiences at class IX-X level in backward areas), thereby forcing these children to go in for the so-called "softer" options. This practice has a significant negative impact on the aspirations of the masses for upward social mobility for their children.

Work and Education

The CABE Committee on USE expresses its deep concern with respect to the exclusionary character of education in general and secondary education in particular based upon the report (April, 2005) of the National Focus Group on Work and Education constituted by the NCERT as part of its exercise of National Curriculum Framework-2005.

This is founded on the artificially instituted dichotomy between work and knowledge. Those who work with their hands and produce significant wealth are denied access to formal education while those who have access to formal education not only denigrate productive manual work but also lack the necessary skills for the same. Accordingly, the Committee recommends the following two-fold strategy for a major curricular reform: Productive work (and other forms of work as well, including social action and engagement) may be introduced as a pedagogic medium for *knowledge acquisition, developing values and multiple-skill formation*.

Common Core Curriculum

A common core curriculum incorporating work-centered pedagogy initially until Class X and, within the foreseeable future, up to Class XII for all children, should be the objective. A set of work-related generic competencies (basic, inter-personal and systemic) may be pursued and also inform the redesigning of evaluation parameters as well as the assessment system, including the public examinations.

Generic competencies will include, among others, critical thinking, transfer of learning, creativity, communication skills, aesthetics, work motivation, work ethic of collaborative functioning and entrepreneurship-cum-social accountability. This will provide a firm foundation for building up a programme of '*Vocationalised* Education' (to be distinguished from '*Vocational* Education') at the secondary/ senior secondary stages. Vocational Education and Training (VET) may be conceived as a *major national programme in the mission mode* and be structurally and administratively placed *outside* the school system. VET in this new perspective will be built upon the *bedrock of 10-12 years of work-centered education in the school system*, unlike the prevailing notion of vocational education 'hanging' in vacuum. VET will include:

- flexible and modular certificate/ diploma courses of varying durations;
- multiple entry and exit points with in-built credit accumulation facility;
- vertical and horizontal linkages with the academic, vocational and technical programmes;
- accessibility all the way from the level of village clusters to the Block and District levels, and also in urban areas;
- provision for carving out 'work benches' in the neighbourhood out of the existing economic activities, production and technical centers;

- scope for engaging local farmers, artisans, mechanics, technicians, musicians, artists and other service providers as Resource Persons or invited faculty; and
- a decentralised accreditation and equivalence programme which will also recognise 'work benches' for the purpose of evaluating and certifying students."

The Committee wishes to emphasise that the above proposal to institutionalise work-centered pedagogy in the school curriculum and building Vocational Education and Training as a programme of national significance for the adolescents and youth can be translated on the ground only if the necessary systemic changes are made. Let us not hesitate in fulfilling this historical expectation.

Common School System

The Education Commission (1964-66) had recommended a Common School System of Public Education (CSS) as the basis of building up the National System of Education with a view to "bring the different social classes and groups together and thus promote the emergence of an egalitarian and integrated society." The Commission warned that "instead of doing so, education itself is tending to increase social segregation and to perpetuate and widen class distinctions." It further noted that "this is bad not only for the children of the poor but also for the children of the rich and the privileged groups" since "by segregating their children, such privileged parents prevent them from sharing the life and experiences of the children of the poor and coming into contact with the realities of life. . . . . . also render the education of their own children *anaemic and incomplete*. (emphasis ours)" The Commission contended that "if these evils are to be eliminated and the education system is to become a powerful instrument of national development in general, and social and national integration in particular, we must move towards the goal of a common school system of public education."

The 1986 policy, while advocating a National System of Education, resolved that "effective measures will be taken in the direction of the Common School System recommended in the 1968 policy." Taking into consideration these policy imperatives and the contemporary emphasis on decetralisation along with the necessary flexibility in the school system to be able to respond to the contextual curricular demands, the concept of the Common School System (CSS) has itself been evolving. Based upon the evolving public discourse on CSS, the following definition of CSS can be constructed: Common school system essentially means a national system of education which is based on the values and principles of the Constitution of India which provides education as a comparable quality to all children irrespective of their caste, creed, language, economic or cultural background, geographic location or gender. This is the perspective articulated by the National Policy on Education- 1986 and further elaborated by the National Curriculum Framework-2005. Such a national system of education will be governed by certain minimum infrastructural, financial and curricular norms.

For instance, in the context of the recruitment and working conditions of teachers, provision for basic resources, and structural flexibility and academic autonomy necessary for innovation are concerned with the spirit of National Policy on Education and the National Curriculum Framework 2005. As per the report of the CABE committee on USE the guiding principles and basic characteristics of a successful programme of Universalisation of Secondary Education are fully consistent with the Common School System as defined above.

The CABE committee report clearly mentions that the kind of paradigm shift discussed here can become sustainable only when it is implemented in all categories of schools, including the privately managed unaided schools, in the whole of the country within a declared timeframe, though a properly phased programme. This essential linkage between curricular reforms and systemic reforms must be understood, before it is too late. And such reforms would be feasible only within the framework of a Common School System.

Three-Language Formula

The three-language formula evolved out of a major political exercise and negotiations in the critical decade of 1950s and the early years of 1960s in response to the rising tensions with respect to different language regions of the country and the question of related cultural identities. In essence, this outcome reflected the federal spirit of our Constitution and the commitment to sustain and promote India's plural character. It is in this background that the 1986 policy made a commitment to implement the three-language formula "more energetically and purposefully. NCF-2005 also reiterates this position and proposes to make a renewed bid to fulfil the commitment.

While, as part of this formula, a crucial responsibility befalls upon the elementary stage of education to promote the mother tongue as a medium of education, it is the secondary/senior secondary stage of education that becomes the real testing ground of the more challenging aspects of the formula. The 1986 policy also acknowledged the "uneven" implementation of the formula. The Hindi-speaking states, with their substantial demographic spread, have a special responsibility in responding to this challenge, especially with respect to the concept of the third language as a modern Indian language from a non-Hindi speaking region. Concrete steps in this direction will provide a new thrust for the non-Hindi speaking states to make a fresh commitment to implement the language policy in letter and spirit. It is here that the political commitment made by the nation's leadership soon after independence to strengthen India's unity and integrity, promote intercultural dialogue and build an enlightened and articulate citizenship, will be redeemed. In this context, the Committee would like to urge upon the Central Government to take the initiative of setting up an effective and adequately funded structure and process for promoting inter-language translation of the highest quality material available in different languages of India. An active role of the States/UTs will be critical to the success of this central initiative. This process must also cover the word class material available globally in the languages of different countries and make it available widely in all major Indian languages. India's capacity in the field of IT should prove to be of special asset in this respect, provided urgent political will addresses this issue. It would be only appropriate if this inter-language endeavor would include Braille and computer-aided facilities for making quality material available to the disabled children also. Apart from enriching communication and understanding among different language regions of the country, the availability of such material in Indian languages will go a long way in enriching the quality of education not just at the secondary/ senior secondary education level but at the higher education level as well.

Teaching –Learning Processes

Curricular structure and course offerings are the necessary condition for quality secondary education. Instructional processes provide the sufficient condition for quality secondary education. Contemporary pedagogical practices are characterised largely by lectures where students are passive listeners. Such kind of processes contribute at best to lower order cognition, memorization and fragile learning; together, they make a grand nexus for large-scale failing in examination. Students lack problem-solving ability, higher order thinking and cognition, and creativity. Most importantly, they miss out on 'learning to know' or learning to learn. If the new generation secondary education sets its targets for students to be able to think critically, solve problems individually and collectively, be creative, teaching-learning must undergo a paradigm shift. Pedagogy must bring students at the centre of stage where they primarily learn to learn through peer interaction, problemsolving, experiential learning, etc. In this new learning scenario, teachers will be facilitators of learning. Research as a tool for learning is quite common all over the world; introduced even at the pre-primary stage. Indeed, by the time students are in the 9th and 10th standards they should become researchers to be able to crack problems, contemplate solutions, explore and experiments alternative and creative ways of problem-solving.

Student Assessment and Evaluation

Secondary education is the turning point for a large majority of students. Not only the certificate one earns after schooling but also the actual learning during schooling is the lifelong resource. Along with building dynamism in curricular framework as well as pedagogy, evaluation must undergo major changes. Conventionally, education system, particularly school education is guided and controlled by concern for results in examination irrespective of the quality of learning —whether fragile or sustainable. The competition, though artificial, for securing percentage of marks in the final examination creates unusual stress in the students leading often to mental break down and suicides. This must change.

Change in the mechanics of examination will be too simplistic a solution, amounting to treating the symptoms, not the disease itself. Examination-stress is directly related to facing the challenge of examination with 'fragile' learning due to memorizing huge stock of information. In order to manage the stress factor in examination it will be necessary to ensure sustainable learning which the function of instructional processes is. Yet, it will be necessary to reconstruct and redesign examination system with attributes like flexibility where a student can achieve mastery learning in a flexible time frame and accumulate credits; eliminating power tests (fixed duration), adopt continuous and comprehensive evaluation. The practice of mark sheets indicating marks in certain subjects must be replaced by a portfolio that would accommodate a student's performance in a variety of domains like life skills, academic/nonacademic and vocational subjects, personal qualities, etc. The portfolio should be comprehensive, revealing of the total being of the student. This aspect is discussed in chapter 5 in detail.

Guidance and Counselling

In this context, it is extremely important to recongnise the role that guidance and counselling play for meeting the needs of adolescent students going through the secondary and higher secondary stages of education. Provision for guidance and counseling is necessary in view of the fact that adolescent boys and girls are facing a fast process of socio-economic and cultural change, and quite often the traditional institutional frameworks provided by the family and community are not adequate for helping the adolescent to cope with the demands made upon him/her. In a society going through a rapid process of institutional change and modernization, facilities for guidance and counseling in every secondary school are necessary. Even as the secondary education system expands towards universalisation, staff for guidance and counseling will be required to ensure that first generation school goers receive adequate coverage in terms of their psychological and personality related needs. Financial allocation necessary for making guidance and counseling a common reality of every secondary school will need to be worked out, and institutional infrastructure necessary for making professional input for such a facility will have to be put in place.

Schooling Facility

There is a lot of disparity in schooling facilities in various regions of the country. There are disparities among the private schools, among private and government schools in the same state, between schools in central sector like Kendriya Vidyalayas(KVS), Navodaya Vidyalayas(NVS), Tibetan Schools, Sainik Schools, etc. Also, there are no specific norms for secondary schools. In view of providing universal quality secondary education, it is imperative that specially designed norms are developed at the national level and then disaggregated for each State/UT keeping in mind the geographical, sociocultural, linguistic and demographic conditions of not just the State/UT but also, wherever necessary, of the Blocks. Also, the disparities among various categories of schools must be reduced. This will require planning of educational facilities, and management of educational services to be streamlined.

RASHTRIYA MADHYAMIK SHIKSHA ABHIYAAN

As a follow-up of the recommendations of the CABE Committee report, the MHRD has launched a scheme for universalisation of access to and improvement of quality at secondary stage in the year 2009 and has brought out a "Framework of implementation of *Rashtriya Madhyamik Shiksha Abhiyaan*". The framework provides a detailed road map for the implementation of access and equity related components of USE and also deliberates upon quality components providing norms largely for infrastructure requirements. Hence, a need was observed by various stakeholders for a document, which provides a vision and multi-layer strategic guidelines on quality improvement of secondary education. The present document on "Vision and Multi-layer Strategic Guidelines for Quality Improvement in secondary education" begins with vision as already set by the CABE report and the RMSA framework and moves ahead to address the quality issues with suggested strategies and action plans.

SECONDARY EDUCATION IN INDIA – VISION

Since Free and Compulsory Elementary Education has become a Constitutional Right of Children in India, it is absolutely essential to push this vision forward to move towards Universalisation of Secondary Education, which has already been achieved in a large number of developed and several developing countries. In this context, the vision for secondary education as follows:

- The vision for secondary education is to make good quality education available, accessible and affordable to all young persons in the age group of 14-18 years.

This vision statement points out towards three A's i.e. Availability, Accessibility and Affordability of secondary education to the target group under the overarching objective of providing quality. India is emerging as the fastest-growing economy in the world. The success depends largely upon human resource development. If we look at the Indian higher education as provider of leadership-manpower in various sectors of economy, we need to tune our secondary education to emerge as the single largest provider of working people in all spheres of national productivity.

Universalisation of secondary education will need to fulfill three major criteria, namely, universal enrolment in the 9th and 10th grades, universal retention achieving zero dropout rate, and universal performance (at a predetermined level, at least 60 per cent of the students of the 10th grade will achieve 60 per cent learning over subjects and other learning tasks) with successful completion by all who are enrolled in the secondary education. Initial questions that need to be resolved are: achieving universal access, equity and social justice.

Whereas universal access may be possible to achieve through expansion of schooling facilities in the formal and unconventional modes, special efforts will be required for achieving equity, social justice and performance of all the diverse groups of learners. Although success in SSA will substantially facilitate the process yet it will take at least another 10 years of committed efforts, in a mission mode approach; universal secondary education should be targeted to be achieved by 2020 and the success in accomplishing this goal will be determined by the synergy among various stakeholders for planning, implementation and execution, political will and support.

VOCATIONALIZATION OF SECONDARY EDUCATION

THE MEANING OF VOCATION

At the present time the conflict of philosophic theories focuses in discussion of the proper place and function of vocational factors in education. The bald statement that significant differences in fundamental philosophical conceptions find their chief issue in connection with this point may arouse incredulity: there seems to be too great a gap between the remote and general terms in which philosophic ideas are formulated and the practical and concrete details of vocational education.

But a mental review of the intellectual presuppositions underlying the oppositions in education of labor and leisure, theory and practice, body and mind, mental states and the world, will show that they culminate in the antithesis of vocational and cultural education. Traditionally, liberal culture has been linked to the notions of leisure, purely contemplative knowledge and a spiritual activity not involving the active use of bodily organs. Culture has also tended, latterly, to be associated with a purely private refinement, a cultivation of certain states and attitudes of consciousness, separate from either social direction or service. It has been an escape from the former, and a solace for the necessity of the latter. So deeply entangled are these philosophic dualisms with the whole subject of vocational education, that it is necessary to define the meaning of vocation with some fullness in order to avoid the impression that an education which centers about it is narrowly practical, if not merely pecuniary. A vocation means nothing but such a direction of life activities as renders them perceptibly significant to a person, because of the consequences they accomplish, and also useful to his associates.

The opposite of a career is neither leisure nor culture, but aimlessness, capriciousness, the absence of cumulative achievement in experience, on the personal side, and idle display, parasitic dependence upon the others, on the social side. Occupation is a concrete term for continuity. It includes the development of artistic capacity of any kind, of special scientific ability, of effective citizenship, as well as professional and business occupations, to say nothing of mechanical labor or engagement in gainful pursuits. We must avoid not only limitation of conception of vocation to the occupations where immediately tangible commodities are produced, but also the notion that vocations are distributed in an exclusive way, one and only one to each person. Such restricted specialism is impossible; nothing could be more absurd than to try to educate individuals with an eye to only one line of activity. In the first place, each individual has of necessity a variety of callings, in each of which he should be intelligently effective; and in the second place any one occupation loses its meaning and becomes a routine keeping busy at something in the degree in which it is isolated from other interests.

No one is just an artist and nothing else, and in so far as one approximates that condition, he is so much the less developed human being; he is a kind of monstrosity. He must, at some period of his life, be a member of a family; he must have friends and companions; he must either support himself or be supported by others, and thus he has a business career. He is a member of some organized political unit, and so on.

We naturally name his vocation from that one of the callings which distinguishes him, rather than from those which he has in common with all others. But we should not allow ourselves to be so subject to words as to ignore and virtually deny his other callings when it comes to a consideration of the vocational phases of education. As a man's vocation as artist is but the emphatically specialized phase of his diverse and variegated vocational activities, so his efficiency in it, in the humane sense of efficiency, is determined by its association with other callings. A person must have experience, he must live, if his artistry is to be more than a technical accomplishment. He cannot find the subject matter of his artistic activity within his art; this must be an expression of what he suffers and enjoys in other relationships — a thing which depends in turn upon the alertness and sympathy of his interests. What is true of an artist is true of any other special calling. There is doubtless—in general accord with the principle of habit — a tendency for every distinctive vocation to become too dominant, too exclusive and absorbing in its specialized aspect. This means emphasis upon skill or technical method at the expense of meaning. Hence it is not the business of education to foster this tendency, but rather to safeguard against it, so that the scientific inquirer shall not be merely the scientist, the teacher merely the pedagogue, the clergyman merely one who wears the cloth, and so on.

THE PLACE OF VOCATIONAL AIMS IN EDUCATION

Bearing in mind the varied and connected content of the vocation, and the broad background upon which a particular calling is projected, we shall now consider education for the more distinctive activity of an individual. An occupation is the only thing which balances the distinctive capacity of an individual with his social service. To find out what one is fitted to do and to secure an opportunity to do it is the key to happiness. Nothing is more tragic than failure to discover one's true business in life, or to find that one has drifted or been forced by circumstance into an uncongenial calling. A right occupation means simply that the aptitudes of a person are in adequate play, working with the minimum of friction and the maximum of satisfaction.

With reference to other members of a community, this adequacy of action signifies, of course, that they are getting the best service the person can render. It is generally believed, for example, that slave labor was ultimately wasteful even from the purely economic point of view — that there was not sufficient stimulus to direct the energies of slaves, and that there was consequent wastage. Moreover, since slaves were confined to certain prescribed callings, much talent must have remained unavailable to the community, and hence there was a dead loss. Slavery only illustrates on an obvious scale what happens in some degree whenever an individual does not find himself in his work.

And he cannot completely find himself when vocations are looked upon with contempt, and a conventional ideal of a culture which is essentially the same for all is maintained. Plato laid down the fundamental principle of a philosophy of education when he asserted that it was the business of education to discover what each person is good for, and to train him to mastery of that mode of excellence, because such development would also secure the fulfillment of social needs in the most harmonious way.

His error was not in qualitative principle, but in his limited conception of the scope of vocations socially needed; a limitation of vision which reacted to obscure his perception of the infinite variety of capacities found in different individuals. An occupation is a continuous activity having a purpose. Education through occupations consequently combines within itself more of the factors conducive to learning than any other method. It calls instincts and habits into play; it is a foe to passive receptivity. It has an end in view; results are to be accomplished. Hence it appeals to thought; it demands that an idea of an end be steadily maintained, so that activity cannot be either routine or capricious. Since the movement of activity must be progressive, leading from one stage to another, observation and ingenuity are required at each stage to overcome obstacles and to discover and readapt means of execution. In short, an occupation, pursued under conditions where the realization of the activity rather than merely the external product is the aim, fulfills the requirements which were laid down earlier in connection with the discussion of aims, interest, and thinking.

A calling is also of necessity an organizing principle for information and ideas; for knowledge and intellectual growth. It provides an axis which runs through an immense diversity of detail; it causes different experiences, facts, items of information to fall into order with one another. The lawyer, the physician, the laboratory investigator in some branch of chemistry, the parent, the citizen interested in his own locality, has a constant working stimulus to note and relate whatever has to do with his concern. He unconsciously, from the motivation of his occupation, reaches out for all relevant information, and holds to it.

The vocation acts as both magnet to attract and as glue to hold. Such organization of knowledge is vital, because it has reference to needs; it is so expressed and readjusted in action that it never becomes stagnant. No classification, no selection and arrangement of facts, which is consciously worked out for purely abstract ends, can ever compare in solidity or effectiveness with that knit under the stress of an occupation; in comparison the former sort is formal, superficial, and cold. The only adequate training for occupations is training through occupations.

The principle stated early in this book that the educative process is its own end, and that the only sufficient preparation for later responsibilities comes by making the most of immediately present life, applies in full force to the vocational phases of education.

The dominant vocation of all human beings at all times is living — intellectual and moral growth. In childhood and youth, with their relative freedom from economic stress, this fact is naked and unconcealed. To predetermine some future occupation for which education is to be a strict preparation is to injure the possibilities of present development and thereby to reduce the adequacy of preparation for a future right employment. To repeat the principle we have had occasion to appeal to so often, such training may develop a machine-like skill in routine lines but it will be at the expense of those qualities of alert observation and coherent and ingenious planning which make an occupation intellectually rewarding. In an autocratically managed society, it is often a conscious object to prevent the development of freedom and responsibility, a few do the planning and ordering, the others follow directions and are deliberately confined to narrow and prescribed channels of endeavor. However much such a scheme may inure to the prestige and profit of a class, it is evident that it limits the development of the subject class; hardens and confines the opportunities for learning through experience of the master class, and in both ways hampers the life of the society as a whole. The only alternative is that all the earlier preparation for vocations be indirect rather than direct; namely, through engaging in those active occupations which are indicated by the needs and interests of the pupil at the time. Only in this way can there be on the part of the educator and of the one educated a genuine discovery of personal aptitudes so that the proper choice of a specialized pursuit in later life may be indicated. Moreover, the discovery of capacity and aptitude will be a constant process as long as growth continues. It is a conventional and arbitrary view which assumes that discovery of the work to be chosen for adult life is made once for all at some particular date.

One has discovered in himself, say, an interest, intellectual and social, in the things which have to do with engineering and has decided to make that his calling. At most, this only blocks out in outline the field in which further growth is to be directed. It is a sort of rough sketch for use in direction of further activities. It is the discovery of a profession in the sense in which Columbus discovered America when he touched its shores.

Future explorations of an indefinitely more detailed and extensive sort remain to be made. When educators conceive vocational guidance as something which leads up to a definitive, irretrievable, and complete choice, both education and the chosen vocation are likely to be rigid, hampering further growth. In so far, the calling chosen will be such as to leave the person concerned in a permanently subordinate position, executing the intelligence of others who have a calling which permits more flexible play and readjustment. And while ordinary usages of language may not justify terming a flexible attitude of readjustment a choice of a new and further calling, it is such in effect. If even adults have to be on the lookout to see that their calling does not shut down on them and fossilize them, educators must certainly be careful that the vocational preparation of youth is such as to engage them in a continuous reorganization of aims and methods.

PRESENT OPPORTUNITIES AND DANGERS

In the past, education has been much more vocational in fact than in name:

- The education of the masses was distinctly utilitarian. It was called apprenticeship rather than education, or else just learning from experience. The schools devoted themselves to the three R's in the degree in which ability to go through the forms of reading, writing, and figuring were common elements in all kinds of labor. Taking part in some special line of work, under the direction of others, was the out-of-school phase of this education. The two supplemented each other; the school work in its narrow and formal character was as much a part of apprenticeship to a calling as that explicitly so termed.

- To a considerable extent, the education of the dominant classes was essentially vocational — it only happened that their pursuits of ruling and of enjoying were not called professions. For only those things were named vocations or employments which involved manual labor, laboring for a reward in keep, or its commuted money equivalent, or the rendering of personal services to specific persons. For a long time, for example, the profession of the surgeon and physician ranked almost with that of the valet or barber — partly because it had so much to do with the body, and partly because it involved rendering direct service for pay to some definite person. But if we go behind words, the business of directing social concerns, whether politically or economically, whether in war or peace, is as much a calling as anything else; and where education has not been completely under the thumb of tradition, higher schools in the past have been upon the whole calculated to give preparation for this business. Moreover, display, the adornment of person, the kind of social companionship and entertainment which give prestige, and the spending of money, have been made into definite callings. Unconsciously to themselves the higher institutions of learning have been made to contribute to preparation for these employments. Even at present, what is called higher education is for a certain class mainly preparation for engaging effectively in these pursuits. In other respects, it is largely, especially in the most advanced work, training for the calling of teaching and special research. By a peculiar superstition, education which has to do chiefly with preparation for the pursuit of conspicuous idleness, for teaching, and for literary callings, and for leadership, has been regarded as non-vocational and even as peculiarly cultural. The literary training which indirectly fits for authorship, whether of books, newspaper editorials, or magazine articles, is especially subject to this superstition: many a teacher and author writes and argues in behalf of a cultural and humane education against the encroachments of a specialized practical education, without recognizing that his own education, which he calls liberal, has been mainly training for his own particular calling. He has simply got into the habit of regarding his own business as essentially cultural and of overlooking the cultural possibilities of other employments. At the bottom of these distinctions is undoubtedly the tradition which recognizes as employment only those pursuits where one is responsible for his work to a specific employer, rather than to the ultimate employer, the community.

There are, however, obvious causes for the present conscious emphasis upon vocational education — for the disposition to make explicit and deliberate vocational implications previously tacit. In the first place, there is an increased esteem, in democratic communities, of whatever has to do with manual labor, commercial occupations, and the rendering of tangible services to society. In theory, men and women are now expected to do something in return for their support — intellectual and economic — by society. Labor is extolled; service is a much-lauded moral ideal. While there is still much admiration and envy of those who can pursue lives of idle conspicuous display, better moral sentiment condemns such lives. Social responsibility for the use of time and personal capacity is more generally recognized than it used to be.

- In the second place, those vocations which are specifically industrial have gained tremendously in importance in the last century and a half. Manufacturing and commerce are no longer domestic and local, and consequently more or less incidental, but are world-wide. They engage the best energies of an increasingly large number of persons. The manufacturer, banker, and captain of industry have practically displaced a hereditary landed gentry as the immediate directors of social affairs. The problem of social readjustment is openly industrial, having to do with the relations of capital and labor. The great increase in the social importance of conspicuous industrial processes has inevitably brought to the front questions having to do with the relationship of schooling to industrial life. No such vast social readjustment could occur without offering a challenge to an education inherited from different social conditions, and without putting up to education new problems.
- In the third place, there is the fact already repeatedly mentioned: Industry has ceased to be essentially an empirical, rule-of-thumb procedure, handed down by custom. Its technique is now technological: that is to say, based upon machinery resulting from discoveries in mathematics, physics, chemistry, bacteriology, etc. The economic revolution has stimulated science by setting problems for solution, by producing greater intellectual respect for mechanical appliances. And industry received back payment from science with compound interest. As a consequence, industrial occupations have infinitely greater intellectual content and infinitely larger cultural possibilities than they used to possess. The demand for such education as will acquaint workers with the scientific and social bases and bearings of their pursuits becomes imperative, since those who are without it inevitably sink to the role of appendages to the machines

they operate. Under the old regime all workers in a craft were approximately equals in their knowledge and outlook. Personal knowledge and ingenuity were developed within at least a narrow range, because work was done with tools under the direct command of the worker. Now the operator has to adjust himself to his machine, instead of his tool to his own purposes. While the intellectual possibilities of industry have multiplied, industrial conditions tend to make industry, for great masses, less of an educative resource than it was in the days of hand production for local markets. The burden of realizing the intellectual possibilities inhering in work is thus thrown back on the school.

- In the fourth place, the pursuit of knowledge has become, in science, more experimental, less dependent upon literary tradition, and less associated with dialectical methods of reasoning, and with symbols. As a result, the subject matter of industrial occupation presents not only more of the content of science than it used to, but greater opportunity for familiarity with the method by which knowledge is made. The ordinary worker in the factory is of course under too immediate economic pressure to have a chance to produce a knowledge like that of the worker in the laboratory. But in schools, association with machines and industrial processes may be had under conditions where the chief conscious concern of the students is insight. The separation of shop and laboratory, where these conditions are fulfilled, is largely conventional, the laboratory having the advantage of permitting the following up of any intellectual interest a problem may suggest; the shop the advantage of emphasizing the social bearings of the scientific principle, as well as, with many pupils, of stimulating a livelier interest.
- Finally, the advances which have been made in the psychology of learning in general and of childhood in particular fall into line with the increased importance of industry in life. For modern psychology emphasizes the radical importance of primitive unlearned instincts of exploring, experimentation, and "trying on." It reveals that learning is not the work of something ready-made called mind, but that mind itself is an organization of original capacities into activities having significance. As we have already seen in older pupils work is to educative development of raw native activities what play is for younger pupils. Moreover, the passage from play to work should be gradual, not involving a radical change of attitude but carrying into work the elements of play, plus continuous reorganization in behalf of greater control. The reader will remark that these five points practically resume the main contentions of the previous part of the

work. Both practically and philosophically, the key to the present educational situation lies in a gradual reconstruction of school materials and methods so as to utilize various forms of occupation typifying social callings, and to bring out their intellectual and moral content. This reconstruction must relegate purely literary methods — including textbooks—and dialectical methods to the position of necessary auxiliary tools in the intelligent development of consecutive and cumulative activities.

But our discussion has emphasized the fact that this educational reorganization cannot be accomplished by merely trying to give a technical preparation for industries and professions as they now operate, much less by merely reproducing existing industrial conditions in the school. The problem is not that of making the schools an adjunct to manufacture and commerce, but of utilizing the factors of industry to make school life more active, more full of immediate meaning, more connected with out-of-school experience. The problem is not easy of solution. There is a standing danger that education will perpetuate the older traditions for a select few, and effect its adjustment to the newer economic conditions more or less on the basis of acquiescence in the untransformed, unrationalized, and unsocialized phases of our defective industrial regime.

Put in concrete terms, there is danger that vocational education will be interpreted in theory and practice as trade education: as a means of securing technical efficiency in specialized future pursuits. Education would then become an instrument of perpetuating unchanged the existing industrial order of society, instead of operating as a means of its transformation. The desired transformation is not difficult to define in a formal way. It signifies a society in which every person shall be occupied in something which makes the lives of others better worth living, and which accordingly makes the ties which bind persons together more perceptible — which breaks down the barriers of distance between them. It denotes a state of affairs in which the interest of each in his work is uncoerced and intelligent: based upon its congeniality to his own aptitudes. It goes without saying that we are far from such a social state; in a literal and quantitative sense, we may never arrive at it. But in principle, the quality of social changes already accomplished lies in this direction. There are more ample resources for its achievement now than ever there have been before. No insuperable obstacles, given the intelligent will for its realization, stand in the way. Success or failure in its realization depends more upon the adoption of educational methods calculated to effect the change than upon anything else. For the change is essentially a change in the quality of mental disposition — an educative change. This does not mean that we can change character and mind by direct instruction and exhortation, apart from a change in industrial and political conditions. Such a conception contradicts our basic idea that character and mind are attitudes of participative response in social affairs. But it does mean that we may produce in schools a projection in type of the society we should like to realize, and by forming minds in accord with it gradually modify the larger and more recalcitrant features of adult society. Sentimentally, it may seem harsh to say that the greatest evil of the present regime is not found in poverty and in the suffering which it entails, but in the fact that so many persons have callings which make no appeal to them, which are pursued simply for the money reward that accrues. For such callings constantly provoke one to aversion, ill will, and a desire to slight and evade. Neither men's hearts nor their minds are in their work. On the other hand, those who are not only much better off in worldly goods, but who are in excessive, if not monopolistic, control of the activities of the many are shut off from equality and generality of social intercourse.

They are stimulated to pursuits of indulgence and display; they try to make up for the distance which separates them from others by the impression of force and superior possession and enjoyment which they can make upon others. It would be quite possible for a narrowly conceived scheme of vocational education to perpetuate this division in a hardened form. Taking its stand upon a dogma of social predestination, it would assume that some are to continue to be wage earners under economic conditions like the present, and would aim simply to give them what is termed a trade education — that is, greater technical efficiency. Technical proficiency is often sadly lacking, and is surely desirable on all accounts — not merely for the sake of the production of better goods at less cost, but for the greater happiness found in work. For no one cares for what one cannot half do.

But there is a great difference between a proficiency limited to immediate work, and a competency extended to insight into its social bearings; between efficiency in carrying out the plans of others and in one forming one's own. At present, intellectual and emotional limitation characterizes both the employing and the employed class. While the latter often have no concern with their occupation beyond the money return it brings, the former's outlook may be confined to profit and power. The latter interest generally involves much greater intellectual initiation and larger survey of conditions. For it involves the direction and combination of a large number of diverse factors, while the interest in wages is restricted to certain direct muscular movements. But none the less there is a limitation of intelligence to technical and non- humane, non-liberal channels, so far as the work does not take in its social bearings. And when the animating motive is desire for private profit or personal power, this limitation is inevitable. In fact, the advantage in immediate social sympathy and humane disposition often lies with the economically unfortunate, who have not experienced the hardening effects of a one-sided control of the affairs of others. Any scheme for vocational education which takes its point of departure from the industrial regime that now exists, is likely to assume and to perpetuate its divisions and weaknesses, and thus to become an instrument in accomplishing the feudal dogma of social predestination. Those who are in a position to make their wishes good, will demand a liberal, a cultural occupation, and one which fits for directive power the youth in whom they are directly interested. To split the system, and give to others, less fortunately situated, an education conceived mainly as specific trade preparation, is to treat the schools as an agency for transferring the older division of labor and leisure, culture and service, mind and body, directed and directive class, into a society nominally democratic. Such a vocational education inevitably discounts the scientific and historic human connections of the materials and processes dealt with. To include such things in narrow trade education would be to waste time; concern for them would not be "practical." They are reserved for those who have leisure at command—the leisure due to superior economic resources. Such things might even be dangerous to the interests of the controlling class, arousing discontent or ambitions "beyond the station" of those working under the direction of others. But an education which acknowledges the full intellectual and social meaning of a vocation would include instruction in the historic background of present conditions; training in science to give intelligence and initiative in dealing with material and agencies of production; and study of economics, civics, and politics, to bring the future worker into touch with the problems of the day and the various methods proposed for its improvement. Above all, it would train power of readaptation to changing conditions so that future workers would not become blindly subject to a fate imposed upon them. This ideal has to contend not only with the inertia of existing educational traditions, but also with the opposition of those who are entrenched in command of the industrial machinery, and who realize that such an educational system if made general would threaten their ability to use others for their own ends. But this very fact is the presage of a more equitable and enlightened social order, for it gives evidence of the dependence of social reorganization upon educational reconstruction. It is accordingly an encouragement to those believing in a better order to undertake the promotion of a vocational education which does not subject youth to the demands and standards of the present system, but which utilizes its scientific and social factors to develop a courageous intelligence, and to make intelligence practical and executive.

6

Audio-visual Aids in Home Science

By audio-visual aids, we usually mean the most modern or the most recently used of these methods. This is a summary identification of very old methods and very modern instruments, and one should react against it. Visual aids are far older. They correspond to a profound tendency among the immense majority of men: to materialize their thoughts in the form of graphic or sonorous images or to give their thoughts a concrete frame of reference. Plato himself took care to set the scenery of his dialogues, and he used concrete words and concrete comparisons as foundations for his most abstract ideas. In France, the *Très riches heures du duc de Berry* bring out the importance which 'illustration' can take in a work which would have otherwise sunk into oblivion. Xylographic images preceded the printing press by three-quarters of a century and the first illustrated book by nearly a century.

The tremendous success of the 'images of Epinal' in books peddled from door to door in France was only a manifestation of popular taste in a society where illiterates continued to be in a majority and where images went with oral literature. Films, radio and television, considered as educational instruments, have merely developed – at a rapid rate – alongside older means whose importance remains considerable. Their common denominator lies in their function as aids.

This is not a theoretical conclusion, for it is confirmed by the very attitude of the educator. The educator basically must contribute to the training of the individual with a view to his integration into a given society and teach new ideas, facts and techniques to a specific public. It is thus relatively easy to define the goals at which the educator aims.

Achieving these goals is another task which brings him face to face every day with the basic problem of pedagogy – that of transmitting or communicating ideas or information. To solve this problem, the educator resorts to infinitely varied means, among them audiovisual aids. If our purpose, therefore, is to aid the educator, we must then offer him as complete an arsenal as possible of these means. But it is the educator and the educator alone who chooses the means which is best adapted to his subject, his audience and his circumstances.

It is thus clear that audio-visual aids cannot be separated from educational materials in general.

This tendency toward the use of concrete examples has developed through a complex process. At first, graphic representation was probably only a way to enable man to capture fleeting thoughts and the sole way of transmitting thoughts, compared to oral transmission which was subject to rapid distortion. The invention of writing, a perfect example of a visual aid at its origin, proceeded from the same necessity. It would be interesting to study, for example, in the light of Mayan writing – of the Codex Troano – how man progressed from the talking image to the letter. We can therefore conclude that 'illustrations' were looked upon at first, at least by the most educated persons, as a minor complement to thought.

The entire history of publishing until the end of the eighteenth century confirms this. But, in the twentieth century, powerful means of reproduction, associated with radio, cinema and television, have changed the aspect of the problem. Sound and visual 'illustrations' are no longer mere minor complements to thought but they directly influence the thoughts and the very conduct of millions of individuals. It was therefore inevitable that a desire should spring up to master such a powerful instrument, to discipline it for better or for worse. But this coveted mastery is still rather crude: it is often reduced to the creating of a few conditioned reflexes, satisfying the merchant but not the educator. Certain of these audio-visual aids are both means of education and media for information and propaganda, and it is not always easy to draw the line between what belongs to the educator and what is within the province of information or propaganda. It is also probable that the child is more affected by the violence of street posters and by the shock techniques of radio and television at home than by the visual aids used in school. Should we conclude then that these means are harmful and should we condemn them? This negative attitude would be most unrealistic.

The only possible conclusion is to accept the need for basic research in these fields. It should bear essentially upon psychology and upon the home science. We educators have already ventured forth, but timidly, onto this terrain. Systematic establishment of contacts with research workers and specialized institutes is the duty of all those who are responsible at the national level for audio-visual services.

It can be reasonably hoped that this basic research will lead to a better use of audio-visual aids and to more scientific pedagogy based upon them. It is not difficult to observe that their use is continuing and developing outside the pale of any research. As a result, a pragmatic pedagogy is taking shape and not necessarily in contradiction to the results of the most scholarly research. Establishing or stimulating closer collaboration between research workers and educators, stimulating the writing of theses or documents containing the fruits of the work of both, and publishing and distributing the results of this work should also be the common task of pedagogical and audio-visual services.

Until now, the problem of the use of audio-visual aids has been examined from an intellectual angle. It also includes important practical and technical aspects. To tell the truth, techniques cannot and should not be separated from pedagogy. We have seen that audio-visual aids cannot be separated from educational materials as a whole, this conclusion being thrust upon us by the attitude of the user when confronted by these materials. Now this same user – whether a teacher, a professor or an adult educator – does not act any differently when pedagogy and techniques are involved. He can never be purely a pedagogue or purely a technician. It is clear, therefore, that the pedagogy of audio-visual aids cannot be separated arbitrarily from audio-visual techniques. No one can hope to achieve good results unless he is a sensitive pedagogue and a skilled technician. The problem must be solved globally.

Unfortunately, this initiation into techniques is not always carried out in the institutions where future educators are trained. In underdeveloped countries, the lack of qualified personnel is the most frequent obstacle to such an initiation. But it is not the only one because similar shortcomings are often found in more favoured countries. Routine, lack of initiative and administrative delays are the main factors responsible for educational sluggishness. There is no doubt that audio-visual aids produce their best results when they are used in connexion with active teaching methods. Here, the task of educators is to draw the attention of their governments to these methods and to the recommendations of previous seminars concerned with the introduction of an initiation into film and radio techniques into normal schools and similar institutions.

Finally, there are other questions which should be taken up in thorough and specific studies. They are related to the use of radio and television in the teaching of reading and writing and of languages. A great deal has been said about the 'singular, specific and irreplaceable services' which can be rendered, for example, by 'teaching by radio'. A great many hopes were stirred as a result of statements repeated with such warm conviction that one could have believed them to be dictated by experience.

First of all, we should note the ambiguity of the term 'teaching'. In the context of the statements to which we refer, this term covers both the teaching of subjects such as home science and history as well as the teaching of reading and writing. One of the greatest problems which remains to be solved is the liquidation of illiteracy. Following hasty conclusions, a belief has grown that, thanks to radio, illiteracy can be liquidated quickly, easily and cheaply. But what do we know about it objectively? Until now, the number of experiments has been limited. Some of them were frankly admitted failures. Fortunately, we will soon be in possession of an exhaustive report of the results obtained during the best known of these experiments, the one at Colombia. One of our experts has made a global study of these results from which we think that we will be able to derive valuable lessons, if not definitive conclusions.

A few complimentary remarks should be made here. The first concerns the basic difference between teaching notions of history, geography, home science, etc., by radio and the teaching of reading and writing. We say teaching by radio because the problem of teaching reading and writing by television is infinitely simpler and the results already acquired are sufficiently convincing. At any rate, it can never be said too often that the global use of audio-visual aids always gives the best results. Opposing radio to television or both to films is a typical example of a false problem. In an educational campaign organized and carried out at a national level, all complementary means must be used if possible. It is also virtually certain that results are proportionate to the means employed in a geometrical, not an arithmetical, progression. In other words, overly strict economy does not pay.

There lies a source of misunderstanding. Too often, it has been believed that making an expert and $10,000 worth of equipment available to a government was enough to solve the problem of audio-visual aids in a given Member State. Audio-visual aids do not have this magic quality. They require serious study and, first of all, serious thought about the place which they should occupy in a budget. Pedagogical problems always end up by leading into budgetary problems – that is, in the long run, economic, social and political problems. The educator must play his pedagogical role.

The tool which is offered to him – and this is the case of audio-visual tools – can multiply the activity of the educator in large proportion. Therefore, the political authorities must be convinced of the necessity of a financial effort which is often considerably large. That is a point of view which often escapes the educator: he must also educate administrators and political authorities. Many mistakes begin here.

So far, we have talked about audio-visual 'aids' and 'means'. Educators obviously consider them from this angle in the best of cases. But will this tremendous development of mass information media which we continue to allow itself to be domesticated? Let us go to the heart of the matter: must we continue to consider these information media as blind forces whose unleashing – and, as far as the educator is concerned, the unleashing begins where his own control ends – would be an educational and cultural catastrophe? Or, to put things in a less impressive but equally embarrassing way, cannot audio-visual 'means' be allowed to play their role without the help or simply the intervention of the educator? Before issuing a condemnation without any possibility of appeal, perhaps it might be wise to remember that films, radio and television can only be arbitrarily separated from the social, economic and cultural context which gives them their means of existence. No doubt, the study of these problems takes us a long way from modest film strips, flannelgraphs, and even traditional black-boards which are still a luxury for thousands of schools.

Let there be no misunderstanding. We know the importance of pedagogy in the use of audio-visual aids. We know that the training of good educators – in this case, good users of these didactic means – is a long and difficult matter. We know that we must think about the desperate problem of training teachers. But pedagogy itself is only a means whose end is education. And education, in the long run, is only a contribution – naturally, of capital importance – to the integration of the individual into a given society. It is in this perspective – from their production to their final use – that we must look at audio-visual aids and the various questions which they raise.

7

Film, Radio and Television as Educational Forces in Modern Civilization

FILM, RADIO AND TELEVISION AS EDUCATIONAL INSTITUTIONS

Film, radio and television are usually discussed under the heading of the customary educational and teaching aids, i.e., on the same level as abaci, wall maps, sand trays or sets of pictures, for the reason that films and tape recordings can be used in education in a way similar to the projection of slides. However, to lump them together with the traditional aids is to mistake completely their true importance and to ignore the social and psychological value of mass media in present-day civilization. A revision of thinking about modern mass media is needed. Far from existing somewhere on the fringes of modern educational thought, they are right at the centre.

Television, for example, is not just an alternative method of demonstration, but an independent and organically complete educational institution, like the school itself. It should be regarded as such and not simply as a vehicle for entertainment, political propaganda or commercial advertising. Educational subject- matter of the most varied kind falls within its range to a far greater extent than is generally realized. It is significant that most television organizations are themselves aware of this.

The large American broadcasting corporations, ABC, CBS and NBC, when questioned, described a large proportion of their programmes as educational. Indeed, the NBC view is that programmes should be adjusted to the possibilities of development and self-realization of individuals and should constantly serve the purposes of education.

A passage in the American Television Code in addition, stipulates that television networks, advertising agencies and, particularly significant, financial backers, must deliberately seek opportunities for the inclusion in broadcast programmes of factual material which will contribute to the enlightenment and education of the American public. The situation in Germany is similar. An analysis of German afternoon programmes in the first half of 1960 shows that out of 203 programmes monitored, 104 were educational. Even among the 406 evening programmes viewed during the same period there were at least 155 with an educational slant. If television plays, and all theatrical and operatic performances are added, as they have some claim to be, our overall view of television almost suggests an educational bias, which may well be in conformity with the true nature of the medium.

The situation is possibly even more favourable with regard to sound broadcasting, although it is naturally completely different in the case of the film. The great majority of broadcasting stations, particularly in Germany, France and England, are public services of high standing. The cinema on the other hand is an industry guided by the profit motive; and while this does not necessarily restrict its practical educational influence, it does modify it in the sense that the educational responsibilities of the cinema are completely vague.

THE *EQUNOCAL* NATURE OF THE MASS MEDIA

The assimilation of mass media by public education cannot be considered complete; in a deeper sense, it is only just beginning. Indeed, it is now being seriously overshadowed by large-scale public and expert criticism of these media, on medical and biological, psychological and sociological and aesthetic, cultural and educational grounds. Such criticism ranges from naive and ill-informed attacks to extremely subtle analyses like those of Giinther Anders and Adorno.

More particularly, the opposition of teachers to the impending threat of school television has recently been increasing. However, one good result of this has been to produce specific affirmations and objections which it thus becomes possible to refute. What is particularly feared in connexion with school television is the encouragement of passive acceptance, educational impressionism, the growth of a dangerous type of conformity, the paralysis of creative imagination through the intensification of artificial stimuli, the replacement of first-hand by second-hand experience, loss of individuality, the mechanization of the pupil/teacher relationship, and the standardization of educational activity.

These objections are by no means to be lightly dismissed, for some of them are valid expressions of educational philosophy; nor can they easily be refuted by purely educational arguments.

The following are, however, useful criteria for establishing the value of visual documentation centres: reasoning based on cultural history and educational sociology, which goes beyond purely educational arguments and sets out to demonstrate the cultural legitimacy of the media; and a critical analysis of the very remarkable educational potential of these forms of communication, from which it might be possible to deduce methods of organizing them and using them for educational purposes.

Scientific and historical research provides ample evidence that the attitude of Europeans as to their surroundings, and their consciousness of the world have changed since the Renaissance, in the sense that the archaic, mythological outlook has gradually made way for the development of empirical and realistic ideas and concepts. The rapid expansion of the natural home sciences is the most impressive intellectual reflection of this development.

This gradual development culminated in a consistent, if sensational way, though at a level beyond art, with the arrival of photography. This is the aesthetic correlation of a type of consciousness that has learned to think in terms of reality.

Photography projects a picture of the world as seen 'through the camera's eye' which has undoubtedly become representative of the twentieth century. Our consciousness has a strongly realistic bias and the greater the extent to which things and situations can be made to seem real or actually experienced, the more significant they will appear to us. It is this illusion of reality that film and television photography can create for us. Considered from the aspect of cultural history, all of us are at home in front of the screen and willingly become receptive to its influence.

The auditory stage of sound broadcasting is no exception to this rule, for the photographic or electronic camera lens and the radio microphone operate on the same aesthetic and psychological levels, though on different sensory levels. Our reality-bound consciousness regards them as identical instruments and, particularly in sound films and television, they have for a long time been fused in an excellent synthesis with an outstanding power of aesthetic and intellectual suggestion.

This evolution of consciousness and its aesthetic consequences may be regretted or may even be interpreted as a sign of regression. Nevertheless, along with the help of mass media, it is now enabling us to make the world our own, both physically and spiritually, and on occasion to render it transparent. The French cinema theorist Henri Agel correctly refers in this regard to a spiritual realism for which the film is something that can also dematerialize the world. In this connexion, if we consider that educational thought from Ratke and Comenius up to the American pragmatists of the Dewey school has followed a very similar road, even the most sensitive and conscientious educators should no longer find it too difficult to assimilate these media.

THE ARGUMENTS OF THE EDUCATIONAL SOCIOLOGISTS

The evolution of Western consciousness has been paralleled by a far-reaching social and cultural transformation of our lives, which in recent years has been proceeding at a staggering pace, owing to the all-pervading influence of technology. Sociologists are fond of describing this as a process of cultural change no longer conceived of as a normal periodic change in style but as a step through the gateway into a completely new cultural era. Whether this is true or not, we are now being subjected to the pressure of a vast process of cultural disintegration. However, this is accompanied by a no less intensive building-up process, something which that is often forgotten. This latter process has already resulted in far-reaching changes in our work and consumption habits and in our social, ethical and cultural attitudes.

In the wake of these new living and world conditions, there are people who up until now have existed merely as pawns in a game of historical power and whose intellectual and political maturity has been gained at the rather dangerous moment when their own world is threatened with the collapse of its scale of values. Since becoming active on the historical scene, these masses have become shouldered with responsibilities and are conscious of educational needs which hitherto arose only in the training of an élite. This process, which Karl Mannheim has described as the 'fundamental democratization' of our society, can bear fruit only if the masses are provided with educational and teaching aids of a completely new type.

In this connexion, the mass media are already playing a tremendous part. For the masses, they really constitute signposts to a real and yet boundless world. They have become so because they make use of an audiovisual language that is understood internationally.

Mass media are, in fact, the catalysing agents in a vast process of cultural change, which they reflect and constantly further and modify. It is precisely this which makes them so outstandingly important for education, regardless of the direction in which their influence may radiate. They have contributed to the development of a revolutionary situation in education, which makes demands on the general educational perception of modern teachers-demands which cannot be ignored.

Cinema, broadcasting and television appeared in that order at almost exact quarter-century intervals, beginning at the close of the nineteenth century. At the same time, their educational and aesthetic potentialities became gradually enriched by increasing technical progress. For example, as camera work and cutting-room techniques progressed, various standard types of film were created-narrative feature films, informational short subjects, educational films and documentaries. The film thus developed into a classical medium of concentrated narrative conveyed in visual and acoustic images.

The novelty of sound radio lay not so much in the fact that it created its own appropriate forms of presentation, as that it possessed practically unlimited possibilities for the diffusion of its message due to communication through electronic radiation. Its primary feature is-reduced to a formula-its ubiquity, i.e., the omnipresence of its broadcasts, whether in the form of original radio programmes or of concert relays. What matters is its reception at the greatest possible number of places simultaneously.

Television may be regarded as a kind of synthesis of these two stages of historical development. It has taken over both the ubiquity of electronic radiation and camera and cutting techniques and has therefore developed into a fully equipped universal stage for an era which in practice can draw upon the whole store of forms known to present and past civilizations. The television screen possesses an adaptability which is unlimited. This is why television is the richest and most versatile of the mass media when it comes to presenting a photographic and auditory picture and interpretation of the universe.

This quality of differentiation naturally has educational consequences which are easy to recognize in connexion with the use of these media in teaching. Every audiovisual expert and every teacher discovers this as soon as he makes a serious study of either films or television.

THE EDUCATIONAL POTENTIAL OF THE MASS MEDIA

In spite of this differentiation in working with the mass media, the audio-visual expert and the teacher will time and again be referred back to an identical system of communication which is equally valid in all of its three variants-film, radio and television and which covers material as widely divergent as plays, sports reports, dance programmes, political reviews, interviews, quiz programmes and even religious services.

Adorno and Horkheimer, in their 'Dialektik der Aufklärung', show ironically that the complaints made by many art and culture historians about the disintegration of the power of stylistic invention in Europe are completely unfounded, as the stereotyped reduction of all the material communication into a form suitable for mechanical reproduction is something more rigorous than the demands of any genuine style. So far as our subject of discussion is concerned this means that things, faces, situations and events are so filtered for purposes of translation into audiovisual language of the mass media that they positively enforce a specific type of experience. The special effectiveness of these media is therefore to be sought in what has become a technical audio-visual language.

One of the basic qualities of this language is its practically unlimited capacity for expressing and rendering virtually every aspect of the world. We all know that anything in this world that is designed to achieve significance and to arouse public consciousness -whether in politics, art, beauty contests, sports records, ideas or even historical events-is compelled to employ this language. The universal appeal of these mass media has become so great that it can be accepted as an uncontested, basic feature of all mechanized communication.

In addition to this unlimited capacity, analysis of the phenomena involved brings to light other exceedingly important characteristics. For it is chiefly the combination of these that produce what may be called the educational potential of the mass media; and it is with this that we are really concerned.

Reduced to four concepts, we have the following: the power of attraction of the audio-visual language, the almost unlimited extent to which it can be manipulated; its tendency towards the accumulation of stimuli which can be called in short the accumulation phenomenon and finally the topicality principle. These features are common to all mass media.

The four phenomena thus roughly defined are the essential structural principles of mass media. They are active at all levels, in programming, in production and presentation, in the action of the media on the public and, not least of all, in our own educational work. Indeed, they are the universal principles of modern communication and therefore deserve closer study and interpretation.

THE POWER OF ATTRACTION OF THE AUDIO-VISUAL LANGUAGE

The remarkable power of film fascination is probably the first thing we notice in considering mass media. This fascination is not merely a kind of diffuse moment of interest, but a very specific effect arising from the technological depiction of the world. In addition, we must remember not only the visual aspect but also the auditory components, which possess their own brand of fascination, principally of an emotional type.

This relationship of photography to our reality bound consciousness acts most powerfully through the fully-developed dynamism of film photography and television, in which it raises fascination to its ultimate level. In his research, Herbert Wölker proved empirically that the film multiplies the intensity of experience many times over, and thus facilitates identification with the matter shown. The influence of identification on the social process of learning has been made clear to us by Karl Heinrich's latest work on the effect produced by ñims.

The intensification of experience depends essentially on the visual and acoustic impact of photography. For that reason, in an age of increasing abstraction, increasing intellectualization and declining sensibility, as Gehlen calls it, film and television, through their power of making things concrete, have a compensatory function. By attracting audiences to the images and the stark graphic descriptions of commercial cinema and television, this function sometimes has a very negative effect; but it nevertheless retains an authentic and indispensable therapeutic quality.

Moreover, the relationship of photography to the world is not confined to this power of making things concrete. The subjects photographed have their own authenticity and documentary value. Photography always relates to facts, to something that has actually happened or really existed. This enhances its fascination, but weakens its power of symbolism. According to Cassirer's theory of symbols, .photographs is never symbols used to express an intnnsically spiritual concept. They are signals pointing to some concrete fact. Therefore, the weak point of photography as a means of conferring reality and exercising fascination lies in its dubious relationship to abstraction. Here we come to an argument applicable to ail mass media and one which recurs in a variety of shapes. Photography makes possible a maximum of what English theorists call involvement, an entering into contact with the outside world; but it holds the mind captive in concrete situations. By drawing on real situations, it promotes what might be called emotional commitment, but at the same time weakens thought by making an assault on our senses. This sometimes appears in a crude form in popular home science broadcasts, where lavish visual display, an abundance and complexity of pictorial matter, very easily gives the illusion of understanding, though in reality it merely builds up visual dummies in our consciousness. The intellect is frequently quite untouched by such visual exploits.

Educational responsibility and imagination must not capitulate in face of this dilemma. Indeed, they must use it consciously and even orient their educational activities on that basis, e.g., by using films and broadcasts in teaching. Through their power of fascination, these are particularly suitable in the initial stages of a learning process, where the great thing is to give a powerful motivation and awaken interest from the start. The mass media are 'magnificent gateways', as the English publicist Hoggard once called them. However, they may prove to be a hindrance where abstractions and generalizations are concerned. In such cases, they may almost act as barriers. O n the other hand, visual barriers of this kind can be set up deliberately, to goad pupils into using their brains. Where an accurate observation of detail is the prerequisite for the correct training of perception, as in geology and geography, the use of films can be exceedingly profitable. It is also must valuable in the 'deepening stage', in the sense in which the term is used in Herbart's theory of phases. O n other grounds, it is also valid for the teaching of politics and civics which, because of their abstract nature, are difficult to present in visual form. Here the mass media are absolutely essential.

The effect of the visual attraction of photography, as a means of realistic presentation and information, upon the film consumption of young people is best known to those who use films in teaching. A profit hungry industry exploits photography's power of attraction and conviction mainly to lend the unreal world of mediocre authors a semblance of reality and to draw the imagination of the audience into a dream world clothed in the garb of reality.

We realize that there is at present no way of overcoming this evil except by preventive educational methods designed to immunize pupils against this form of mental poison. The ability to illustrate is transformed into the power to seduce. The basic meaning of the Latin word fascinare is 'to bewitch'. This conveys an echo of the assault on our senses and, let us be honest, is not this power of enchantment present to some extent in every film and in every radio or television programme?

FACILITY OF MANIPULATION

The adaptability of mass media is a property which makes of them well-forged and efficient tools in the hands of experts. It gives them their wealth of expression and ensures their suitability for all purposes. However, its values are neutral and it may serve either truth or falsehood.

The concept itself is used here in a very broad sense, which makes it possible for us to penetrate to the reality underlying every phase of film and radio production. Facility of manipulation is a universal phenomenon in the mass media and is displayed in a great variety of ways.

Perhaps the clearest way of demonstrating it is by reference to the work of the film cutter, whose sole function is to cut and re-join single parts of film into intelligible sequences. The purpose in this case is to create sense. Cutting and mixing images in film and television are primitive forms of manipulation. They may be used to tell the truth, to lie, to camouflage, to excuse or anything else.

The early Russians were well aware of the power that lay in cutting and had good reasons for regarding it as the fundamental principle of film art. But manipulation begins as early as the shooting stage, in focusing, in lighting, in camera angles. No photography is possible without perspective. Even a snapshot is a form of interpretation.

Nowadays, the problem of manipulation also appears on an entirely different level in television, in the person of the interpreting speaker. Speech within the framework of a visual medium has in this way become a manipulatory power of the first rank. The oral description given in a visual broadcast establishes a very pronounced emotional accent. This is a very effective form of primitive manipulation.

It must however be granted that, on a higher level, television is nowadays campaigning for a new word picture relationship. This takes the form of an extremely interesting process where idea and observation are fused in a single simultaneous act. Words become concrete in picture sequences and images are intellectualized by the medium of the interpreting word.

This cultural phenomenon is of great importance and novelty and is rendered possible only through the medium of television. This experience gives an indication of educational resources which are still untapped but which will one day radically alter the educational style of television.

On the highest level, again, the manipulation process is relentlessly carried through in radio programming and in the planning centres of the film industry. Here, decisions about spheres of influence are made, and whole populations are exposed to the magical influence of planned films. In this regard, everything depends on the personality of those who occupy these posts of command. At this point, the phenomenological method of examination ought to make way for a true sociological analysis of the balance of power in the 'brains trusts' who control the broadcasting organizations and the film industry. In any event, a study of this power of manipulation at every stage of film and radio production might well provide a most valuable contribution to our knowledge of the inner educational structure of these systems. Manipulation is also important at a much humbler level, e.g., in the preparation of our educational films. Here the problem is one which causes us great concern.

Should we take as our model the perfect educational film, which traditionally constitutes a system of knowledge so compact and as completely adaptable as almost to render superfluous both the teacher and any further work on the material? Or should we produce open fragments of film, where the subject matter is accompanied by questions, so that pupils are placed in a working situation which in terms of modern teaching theory is educationally ideal? Here we come up against the same ambivalence and qualitative difficulties as were encountered in considering the problem of fascination. In this case too, the search for truth or falsehood, the encouragement of sense or nonsense, the offer of an opiate or a challenge, are effected by the same method-the power of manipulation- and by that alone.

What educational maxim can we derive from this? Manipulation must always be uncovered. This must happen in two directions. In the first place, the manipulation of sense in the cinema must be discerned, i.e., we must learn how to understand films. In the second place, it must be exposed. Whether we are concerned with exposing a dream structure or with seeing through the visual perfection and manipulation of the newsreels of the Third Reich and laying bare its ideology, we should be constantly engaged in an effort to uncover the serious consequences of manipulation.

THE CUMULATIVE EFFECT

The cumulative tendency, i.e., the tendency to pile up stimuli, is something mass media share with the other constituents of modern civilization, which suffer in general from a plethora of facts, stimuli, material and opinions. Owing to their unlimited capacity, however, these media are predestined to a boundless accumulation of stimuli, precisely because the technique of providing them is so easily mastered.

In this regard, the thematic, visual and sound overloading of television broadcasts and films is typical of the production style of all the mass media. It is claimed that this ultimately induces a permanent blockage of the audience's capacity to take in what it sees and hears. It has been said that television broadcasts are nowadays only looked at, but no longer seen. The onlooker develops a layer of undigested secondary experiences, a hydrid form of consciousness, which believes that it knows everything but in actual fact merely contains masses of experience which can lead to absolutely nothing. However, those who tend to frown upon the endless piling on of stimuli are overlooking the fact that it originates in a genuine spiritual need which is only awaiting satisfaction. This is the need for an expansion of consciousness and a widening of the horizon, without which it is becoming increasingly difficult to find our way and to act constructively in our complex world. In the recent development of Europe, our consciousness has altered not only qualitatively but quantitatively.

Educational theory seems at the moment to have no proposals for satisfying its demands. Even the schools are running aground at this point. If we consider seriously, even for a moment, what Henry Cassirer, head of the Unesco television part, put forward at the London Television Conference in 1957, namely that a revival of the universal mystic thought of the Renaissance, as represented by Leonardo, Michelangelo and Machiavelli, was required on sociological grounds, not merely on the level of genius but among the broad masses, we cannot casually dismiss television's possibilities in that direction. If there is any way out of the educational bottleneck that now exists all over the world, it must be by means of the mass media, which possess not only the technical capacity for the task, but also the methodical facilities for implementing it.

THE PROBLEM OF TOPICALITY

This problem is of the same magnitude as that posed by the power of fascination of the mass media. Topicality and the trend towards it have come to set the pattern for television. Live broadcasts are among the high points of television programmes.

Arnold Hauser, in his Sozialgeschichte der Kunst und Literatur tries to account for the power of attraction exerted on the minds of spectators by the impression of spontaneity resulting from the coincidence of perception and event, and attempts to explain why the modern mind has this peculiar sensitivity towards actual events.

We may agree with Hauser that this is not so much a fashionable contemporary whim as a profound metamorphosis of our attitude to life, which experiences the world primarily as a process in which we can genuinely participate only through grasping significant moments-a truly Heraclitean view of the universe !

It seems that the television set has already become a concrete symbol of this process of simultaneous experience, for it provides a synchronized record of life as it flows by. Television enables millions of people to participate in all kinds of topical events, even if most of them are not 'Heraclitean' moments. This is not the place for an assessment of the value of this form of modern topicality. However, even if we regard it as no more than a potentialy important anthropological phenomenon, we are faced with the introduction of completely new elements into our already complex world. Naturally, our educational thinking as a whole cannot remain unaffected. Try to imagine contemporary events becoming a legitimate, even an integral feature of modern general education. The schools would then be faced with a task for which their organization and present attitude towards teaching does not yet equip them.

Only the mass media, and television in particular, are already prepared to cultivate a relationship with the outside world that could conform to this topical pattern.

RIVAL EDUCATIONAL PATTERNS

Film, radio and television are cultural institutions which obviously cannot be considered as educationally neutral. On the contrary, they exert a lasting formative influence on character, though this is often involuntary on the part of their organizers.

Within the framework of their influence a completely novel educational situation has developed, because they use for their own purposes a technical audio-visual language that has created an entirely new educational atmosphere. Their boundless capacity for manipulation, their fascination for the senses, their tendency to intensify stimuli and their accent on topicality reveal the mass media as means of communication in which a hitherto unknown educational ideal has been given an institutional structure which seems clearly opposed to the traditional conception of the school.

We should be wise to accustom ourselves to the idea that we are now dealing with two rival forms of education, which not only follow different ideas of teaching but have become embodied in different social structures. On the one hand we have the state school system from kindergarten to university and on the other the large, more or less government-controlled broadcasting stations.

W e need not hesitate to regard television stations as setting the pattern for the new type of teaching, as they not only embody a new educational trend but also display certain cultural, social and aesthetic developments in a representative combination. It is perhaps too soon to attempt an accurate definition of the differences between the two educational patterns, for the whole development is still in a state of flux. However, some of the differences are already beginning to emerge.

Television clearly supports an extensive concept of teaching, in which broad surveys, a wealth of facts, the piling up of stimuli, a receptive attitude towards information, topical value and the establishment of a pattern of learning with particular orientation are the decisive factors.

Schools, on the other hand, embody the ideal of an intensive, selective education, based on the independent activity of pupils, in which exemplary teaching conditions and methodical thoroughness are the valid objectives. They want to and must develop exemplary learning methods. Both types of education are based on the genuine needs of modern civilization. For a long time, our society has been subjected to spiritual and psychological stresses which find their concrete expression in this educational duality.

As a result, these two types in conjunction form the first integrated educational system of modern times. The natural relationship between school and television might therefore be described as a sort of competitive co-operation, as in the long run schools will be unable to avoid making use of current educational material from outside.

However, the screen requires spectators who have been subjected to school educational methods and are equipped with faculties of comprehension without which the fluctuating world depicted in the daily flood of images cannot be intellectually revealed. This demands the cultivation of new educational qualities which until now have perhaps appeared suspect.

Television requires promptness in orienting ourselves to a large mass of stimuli, alertness in our observance of rapid sequences of pictures, preparedness for the interpretation of quickly-changing superficial appearances and the ability to hold aloof from the assault on our senses. It cannot be denied that such factors should be included in the spiritual and intellectual equipment of contemporary human beings even if only a few of us are prepared to admit that we already possess a training ground for these qualities in the form of the television screen.

It is therefore strange that, at any event in Germany, these two educational institutions still profess to ignore each other officially-though, paradoxically enough, they are already surreptitiously linked by the fact that schoolchildren participate in both.

This temporarily illicit relationship need only be legalized at the level of educational policy to bring about a situation which could well be decisive for the future of education in our country.

School television broadcasts might possibly be one way of bringing about a temporary link, as is already the case in many countries. However, there are other possibilities, some of which are quite revolutionary. Developments in the United States are to some extent a model for the future everywhere. There, television stations have simply incorporated the school system, with its methods and curriculum content. The early-morning broadcast 'continental classroom' is an example of this, as is the Italian 'telescuola'.

Moreover, some schools have begun to set up regional television systems of their own, with the help of which they are arranging a rich variety of educational programmes and are thus entering into competition with the television stations, partly through the adoption of radio methods. The head of an audio-visual centre should be responsible for an organ serving both types of education and both educational institutions. He represents the school and its classical teaching traditions and at the same time the novel requirements of the mass media. He leads an amphibian existence, which in this situation may be a valuable stimulus for a far-seeing government educational policy, as authorities cannot remain unaffected by these developments.

We must wait and see if they will know how to make best use of them. At any rate, the audio-visual centres are the appropriate clearing houses for these problems, the specialized agencies in a process which is only just beginning but which will become of national importance.

8

Multimedia as an Educational Tool

For many of us, the lure of computers is a powerful one. However, many of us also refrain from using computers for fear of failure. We want to hone computer skills, but are scared to make the effort because we lack those very skills. Too many of us, especially in the field of learning, are caught in this modern tug-of-war.

Throughout the 1980s and 1990s, the concept of multimedia took on a new meaning, as the capabilities of satellites, computers, audio and video converged to create new media with enormous potential. Combined with the advances in hardware and software, these technologies were able to provide enhanced learning facility and with attention to the specific needs of individual users.

A primary application of the interactive multimedia for instruction is in an instructional situation where the learner is given control so that he/she may review the material at his or her own pace and in keeping with his/her own individual interests, needs, and cognitive processes. The basic objective of interactive multimedia material is not so much to replace the teacher as to change the teacher's role entirely. As such, multimedia must be extremely well designed and sophisticated enough to mimic the best teacher, by combining in its design the various elements of the cognitive processes and the best quality of the technology. With today's multimedia courseware, once a programme has been designed and built in with the appropriate responses, it should be flexible and permit change and alteration.

We shall look at the usage, advantages and disadvantages of multimedia in education and training. Some of the prototype multimedia lessons are also given at the end as examples.

DEFINITIONS

Multimedia. is a term frequently heard and discussed among educational technologists today. Unless clearly defined, the term can alternately mean .a judicious mix of various mass media such as print, audio and video. or it may mean the development of computer-based hardware and software packages produced on a mass scale and yet allow individualized use and learning. In essence, multimedia merges multiple levels of learning into an educational tool that allows for diversity in curricula presentation.

Multimedia is the exciting combination of computer hardware and software that allows you to integrate video, animation, audio, graphics, and test resources to develop effective presentations on an affordable desktop computer. (Fenrich, 1997). .Multimedia is characterized by the presence of text, pictures, sound, animation and video; some or all of which are organized into some coherent program. (Phillips, 1997).

Today's multimedia is a carefully woven combination of text, graphic art, sound, animation, and video elements. When you allow an end user, i.e. the viewer of a multimedia project, to control 'what' and 'when' and 'how' of the elements that are delivered and presented, it becomes interactive multimedia.

As such multimedia can be defined as an integration of multiple media elements (audio, video, graphics, text, animation etc.) into one synergetic and symbiotic whole that results in more benefits for the end user than any one of the media element can provide individually.

Specific uses of multimedia include:

- drill and practice to master basic skills
- the development of writing skil
- problem solving
- understanding abstract mathematics and home science concepts
- simulation in home science and mathematics
- manipulation of data
- acquisition of computer skills for general
- purposes, and for business and vocational training
- access and communication to understand populations and students
- access for teachers and students in remote locations
- individualized and cooperative learning
- management and administration of classroom activities

THE NEED FOR MAKING MULTIMEDIA COURSEWARE

Why use multimedia at all? Of what use is multimedia in education? The answers to these questions could be sought through an understanding of the capabilities and limitations of the medium.

Besides being a powerful tool for making presentations, multimedia offers unique advantages in the field of education. For instance, text alone simply does not allow students to get a .feel. of any of Shakespeare's plays. In teaching biology, an instructor cannot make a killer whale come alive in a classroom. Multimedia enables us to provide a way by which learners can experience their subject in a vicarious manner. The key to providing this experience is having simultaneous graphic, video and audio, rather than in a sequential manner. The appeal of multimedia learning is best illustrated by the popularity of the video games currently available in the market. These are multimedia programmes combining text, audio, video, and animated graphics in an easy-to-use fashion.

Moreover, under conditions of chronic under-funding, multimedia can provide an enhanced or augmented learning experience at a low cost per unit. It is here that the power of multimedia can be unleashed to provide long-term benefit to all. Multimedia enables learning through exploration, discovery, and experience. Technology does not necessarily drive education. That role belongs to the learning needs of students. With multimedia, the process of learning can become more goal oriented, more participatory, flexible in time and space, unaffected by distances and tailored to individual learning styles, and increase collaboration between teachers and students. Multimedia enables learning to become fun and friendly, without fear of inadequacies or failure.

ADVANTAGES OF MULTIMEDIA

The pedagogical strength of multimedia is that it uses the natural informationprocessing abilities that we already possess as humans. Our eyes and ears, in conjunction with our brain, form a formidable system for transforming meaningless sense data into information. The old saying that "a picture is worth a thousand words" often understates the case especially with regard to moving images, as our eyes are highly adapted by evolution to detecting and interpreting movement. For example, a photograph of Ganges in Varanasi, apart from being aesthetically pleasing, can contain a wealth of information relating to the culture, religion, geography, geology, climate, history, and economics of the area. Similarly, a recording of a politician's speech can allow us to discern significant semantic features not obvious in a written transcript.

For the student, one advantage of multimedia courseware over the text-based variety is that the application looks better. If the courseware includes only a few images at least it gives relief from screens of text and stimulates the eye, even if the images have little pedagogical value. More often than not, the inclusion of nontextual media into courseware adds pedagogical value to the application. For example, a piece of courseware describing a dig at an archeological site would be more valuable to the student, if it included images of the site, such as enhanced aerial images showing features like old field boundaries, or diagrams illustrating where the digging and scanning took place. In this respect, using the text only, even in a creative way, has obvious limitations as compared to the use of both text and pictures.

PRACTICAL DISADVANTAGES OF MULTIMEDIA

Multimedia requires high-end computer systems. Sound, images, animation, and especially video, constitute large amounts of data, which slow down, or may not even fit in a low-end computer. Unlike simple text files created in word processing, multimedia packages require good quality computers. A major disadvantage of writing multimedia courseware is that it may not be accessible to a large part of its intended users if they do not have access to multimedia-capable machines. For this reason, courseware developers should think very carefully about the type of multimedia elements that need to be incorporated into applications and include only those that have significant value.

Multimedia has other weaknesses too. While proponents of this new technology are very enthusiastic about its potential, they often leave the financial and technical issues unattended. Development costs in multimedia are very high and the process of developing effective multimedia takes time. Time spent on developing the multimedia package requires money so that the true cost of an interactive programme mounts with each delay.

Further, if the prerequisites for using multimedia include access to computers with related software, the user must possess a minimum level of computer literacy in order to exploit the capabilities of this medium for learning. And finally, training of the educator who is unfamiliar with the production and design of multimedia courseware or packages can be equally complicating.

The critical question, then, is: How do we overcome some of the identified barriers and begin the process of multimedia implementation alongside the instructor, textbook, and blackboard? It is the barriers rather than the technologies which we must address before multimedia, or for that matter, any media technology becomes as accepted as the printed text or guidebook.

USE OF MULTIMEDIA IN AN EDUCATIONAL SETTING

Let us look at some examples of what is called .innovative use.. Let us say a student wants to write a paper on desert animals. Traditionally, the primary source for obtaining information would be the encyclopedia generally available in the library. With access to interactive multimedia, the student would collect various textual materials about the camel from sources on a CD-ROM. In addition, the student may be able to copy a diagram or the skeleton and muscular structure of the camel and the ostrich to study what is common about the two creatures. With a multimedia approach, the student could also access Web sites on the Internet to get more information. The student could then add film clips on these animals in their natural habitat (all may be from the same CD-ROM) and blend them into a report. Then by adding titles and credits, the student now has a new and original way of communicating his/her own individual perspective.

Besides student use, teachers should find multimedia of great use in delivering their lessons. For example, a history teacher could use a multimedia CD to create a lecture on the non-violence movement by using film clippings and audio tapes on Mahatma Gandhi or Martin Luther King, also by incorporating other audio visual information with text to make the subject come alive. All this material would be available on a videodisc. Similarly, a university professor might use a multimedia CD to prepare or to update information or to teach so as to enliven and also add insight to his/her teaching, thereby improving the quality of the course. The uses of multimedia need not be seen as a tool for classrooms only. In an industry dealing with hazardous materials, workers need to be trained. It could be risky to provide hands on training. In this case, simulated learning can take the place of actual hands on training by using all the features of interactive multimedia. Training can thus take place individually at the learner's pace and on his/her own time. Medical procedures, first-aid training and instruction of paramedics or even surgeons are made both simple and interesting through the use of multimedia. The doctor or paramedic can run through a complete procedure on videodisc and analyze all the possible outcomes and can evaluate the possibilities before treatment of the real life patient starts.

In all the instances, the user can and normally does work individually and in an interactive mode with the medium.

9

Web Based School Education in India

INTRODUCTION TO WEB BASED LEARNING

As the Internet technology is introduced it makes a new revolution in information technology. The wide use of Internet also affected the methods of education. It is a global network and gives the concept of global classroom where any number of students can interact with each other at any time. Goodbye classes, goodbye books and Goodbye teachers' is possible with the webbased education. The WWW gives attractive features to Web Based Education, which are:

- The ability to have multimedia documents
- The hypertext/hypermedia capability
- WWW network basis, allowing for distance learning.

In web based education we have two different types, asynchronous and synchronous learning:

- In asynchronous the educational module is to be installed from a particular web site and then you can unpack it offline on your machine. In this case there is no mutual interaction of student with teacher.
- In synchronous type there is synchronization among the students and teacher on-line. This synchronous Web based education provides the most emerging concept of E-learning. E-learning is not a web delivered a common misunderstanding.

E-Learning is an interactive experience with access to on line tutors and can be done from any computers once you have your password. Access is through web browsers such as Internet explorer and Netscape Navigator. With ELearning training is organized in the form of modules. The modules are approximately onehour session that focuses on specific subject of training. Using E-Learning the training can be brought right to your desktop. This makes technical training more convenient.

During the live E-Learning module, participants will have the ability to ask the instructor questions, get answers and interact with other students — all on line. We have discussed problems, considerations & approaches to WBL in India along with important Features of Web-Based Learning Environment. In what follows, part second explains the scope for improvement in school education by using Information Technology, third part explains tools of Information Technology useful for school education, fourth part explains Web Based Education: Considerations and Approaches, fifth on problems to be faced while implementing IT in school education in Indian context sixth part explains important Features of Web-Based Learning Environment and finally last part gives conclusion.

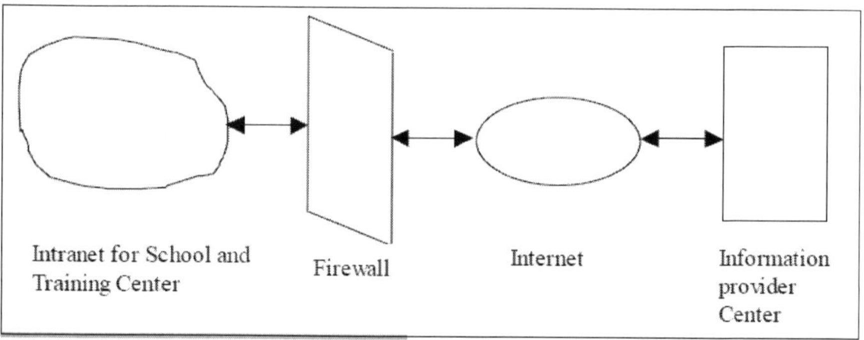

SCOPE FOR IMPROVEMENT IN SCHOOL EDUCATION BY USING IT: WEB BASED EDUCATION

If Information Technology is used in school education it provides:

Flexibility, Accessibility, And Convenience

With a very short period of training the student can access the learning material when their schedule allows. No separate distribution mechanism needed (WBL), can be accessed from any computer anywhere in the world, keeping delivery costs low, this leads to cost saving.

Enhanced Learning

Cognitively, active and context-based ("real world") learning activities, the highly interactive nature of well designed online learning, flexibility to review course material at any time, all improve learners abilities to synthesize and retain information.

Many learners also find it easier to ask questions via E-mail because they have the privacy of direct contact with the instructor and avoid the classroom fear of "exposing" ignorance.

Ease and speed of Update

WBL allows for efficient and quick updates to course material for frequently changing information. The changes are made on the server program. Everyone worldwide can instantly access the update.

Consistency of learning material

Each learner gets identical instructions to ensure the consistency and quality of the message by using WBL.

Cross Platform

WBL can be accessed by web browsing software on any platform Windows, Mac, UNIX etc. All these factors contribute to improve the quality of school education by overcoming factors like social background of students, parents, different standards of teaching and teachers training programs, all teachers cannot deliver the same message to all learners. Also by using WBL students can do their self –assessment & management has access to progress reports & assessment data of individual learner.

TOOLS OF INFORMATION TECHNOLOGY USEFUL FOR SCHOOL EDUCATION

System Implementation Structure

To implement the WBE we propose the system implementation structure. The school classrooms, office and training centers are connected through Intranet. This Intranet is connected to the Internet by using network operating system. Firewall is introduced between Intranets and Internet in order to provide security.

System Description

In initial stage of school education the students are not expert in reading and writing. Subject understanding increases if they learn the things through visualization. With the help of multimedia or Rich Media, which includes, Audio, video, graphics and Java Applets have made WBE very effective. We propose Multimedia content database scheme as shown in fig.

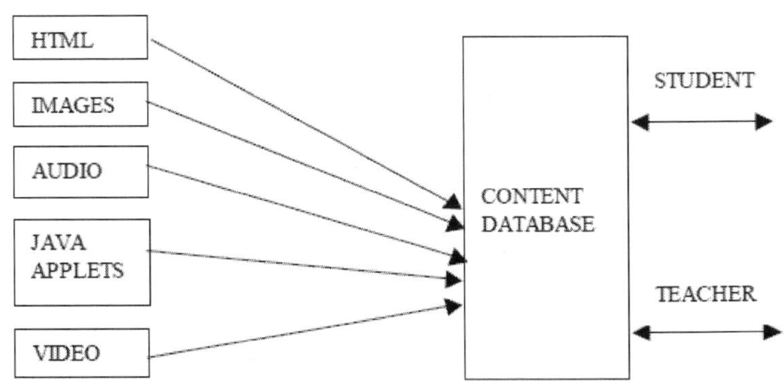

In this database contents the data about educational centers, courses, tutors, students, examinations as well as some story books and games in the form of html pages, audio and video files, Images and Java Applets. Student and teachers can access this database for learning as well as for teaching.

In the primary stage students don't have good knowledge of English. Therefore the presentation should be available in their mother tongue for the better understanding, which is also helpful in improving their pronunciation. This is possible by developing Natural Language Interface to database.

One important device called, as "Tech Commander" is also useful for teachers to identify students potential by viewing any students computer display on his own monitor. If he finds something that everyone should see he could set everyone's monitor to display it.

Web Based Education: Considerations and Approaches

- Conversion of Existing Material: In order to shift from traditional education to WBE we have to convert the existing school educational material to the Web. The important points to consider are bandwidth, design, usability, and the necessity of high quality media elements & consistency of material across the mediums.
- Authoring for Multiple Delivery Environments: We have to provide consistency of interface & ease of authoring & design of an effective multi platform course.
- Using the Web for student/Teacher Interaction: Web site can be used for posting of assignments, student work & marks, along with the ability to submit work on-line through the site, also JavaScript & JAVA applets to demonstrate course concepts interactively. This means that course delivery on the Web must be dynamic & truly interactive between the instructor & the students.
- Faculty Support and Training: We have to provide centralized support & training resources for training the teachers initially.

Problems to be faced while implementing WBE in school education in Indian context: Looking at how to use Information Technology in school education, its different tools, the system structure as defined & described it is obvious that we will face some problems while implementing WBE in school education in India. The major problems we will be facing are:

- Intensive Training to Schoolteachers: Schoolteachers are not introduced to the web based education. Therefore training should be given in order to create a learning environment that will itself train and spur students on the one hand to turn the learning experience into useful, practical and personal knowledge.
- WBL awareness & Workshops: In rural area parents are not much knowing about WBL. So the demonstration, seminars & workshops

needs be conducted for society in order to understand the importance of it.

- Bandwidth Limitations: Limited bandwidth of Internet connection gives slower performance for sound, video and intensive graphics, causing long waits for downloads that can affect the ease of the learning process. Improved bandwidth will help the teacher to solve his problem.
- Effect on Teachers: WBL will lead to reduction in manpower as per as teachers are concerned. This will lead to agitations by teacher's organization.
- Effect on Students: Although the students will be benefited by WBL there will some part of students opposing this introduction of technology in education.
- Infrastructure: WBE will primarily require free access to Web to all the learners and hence government of India will have to setup nation wide Fiber Optic Cable network.
- Access: Every school will not have equal opportunity to information because of access issues. The schools with fewer budgets will always face this problem. This is the major problem as per as India is concerned, as there is big gap between poor & rich communities in India.
- Download: The learning material that appears on web needs to be downloaded will require more time. The speed depends on the transmission methods & bandwidth, which is problem as per as India is concerned.

Important Features of Web-Based Learning Environment

While designing Web-Based Learning sites the following important features should be kept in mind:

- The Online Syllabus: An online syllabus provides the instructor with a way to change course material easily and as per the requirements in industry, and the student will have a complete and up-to-date picture of the course requirements. Hypertext links to sample relevant disciplinary web sites may be helpful in giving students (and also prospective students) a sense of the disciplinary context for the course.
- Personal Home Pages: Personal home pages can be used to foster the sense that the class is not just a collection of isolated individuals but a community of learners who can profit from interacting with one another. Home pages encourage students to learn about each other so as to encourage contact and mutual interests. This helps the learners to create a group with common interest.

- Interactivity: Adding discussion forums and chat sessions to your online course is a common way to add an interactive component to a web-based course. There are many implementations of bulletin board and chat session software to choose from. A second method of interactivity is, of course, email. It's a good practice to have an online list of the e-mail addresses of all registered students, the professor, and teaching assistants. This is possible with an e-mail subscription mechanism included in your Online Syllabus.
- Assignments: The web page listings of homework assignments, upcoming events and exams can be more interactive than the familiar print counterparts. If some homework assignments, for example, are based on online materials, they can be directly linked to the class schedule. This helps the students to plan the preparations for the examination in systematic way.
- Announcements: To be effective, announcements need to be read; for that to happen, students need to know when a new announcement has been posted. Alert sounds or perhaps a blinking link added to a page can let students know of new announcements, or perhaps, even a mass e-mail to all students in the course.
- For a home page, or a long life syllabus, various software tools can be used for the subscribers announcement about page changes. All these techniques will attract the learner's attention towards announcements.
- Testing: Online drill or practice testing can be used to reinforce material, even if the results are not used as part of a grade. Reading comprehension questions, for example, in short answer or multiple choice formats can provide students with an assessment of their level of understanding of text. This facilitates the students to measure his level of understanding and through continuous assessment he can try to improve his performance.
- Course Management: Software should be available to add or delete students from the course, assign user Ids and passwords, create or edit home pages, and manage any open discussion groups. This helps to keep up to date records of students admitted for various courses.
- Content: Perhaps the most difficult part of developing a web-based course is creating the online contents. You can begin by transferring your basic lecture materials to the web and integrating media such as sound, images, and video. Remember, to experiment with incorporating some of the new web-based learning paradigms. And finally, come back and rebuild the lecture building its graph structure and using more html facilities.

Other Features of a Web-Based Learning Environment

- Managing cognitive load — the amount of information people can process — is essential to effective teaching or training. Bombarding learners with too much information at once, called cognitive overload, is one of the chief obstacles to learning.
- This indicates that we should provide only required information in order to avoid cognitive overload.
- Dividing each tutorial lesson into segments (Classroom, Quiz, Lab, etc.) and then further subdividing these segments into a manageable number of chunks allows users to digest new concepts and skills in a manner that prevents overload.
- Web-based tutorial: Users will also enjoy a great deal of flexibility in managing their cognitive load, selecting instructional tasks from a menu of lessons, depending upon the amount and kinds of skills they bring with them, and once engaged in a lesson, selecting which portions of that particular lesson they wish to complete. This allows the students to learn the topics in proper sequence and according to his ability of understanding.
- Because the limited capacity of working memory is rapidly overwhelmed by large amounts of new information, frequent opportunities to practice are important. Rehearsal encodes or moves information into long-term memory.
- The practice assignments can be presented with practice opportunities throughout the classroom portion of the lesson and is also encouraged to complete the practice portion of each lesson. This allows the student to find out how much he has understood at the end of learning a particular module.
- Finally, online testing is used to reinforce material. Elaborative rehearsal involves presenting questions, which allow the user to apply knowledge in an appropriate context, thus encoding it into permanent memory.
- Quiz questions are designed to provide an authentic assessment of user skill levels by calling on the user to apply the appropriate techniques and practices from the lesson.

CONCLUSION

With introduction of Web Based Education at school level our children and youngsters will grow as "Computer kids". Their exposure will get increased due to which the Knowledge level will get definitely improved.

Use of Internet for education has a potential to change many aspects of our lives. In conclusion we can say that WBE is Platform independent, convenient in access, cost saving, easily updated contents and with emerging technologies it can be made more effective. Web-Based Learning adds human support through on-line tutor, thereby extending the scope of what can be effectively taught into many new subject areas. In addition more supporting material can be made available through web site links to other documents and systems.

With all these important features incorporated in Web-Based Learning system it will enhance the quality of education in our country at all levels i.e. Primary, Secondary and Higher Education.

10

Organization of the Syllabus Into Units for the Year

CURRICULUM DESIGN

A curriculum is a series of activities in which students engage with subject matter. Because everything cannot be studied at once, these activities must be orchestrated in some way. This arrangement is called curriculum design. Whether the subject is geometry, visual arts, or map skills, it is arranged in ways that emphasize some aspects and implications of the subject and neglect others. In this way, curriculum design is among the most powerful tools educators can use to influence what students learn. Curriculum design can be viewed as an arrangement of materials prepared in advance and intended for instruction. Alternately, it can be considered as what emerges from interactions among teachers, students, and materials.

In either case, however, a given design suggests conscious planning and brings with it a predisposition to what subject matter and instructional arrangements count as educationally significant. No definitive taxonomy of curriculum designs exists. Several design types, which are among the best known, are considered here: school subjects, social, personal relevance, and intellectual development.

Designing a school curriculum should always include the state or national standards that support them—or both. Think of standards as tree limbs, and the good curriculum that results as the buds and blossoms that grow out of them. School curriculum is an outgrowth of sound standards, and students grow and learn from organized and engaging curriculum that aligns with important standards.

- Identify the social studies learning standards for the state you are constructing the curriculum for. Each state's Department of Education website has them. In addition, the national associations for core instructional areas have sets of common standards for all states, such as the National Council of Teachers of Mathematics, the National

Council of Teachers of English, and National Council for the Social Studies, the National Science Association and the International Reading Association.

- Develop a set of differentiated benchmarks for students to reach that align with the state or association standards. For example, if a social studies standard states, "Students will know what tools were used for early human survival," a differentiated benchmark would say, "Students will research and create three early human survival tools, measure and compare their mass, and then graph out the results." Benchmarks help students to take learning to the next step through action.
- Develop a list of student objectives that set forth what students will know and be able to do. For example, an objective for social studies might say, "Students will be able to understand that life is influenced by culture and environment," or "Students will interact in a variety of environments to discover cultural influences." With strong objectives in place, students become involved in active learning.
- Includes lesson samples and activity ideas that include strategies and techniques with a lot of different "doing" activities. Pair up the activities with the standards they support. For example, "Students will be able to understand that life is influenced by culture and environment" could involve activities with students comparing and contrasting different cultures, researching other cultures and writing essays, reports and stories.
- Include a listing of supplemental resources and tools to be used with the activities and benchmarks. Include a range of resources, such as encyclopedias (online or text), magazines, newspapers, internet sites, guest speakers, authors, fiction and non-fiction trade books, alternative text written at various reading levels, maps and artifacts

FACTORS THAT INFLUENCE CURRICULUM DESIGN

Objectives

- Child psychology.
- Economic factors
- Environmental factors
- Political factors
- Social factors
- Technological factors

Content

- Influence of politics on curriculum
- Influence of society on curriculum

- Influence of economy on curriculum
- Influence of technology on curriculum
- Influence of environment on curriculum
- Influence of child psychology on curriculum.

How Political Factors Influence Curriculum Design

- From your experience as a student and teacher, you may have noticed how politics influence education. This is why education is regarded as a political activity.
- National ideology and philosophy have a tremendous influence on the education system because:
- Politics determine and define the goals, content, learning experiences and evaluation strategies in education.
- Curricular materials and their interpretation are usually heavily influenced by political considerations.
- Political considerations may play a part in the hiring of personnel.
- Funding of education is greatly influenced by politics.
- Entry into educational institutions and the examination systems are heavily influenced by politics.

How Social Factors Influence Curriculum Design

When you examine the curriculum being offered in your country, one question you may need to deal with is the extent to which social factors or social considerations influenced the design of the curriculum. Society has its own expectations about the aims and objectives that should be considered when designing the curriculum. It also has a perception of what the product of the school system should look like. It is therefore necessary for curriculum designers to take into account these societal considerations. If this does not happen, the curriculum becomes irrelevant.

As you know, a number of religions co-exist in countries in the SADC region. Your own community may include Christians, Muslims, Hindus and adherents of other religions. Their views must be considered when designing a curriculum. In Zimbabwe, for example, subjects such as sex education and political economy have proved difficult to include in the curriculum because of the resistance from some religious groups. These groups feel that including these subjects in the curriculum will undermine their belief systems.

The same groups of people would not tolerate a curriculum that does not include religious and moral education. The design of curricular materials and their presentation should accommodate the culture of the society that the curriculum is seeking to serve. You should, however, be sensitive to the fact that the curriculum can be used to perpetuate inequities. You may have a curriculum that is gender biased against female children because it includes instructional materials that portray negative attitudes towards women and girls. It is therefore possible for culture to have both positive and negative influences on the curriculum. Pause for a moment and consider the number of groupings in the society in which you live. These can be professional associations, cultural groups and religious organizations. The list is endless. These groups can bring their views to bear on curriculum design. This is so because any curriculum of value must result from the broad consultation of a wide range of stakeholders

How Economic Factors Influence Curriculum Design

One of the reasons why education is financed by governments is to improve the country's economy. Therefore, the national curriculum should concern itself with the requirements of the economy. Perhaps you are wondering how the economy of the country affects the curriculum. The children you teach will need to be employed. The skills needed by industry should be translated into the content and learning experiences of these children. The skills, knowledge base and attitudes required by industry should be developed in the classroom.

You might have noticed some advertisements for vacant posts in your local media. Employers have basic requirements. Educational institutions find themselves working to meet these basic requirements academically and professionally. As you are reading this unit, you might be thinking of acquiring a higher academic or professional qualification. This would enhance your upward social mobility. The market forces dictate what should be included in the national curriculum. It also subtly determines the quantity of learners at different levels.

As a teacher, you require classroom supplies such as:

- Textbooks,
- Charts,
- Equipment, and
- Chemicals for science experiments.

These materials are products of industry. Without these materials, learning is compromised. It is therefore crucial that serious consideration be given to economic demands when designing the curriculum.

How Technological Factors Influence Curriculum Design

The computer is the latest technological innovation that will have a significant impact on education and society. If you are not computer literate, you may feel that you are not up-to-date. In your area, you may have noticed that a number of schools have introduced computing as one of the subjects.

The intention is to equip the learners with the requisite computer skills and knowledge. In addition to computers, other forms of electronic media are being used in teaching. These have provided a variety of learning experiences and have facilitated individualized learning. Curriculum designers cannot afford to ignore technology and its influence on the curriculum.

How Environmental Factors Influence Curriculum Design

Over time, people have become insensitive to their surroundings and natural resources. This has affected the sky, the land and the sea. The end result is that humanity is being adversely affected by these in-considerations. Industrial wastes have polluted the world.

For example, the ozone layer in the atmosphere, which protects us from harmful radiation from the sun, is being depleted. People want this redressed. It is through education that remediation can be effected. Consideration for the environment must of necessity influence curriculum design to ensure the survival of future generations.

MODELS OF CURRICULUM DESIGN

Curriculum design is a complex but systematic process.A variety of models of curriculum design in order to make this complex activity understandable and manageable. It is important that as a teacher to understand how the curriculum is being used in schools was designed.

Objectives

- Discuss various models of curriculum design.
- Compare curriculum design models.
- Explain steps in curriculum design in relation to models of curriculum.

Content

- The objectives model,
- The process model,
- Tyler's model,
- Wheeler's model, and
- Kerr's model.

The Objectives Model

The objectives model of curriculum design contains content that is based on specific objectives. These objectives should specify expected learning outcomes in terms of specific measurable behaviours.

This model comprises some main steps:

- Agreeing on broad aims which are analysed into objectives,
- Constructing a curriculum to achieve these objectives,
- Refining the curriculum in practice by testing its capacity to achieve its objectives, and
- Communicating the curriculum to the teachers through the conceptual framework of the objectives, evaluation is done at each stage of the curriculum design.
- Content, materials and methodology are derived from the objectives.

The Process Model

Unlike the objectives model, this model does not consider objectives to be important. Using this model presupposes that:

- Content has its own value. Therefore, it should not be selected on the basis of the achievement of objectives.
- Content involves procedures, concepts and criteria that can be used to appraise the curriculum.
- Translating content into objectives may result in knowledge being distorted.
- Learning activities have their own value and can be measured in terms of their own standard. For this reason, learning activities can stand on their own. It is important to note that in the process model:
- Content and methodology are derived from the goals. Each of them has outcomes that can be evaluated.
- The evaluation results from the outcome are fed into the goals, which will later influence the content and methodologies. Unlike the objectives model, there is no direct evaluation of the content and methodologies.

Tyler's Model

Tyler's model for curriculum designing is based on the following questions:

- What educational purposes should the school seek to attain? What educational experiences can be provided that are likely to attain these purposes?
- How can these educational experiences be effectively organized?
- How can we determine whether these purposes are being attained?

Objectives of Curriculum Studies

The model is linear in nature, starting from objectives and ending with evaluation. In this model, evaluation is terminal.

It is important to note that:

- Objectives form the basis for the selection and organization of learning experiences.
- Objectives form the basis for assessing the curriculum.
- Objectives are derived from the learner, contemporary life and subject specialist.

To Tyler, evaluation is a process by which one matches the initial expectation with the outcomes.

Wheeler's Model

Wheeler's model for curriculum design is an improvement upon Tyler's model. Instead of a linear model, Wheeler developed a cyclical model. Evaluation in Wheeler's model is not terminal. Findings from the evaluation are fed back into the objectives and the goals, which influence other stages Wheeler contends that:

- Aims should be discussed as behaviours referring to the end product of learning which yields the ultimate goals. One can think of these ultimate goals as outcomes.
- Aims are formulated from the general to the specific in curriculum planning. This results in the formulation of objectives at both an enabling and a terminal level.
- Content is distinguished from the learning experiences which determine that content.

Kerr's Model

Most of the features in Kerr's model resemble those in Wheeler's and Tyler's models. However, Kerr divided the domains into four areas: objectives,

- Knowledge,
- Evaluation
- School learning experiences. What you should note about the model is that:
- The four domains are interrelated directly or indirectly, and
- Objectives are derived from school learning experiences and knowledge.

In Kerr's model, objectives are divided into three groups:

- Affective
- Cognitive
- Psychomotor.

The model further indicates that knowledge should be:

- Organized,
- Integrated,
- Sequenced, and
- Reinforced.

Evaluation in Kerr's model is the collection of information for use in making decisions about the curriculum. School learning experiences are influenced by societal opportunities, the school community, pupil and teacher relationships, individual differences, teaching methods, content and the maturity of the learners. These experiences are evaluated through tests, interviews, assessments and other reasonable methods. In his model, Kerr asserts that everything influences everything else and that it is possible to start an analysis at any point.

In designing a curriculum, you need to:

- Establish or obtain general goals of education.
- Reduce the general goals to specific instructional objectives, including

objectives that cover different domains and levels.
- Assess prior student knowledge and/or abilities.
- Break learning into small, sequential steps.
- Identify teacher behaviour.
- Identify student behaviour.
- Write a description of the lesson.
- Evaluate to see if the intended outcomes have been achieved.

If you complete these eight stages, you would have conducted what is generally referred to as the task analysis process.

ADVANTAGES OF THE CENTRALIZED PATTERN OF CURRICULUM DESIGN

Some of the advantages of a centralised pattern of curriculum design are listed below:
- It makes it easy to achieve national goals, since all schools use the same documents.
- Learners can transfer from one school to another without being disadvantaged.
- Entry requirements for universities and colleges can be centrally determined and parity can be ensured
- Communication to schools regarding academic requirements is easy, since the Ministry of Education is directly involved.
- Learning materials can be mass-produced, making them less expensive for both producers and consumers.
- Institutions can be well staffed and richly serviced because they draw from a national pool of expertise and resources.

DISADVANTAGES OF THE CENTRALISED PATTERN OF CURRICULUM DESIGN

Some of the disadvantages of centralising the development of the curriculum are listed below:
- The process takes a long time before the final document is produced.
- The design is insensitive to the needs of some groups within the country.
- There are coordination and communication problems when para-statals are involved in curriculum design.
- There is limited participation by various members of the community, resulting in little commitment during the implementation stage.
- It stifles creativity and initiative on the part of the teacher and other community members.
- Generally, the centralised pattern stresses content, mainly knowledge, at the expense of the development of attitudes and skills. There is a

scramble for certificates, with little regard for the development and demonstration of productive skills.

DECENTRALIZED PATTERN OF CURRICULUM DESIGN

The decentralized pattern of curriculum design occurs when the local authorities or individual states draft their own curriculum. This type of designing is common in developed countries. However, some developing countries with large populations and states, such as Nigeria, use the decentralized pattern of curriculum design. This pattern of curriculum designing has the following characteristics:

- Local communities initiate the changes to suit their local needs.
- Teachers work with the parents to determine the content. The learning experiences are based on what is available.
- Subjects in schools could be the same, but the content will vary from school to school, state to state, or district to district.
- Each school, state or district has its own syllabus that is produced locally.
- Generally, the textbooks may not have been centrally approved.
- Each school, state or district has its own form of evaluation.
- Very few people are involved in curriculum designing.

You can now look at some of the institutions that are involved in designing the curriculum.

State or District Based Curriculum Designing

In principle, these have the same structure as the centralised structure that was discussed earlier in this section. The only difference is that each district or state will have the final approval on content. However, each curriculum produced should meet the national goals. In general, the same types of people involved in the centralised pattern are also involved at the state or district level.

Local Authorities

Institutions and responsible authorities such as town boards and churches may be involved in curriculum development. Normally, they would depend on the teachers, heads of schools, subject specialists, industry representatives, researchers and consultants to draft the curriculum.

Consultants and teachers usually outline the content and learning experiences. Assessment and evaluation are conducted by a board of the local authority's choice.

Continuous assessment is generally the norm in schools with a decentralized pattern of curriculum designing. Like the centralised pattern, the decentralized pattern of curriculum designing has some advantages and disadvantages.

Advantages of the Decentralized Pattern

The following are some advantages of the decentralized pattern of curriculum designing, to which you can add more: The curriculum addresses local needs.

- The local community is directly involved and is committed to its implementation.
- The system encourages creativity and initiative on the part of the teacher.
- It takes less time to produce the curriculum than it would take when a centralised pattern is used.
- Students learn what is relevant to the local community.

Disadvantages of the Decentralized Pattern

The following are some of the disadvantages:

- There is no guarantee that national goals will be achieved.
- Learners cannot easily transfer from one school to another when their families move.
- There is generally a problem in developing or accessing teaching materials which, if available, are expensive to produce.
- There may not be adequate expertise in the local community to develop part of the curriculum

CURRICULUM PRACTICE

SCHOOL-BASED CURRICULUM

In order for you to develop insight into the methods you can use to deliver teaching content, it is important to understand how a school-based curriculum is designed. This is the focus of this unit.

What Is a School Curriculum?

For the purpose of this unit, school shall be defined as a social institution designed to give formal learning to children. As a teacher, you are aware that a school curriculum is a programme of selected content and learning experiences offered by a school and capable of either modifying or changing learner behaviour. Included in this definition are the following ideas:

- There is a source from which content and learning experiences are selected.
- One or more people select content and learning experiences. Their selection is based on specified criteria and/or influenced by a number of factors.
- The learner should experience a change in behaviour after completing a programme. Ideally, the behaviour changes should be those expected by the educators involved in the teaching-learning process.

As the unit unfolds, these ideas will be developed further. Have you ever looked at your own school's curriculum? You should notice that it is a list of subjects and experiences offered by your school to the learners. Have you wondered "Why were those subjects chosen and not others?" Another question may be, "Who chose these subjects and experiences?" These questions will be addressed in this unit. Let us start by looking at why it is necessary to design a school-based curriculum.

Reasons for Designing a School Curriculum

As you are already aware, a school serves the needs of the child. All that is done by the school should be for the good of the child. You as a teacher should not lose sight of this fact. The school is established to improve the community, the environment and the lives of the learners. It therefore becomes the responsibility of the school to develop the following:

- the capacity of the learner
- the manipulative skills of the learner
- the attitudes and value systems of the learner.

If the school fulfils these three responsibilities, a learner will be able to display new behaviours. A school curriculum should help all learners to develop their mental capacity, acquire manipulative or technical skills and develop their emotional state. To accomplish these goals, the school curriculum must meet certain demands.

Factors That Influence a School-Based Curriculum Design

Assuming that the school curriculum developers design their curriculum with the child in mind, there are a number of factors that they need to consider. These are described below.

National Goals of Education

Learning in any country is guided by its national goals and philosophy. These are influenced by political considerations to ensure national identity. Curriculum development can be centralised at the national level or decentralised to the local level.

Number of Subject Options Available

The central pattern of curriculum design is further influenced by the number of subjects in the national curriculum. Normally, a school cannot include on its list a subject that is not on the national curriculum, so the school curriculum is limited to what the national list has to offer.

The Learner

In addition to national goals, the school curriculum is influenced greatly by the mental, physical and emotional requirements of the child. The school curriculum developers look at the child's level of development and maturity. The juniors should be given what they can handle in terms of depth and quantity. For example, in science at the primary level, there is more concern with the systems and processes that affect the learner's life without giving the principles and theories behind them. At higher levels, the physical, chemical and biological systems and processes are described in terms of the principles and theories that explain them. The level of complexity increases as the mental capacity of the learner develops.

Learning experiences increase in intensity and complexity with increased manipulative skills. Thus the physical condition of the learners also influences the selection of subjects and experiences. One cannot teach art appreciation to children in a school for the blind and under normal conditions, one would not teach music to the deaf.

Resource Availability

By resources, we are referring to learning facilities, materials and personal factors such as qualification and experience. A school should not select a subject merely because other schools are offering it. A secondary school should not offer computer science if it has no electricity, or opt for rugby if there are no grounds and trainers qualified to coach the sport. The developers must look at the resources that are available before selecting a subject for the school.

Culture of the People Around the School

At a secondary school, it does not make much sense for the Bible to be taught in a Hindu society or the Koran to be taught in a Christian society. In any country, subjects such as commerce, economics, science and accounting make a lot of sense because they will help the learners to acquire skills needed to produce goods and services. To humanists, it makes sense to include literature, history, science and geography. The content and learning experiences provided by a school should have cultural relevance for its learners.

The School Environment

Planners should consider what the environment could offer to the learner and how the environment can be exploited to facilitate the teaching and learning process. For example, if the school is located in a desert area, you might think of offering a course on crop science and farming in arid environments.

Evaluation System and Strategies

You should also note that the designer of a school curriculum should consider the system and strategy for the evaluation of the curriculum. Practical assessments for certain subjects such as chemistry require special equipment and apparatus that the school might not be able to afford. Learners might be frustrated if they followed a course of study for which they were not assessed, because where there is no assessment, there is no certification. In addition, the instructors teaching these subjects may not take them seriously. Without commitment from both the teacher and the learners, teaching these subjects wastes time and money.

It also would not make much sense to offer a subject in a trade that required industrial testing equipment if the school could not expose the learners to the same environment and conditions found in industry. These examples stress the need to consider evaluation seriously.

The Process of School Curriculum Designing

Formulating a school-based curriculum is not different from designing a curriculum in general. The only difference is that content and learning experiences are more localised. Taba and other writers suggest that the steps below be followed:

- Diagnosis of needs
- Formulation of objectives
- Selection of content
- Organisation of content
- Selection of learning experiences
- Organisation of learning experiences
- Determination of what should be evaluated and the means of evaluation.

You might be wondering what happens at each stage. Let us examine each stage more closely.

Diagnosis of Needs

This is a fact-finding stage in which you assess the needs of society and the available resources. You might need to find answers to the following questions:

- Who are the learners?
- Who are the teachers?
- Why is the programme necessary?
- Where will the programme be implemented?
- How will it be implemented?

The answers to these questions will become the basis for establishing policy or formulating goals.

Formulation of Objectives

Once the goals are established, one needs to determine what the outcomes should be. At this stage, the goals are written as statements of intent that describe the behaviours which children are expected to exhibit as a result of studying the curriculum. Once this is done, you must then identify the content.

Selection of Content

After the intended outcomes have been determined, for example, to produce children with inquiring minds, you need to select content that will help achieve that objective. Subjects such as science, mathematics and geography may be selected. These subjects are based on inquiry. This stage relates the objectives formulated in the second stage to the subjects available from the national curriculum.

Organisation of Content

The third stage is concerned mainly with the identification of content that can be included.

At this stage, the identified content is sequentially arranged to correspond to the maturity and development levels of the learners. Related content is also grouped and all possible relationships established. Once content has been organised, it will be easier to select learning experiences.

Selection of Learning Experiences

This stage is concerned with the identification of relevant learning experiences that will enable the learner to understand and appreciate the content. These are identified in any order and put on paper. When all the selected subjects have been reviewed, one then needs to look at sequencing these experiences.

Organisation of Learning Experiences

Learning experiences are organised in the same manner in which the content is organised. Identified experiences are arranged according to their complexity.

The simple tasks come first and the most complex appear later. This will help the learner to go through the course with ease.

At this point, you should be aware that a school must grade content and learning experiences. This is why subject matter is prescribed for each grade, standard or form. These stages determine what should be taught at what level, and how. After the content and sequence of learning experiences have been determined, evaluation is the final step in the process of designing a school curriculum.

Evaluation

Consideration is made at this stage as to whether the desired outcomes have been met. In order to accomplish this, it is necessary to measure learners' accomplishments and compare them with the objectives identified at the beginning of the curriculum planning process. The results of the evaluation will be used for curriculum improvement.

SYLLABUS DESIGN AND ASSESSMENT

As a teacher, you have used a syllabus to prepare your lessons. Teachers can be more effective in their teaching when they understand and interpret their syllabuses well. This unit discusses the syllabus and its interpretation.

What Is a Syllabus?

Generally, a syllabus is defined as "a course of study offered by a learning institution in a specific period of time". Other authorities have considered a syllabus to be a collection of topics on the same subject matter that are required to meet the course objectives. Farrant defined a syllabus as "a series of statements of what is to be learned".

For the purposes of this unit, a syllabus will be defined as a course outline comprising a collection of topics on the same subject matter and a series of statements of what is to be learned within a given time frame.

A syllabus is a very important document to a practising teacher because it is the basis for the content delivered to the learner. Below are some reasons why it is important to have a syllabus:

- From the syllabus, the teacher can determine what topics are to be taught at each level: class, grade or form.
- The syllabus outlines terminal objectives. It gives the teacher the basis for evaluation, since these objectives specify the expected achievements at the end of the course.
- The syllabus lists concepts to be developed; it tells the teacher what pupils should learn.
- The syllabus outlines the learning experiences and provides notes on the subject to be learned. These help the teacher determine the depth of the content and the expected skills to be developed. The teacher can easily prepare materials needed to deliver lessons.
- The syllabus provides strategies and means of evaluating the learners' understanding of the subject. In some instances, the syllabus may suggest the skills to be evaluated and the weighting of each skill (for example, practical skills 40% and knowledge 60%). The syllabus specifies the number of examination papers and their nature, as in the following:

Three papers will be set in this subject:

- Paper 1: Theory – multiple-choice questions
- Paper 2: Theory – structured and long-answer questions
- Paper 3: Alternative to practicals

Difference Between a Syllabus and Curriculum

The two words 'syllabus' and 'curriculum' are often used interchangeably. As a teacher, you should be aware of the differences between them.

Curriculum:

- Contains a broad description of general goals.
- Indicates overall philosophy of education that applies across subjects.
- Reflects national and political trends.

Syllabus:

- Is a more detailed and operational document of teaching and learning elements.
- Translates the philosophy of the curriculum.
- Is a collection of related topics on the same subject.

A syllabus is derived from the curriculum objectives. A curriculum is general, while a syllabus is more specific and focused on one subject. We can now look at some important elements of a syllabus.

Elements of a Syllabus

Before elements of a syllabus are discussed, it is important to note that syllabuses are designed centrally by panels of specialists and teachers with experience in the subject. A number of consultations are done before the final document is produced. Panellists are given assignments that must be completed before they are reviewed and discussed. When the panels finally produce a document, a lot of effort will have gone into it. This is why the syllabus is able to guide and inform teachers in schools. The common elements found in most types of the syllabus are described below.

- *Course Objectives* outline the learning that pupils should be able to demonstrate at the end of the course. Generally, these objectives concern themselves with the skills, knowledge and attitudes that are to be developed. They are subject-specific, unlike those in the curriculum.
- *Course Content.* In each subject area, there are certain topics that should be included at each level. These topics are listed so that the teacher knows which subject matter to teach and the level at which to teach it.
- *Methods of Evaluation.* This indicates the means and strategies of evaluation, the skills to be evaluated and the number of test papers, including the nature of the papers.

While formats are given in syllabuses, they normally differ from subject to subject. When a school receives the syllabus, the document is interpreted and divided into topics to be taught each term. The grouping of these topics depends on:

- *Complexity of concept within each topic.* Topics with simple concepts are taught before more complex ones.
- *Relatedness of topics.* Topics that are related should come together but be sequentially ordered.

- *Seasons of the year*. Certain topics are best taught during wet or dry seasons. The weather will determine the term in which certain topics are taught. For example, it is most effective to teach about floods during the rainy season and about photosynthesis in biology when the leaves are green.

Scheming

Once the school syllabus is ready, each teacher will be asked to draft a scheme of work. Though you have made and used a scheme of work, let us briefly discuss it.

Generally a scheme is a breakdown of topics into teaching units that are sequentially arranged to facilitate teaching. There are different formats used, depending on the conventions in each school, but all generally include the date, topic, objectives, activities, resources to be used and assignments and evaluation, both general and individual.

There is also a scheme-cum-plan. This type of scheming combines the scheme and the planning of the lessons. This document should be detailed so that anyone can follow it. At this point, it is necessary to review important terms such as 'concepts', 'core messages' or 'major understandings', 'terminal objectives' and enabling objectives', as they are generally used during scheming.

Concepts

Wilson, Robeck and Michael define a concept as "a generalised idea of a group of a class of things". A concept is an abstraction; it does not make relationships explicit. An example of a concept in science is 'states of matter'. In mathematics, you can look at 'addition' and in sociology 'change'. These need to be qualified further. To do this, core messages or major understandings are used.

Core messages or major understandings

These are statements that make relationships explicit. They relate ideas so that their meaning is understood. Using concepts cited above, these examples can be drawn:

- *States of matter*. As a core message, you can have 'a change in the states of matter'. You can now build meaning of movement from one to the other.
- *Change*. In sociology, you can have the core message 'resistance to change'.

To derive meaning from concepts, core messages or major understandings need to be built. Many people, however, have taken core messages to be concepts. In teaching, if you present the core message, then the learners will benefit. However, note that teaching and learning are related but independent processes. Although a teacher may facilitate learning, the learner is responsible for his or her learning.

Objectives

An objective is defined as an intent communicated by a statement describing a proposed change in the learner. In this unit, an objective is a statement of what the learner will do as an outcome of instruction and a statement of change in the behaviour of the learner as a result of the instruction or training. Objectives generally are written in terms of the learner's performance or behaviour. Objectives may be classified as terminal or enabling.

- *Terminal objectives* are statements of intent regarding the learner's achievement at the conclusion of a unit of instruction. Such statements are derived from the content of the unit.
- *Enabling objectives* are statements of intent that make it possible for the learner to arrive at the terminal behaviour. In other words, an enabling objective is a sub-terminal objective.

Also note that learning objectives must be 'SMART':

- Specific
- Measurable
- Achievable
- Realistic/Result-oriented
- Time framed

Objectives are specified because:

- they enable the teacher to select learning materials and teaching methods,
- they guide the teacher in creating the learning environment in which objectives can be accomplished, and
- they show learners what is expected of them.

Evaluation

After the teacher has sequenced the topics, outlined the concepts, specified the learning objectives, identified activities and materials to be used and taught the lesson, it is important to determine whether the instructional and learning intentions have been met. The teacher needs to prepare some means of evaluating materials, learners and methods used in teaching. Evaluation strategies should be specified when the teacher is drafting the scheme of work.

Instruments in the form of self-evaluations, self-assessments and practice activities should be prepared. Normally these are referred to as exercises, homework and tests. In the scheme of work, the teacher should indicate when each type of assessment is given. Guided by the objectives given, it should be easy to make these tests and exercises by basing them on intended outcomes. A record of what happens during teaching should be written under the assessment and evaluation column in the scheme book. Continuous assessment gives the teacher a clear picture of the progress the learners are making. This is very important in teaching

TIMETABLE

Imagine what would happen in your school if you had no timetable and all the teachers wanted to teach the same class at the same time. Would all the teachers be qualified to teach the same class? Would the learners receive the education they deserved? Would there be adequate resources for each class? This unit discusses timetabling and its importance for the smooth running of the school.

Types of Timetables

For the purpose of this unit, we will refer to a timetable as a schedule of events that guides school activities throughout the day, week, term or year. For each activity, a timetable generally specifies a starting time and an ending time. In some cases, it indicates who is involved and how the activity will be conducted. At school, there is a master timetable that is prepared by the head and deputy. This timetable shows when the school day begins and ends. It shows the activities for each day. It further shows which teacher will teach which subject to which class, on what day and at what times. From the master timetable, each department prepares the timetable that should be followed by all the members of the department. This is called a department timetable. Each teacher will note his or her own class and subject times from the department timetable and create a class timetable or individual timetable. For primary schools and small secondary schools, class or individual timetables are extracted from the master timetable. Generally the shortest duration on the timetable is called a period. The length of a teaching period varies from school to school, although the range is normally between 30 minutes and 40 minutes. However, there are schools that use blocks instead of periods. A block is used at the tertiary level more than in high schools because the time span is generally an hour or more. Blocks of periods can also be used to teach science, language, literature and practical subjects when more than one period is needed.

Role of a Timetable in a School

The timetable performs a number of functions in a school. Some of these are discussed below.

Communication

In administration, a timetable is a means of communication for administrators, teachers, students and school staff. Each person is told who does what, when, how and where. All that is needed will be a reminder. Some schools use a bell or siren.

Resource Allocation

A timetable indicates what subject or class should be taught at any given time. The administrator looks at the teachers available and deploys them accordingly. For example, a primary school with four streams at each level from Grade/standard 1-7 may have only 18 qualified teachers. It would make sense to ensure that each level has a qualified teacher. The lower levels and upper levels, whenever possible, should have more qualified teachers where more expertise is needed. By looking at the timetable, it is possible to determine when learning materials would be needed during the year, term or part of the day. The head would know what materials should be given to which people and at what time. For example, an overhead projector may be needed by Mr Bulawa for his history class and Mr Moyo for his English class. The timetable facilitates the distribution of resources. Time as a resource must to be adequately and equitably shared, depending on the recommended number of periods. For example, in Zimbabwe, mathematics requires 320 hours as compared to 70 hours for religious education. Each subject should be appropriately fitted on the timetable so that the instruction is spread over a period of time rather than being crowded into one part of the year or day.

Control

The timetable indicates when an activity should start and when it should end. Teachers plan work to fit the time available. The students are required to do certain activities in specified periods. A student who likes sports will not do sports all day, but other subjects as well. Thus, a timetable restricts or controls the activities occurring within a school.

Accountability

The timetable shows what is to be done, by whom, when and how. If things go well or wrong, it is known who did it, when and where. To the authorities, it justifies the number and responsibilities of teaching staff.

Monitoring Tool

With a timetable, it is easy to monitor events in the school. Teachers can easily plan and monitor their own work and the children's progress. Heads and Ministry of Education authorities can monitor what is happening in their schools. The timetable can indicate what has been taught, who taught it and the learners involved.

Factors That Influence Timetabling

The following are some of the factors that influence timetabling:

- *The length of the school day* determines how many subjects can fit on the timetable. For example, a boarding school can start school at 07:15

hrs and end at 17:30 hrs. It will have more activities fitted on the timetable and can afford to give more time to each period than could a day school which starts at 08:00 hrs and finishes at 15:00 hrs. Timetabling is difficult when a school day is divided into two sessions. The number of hours available for instruction can be greatly restricted in this situation.

- *The number of required contact hours* should also be considered. For example, 320 hors are required to complete a mathematics course at the junior secondary level, while an Africa language course requires 160 hours. Therefore, there will be more mathematics periods than African language periods on the timetable each week.
- *The number of teachers* in the institution will determine the size of the classes and periods on the timetable. In a secondary school, the timetable indicates the number of subjects and classes each teacher will teach. In primary schools, the number of teachers will determine whether there will be multigrade (composite) classes or single classes. This affects the way the timetable is produced.
- *The availability of facilities* will determine whether there will be double sessioning or not. If a school has fewer classrooms than classes, the only way to accommodate all the classes is to have more than one session each day. This scheduling solution, however, creates many other problems.
- *The number of subjects in the curriculum* influences timetabling. Schools with a few subjects might have long periods, while schools with a wide curriculum have short periods in order to accommodate all the subjects they offer. Some schools cannot accommodate sporting activities and social clubs on their timetables, while others can do so easily.

Scheming and Planning

From your experience of scheming and planning as a teacher, you are most likely familiar with indicating times, topics, objectives, methods, teaching aids and activities. In your teaching, a lesson plan indicates the steps to follow, method to use and activities to do with your class. This requires serious and thorough preparation.

RESOURCE ALLOCATION

In that unit, you were informed that allocating time to the teaching of subjects in the school curriculum is an activity that enables teachers to interact with students in the process known as teaching.

The unit you have just started focuses on resource allocation. It deals with the allocation of various types of resources needed to make the teaching and learning process an instrument of achieving national and school curricular goals and objectives. Without resources, these goals and objectives cannot be realised. But you may ask:

- What are these resources?
- How do schools access them?
- Who provides them?

This unit will provide some answers to these questions.

Definition of Resource Allocation

In order to have a full understanding of this unit, it is important that you are familiar with the meaning of the words 'resources' and 'allocation'. Perhaps you have read and heard about these words, but not in the context of curriculum implementation. Before you relate them to the achievement of curriculum goals and objectives at both national and school levels, we will define them.

- Resources are defined by *Longman Dictionary of Contemporary English* as "the means, money, property and skills that are available to someone or an institution for the purpose of achieving specified objectives".
- Allocation is derived from the verb allocate, meaning to decide officially that a particular amount of resources be given to or used for a particular purpose.

In the context of this unit therefore, resource allocation refers to the resources that governments, local authorities and schools make available for the purpose of achieving educational goals and objectives as specified in the curriculum. The ultimate consumers or beneficiaries of these resources are the learners and the society as a whole.

Sources of Educational Resources

You should have identified a number of the sources in the exercise you have just completed. Below are a few of the sources of educational resources that schools are likely to use.

Central Government

As you are aware, the central government allocates huge sums of money to the Ministry of Education to use in its mandate of educating the country's children. Other ministries also allocate funds to carry out their own national mandates or responsibilities. The central government allocates financial resources yearly to various ministries in what is popularly known as the 'Budget'.

Ministry of Education

Once the Ministry has received its share of financial resources from the central government, it has to distribute them rationally to its various divisions or departments with specific responsibilities for the implementation of educational goals and objectives. Each division or department in turn allocates its share to its various components for utilisation, and the process continues until it reaches the teaching and learning experiences at the school and classroom levels.

Local Authority

The local authority can be a recipient of government financial resources and can also generate its own resources and allocate them to schools under its care or jurisdiction. Rural and urban councils are the authorities with this responsibility. The most important resource they allocate to schools is land on which the school buildings and playgrounds are situated. A local authority can also allocate money to individual schools for infrastructural facilities such as classrooms, laboratories, libraries and textbooks. This is done in order to facilitate the teaching and learning process at the school and classroom levels.

The School

The school has many resources at its disposal which it can use in its task of translating centrally planned curriculum goals and objectives into learning activities. Some of the resources a school may have at its disposal include:

- money (school fees, sports fees, levies and government grants)
- time
- physical facilities (classrooms, laboratories, libraries and playgrounds)
- equipment (radios, televisions and computers)
- classroom furnishings (desks, benches and chalkboards)
- teachers
- books (textbooks and exercise books).

A school has to allocate each of these to students in order to realise learning experiences.

Parents

Parents are also a great source of educational resources. In most countries, parents pay fees in order for the school to purchase books and materials needed in the teaching and learning process. In some communities or localities, the parents buy books for their own children.

Parents can also contribute towards the salary of teachers, as is the case in private schools and schools with high fees.

The Teacher

The most important resources teachers have are:

- knowledge,
- skills, and

It is the teachers who translate the curriculum goals and objectives of the nation, the community and the school into learning experiences. It is therefore important that they have adequate time and competencies to do so.

Types of Educational Resources

Now that you know the sources of educational resources, it is necessary to classify these resources as:

- financial,
- human, or
- material.

This section of the unit focuses on how the Ministries of Education utilise these resources. We will examine each of them individually.

Financial Resources

In nearly every Southern African Development Community (SADC) country, the allocated funds are used for:

- meeting teachers' and administrators' salaries,
- providing teaching and learning materials to schools through per-capita allocation to every registered student,
- the training and professional development of teachers,
- building tutorial and teacher residential facilities, and
- administration and maintenance of buildings and facilities.

Human Resources

The human resources Ministries of Education have are:

- teachers, inspectors, and
- administrators.

It is the quantity and quality of the human resources that determine the quality of teaching and learning. The rational allocation of these to different parts of a country is therefore a central function of the Ministry. The Ministry should ensure that there is some equity in the distribution of qualified and non-qualified teaching and supervisory personnel to regions, districts and schools. This ensures that no one area develops at the expense of the others. The allocation of human resources to regions and schools is as important as the allocation of financial resources.

Material Resources

At the Ministry level, material resources include all the equipment, buildings and even vehicles that are purchased and maintained in order to assist schools in their teaching and learning function. These must also be equitably allocated to regions, districts and schools in order to reduce inequalities and inequities among communities in the society.

Resource Allocation at the School Level

It is at the school that resources from the sources you previously identified interact in order to achieve the educational goals and objectives outlined in the curriculum. The school head must recruit qualified and competent teachers. The deployment of these teachers to subject areas and classes is one form of allocating resources at the school level. The school heads should allocate the time, material and human resources at their disposal for the benefit of all. Failure to competently allocate these resources may result in failure to achieve the curriculum goals and objectives the school is set up to achieve.

Resource Allocation by the Teachers

Teachers also have resources that they can allocate to their students. We identified these resources as time, knowledge and skills. In order for the teaching and learning process to take place effectively, teachers must be able to allocate these resources equitably among their students. The teacher is the last person in the chain to make sure that resources allocated at various levels are utilised for the benefit of the students.

Adequacy of Educational Resources

With the high demand for education throughout the SADC region, educational resources are far from being adequate. Central governments are unable to meet the financial requirements of the Ministries of Education. In turn, Ministries are unable to meet the requirements of regions and schools. Therefore, at the school level, heads and teachers must manage the resources they have very efficiently in order to achieve the goals of the prescribed curriculum.

DELIVERY METHODOLOGIES

You learned how educational resources are allocated to Ministries of Education by central governments for the purpose of implementing national educational goals. We also explained how the school can mobilise resources at its disposal in order to translate curriculum objectives into teaching and learning experiences.

This unit will take you through a very familiar area. We will discuss teaching methodologies, which are the methods teachers use to deliver their lessons.

Definitions

As we have done in other units, we will define key words used in this unit.

Teaching

What is your definition of this term? There may be as many definitions of the word as there are teachers. However, Hunter in Beach and Reinhartz defines teaching as "the constant stream of professional decisions that affects the probability of learning: decisions that are made and implemented before, during and after interaction with the students".

According to Beach and Reinhartz, teaching is a complex and multidimensional activity. It includes:

- telling
- explaining
- defining
- giving examples
- stressing critical attributes
- modelling
- demonstrating.

Method

Collins Reference English Dictionary defines method as "techniques of doing something", while *Longman Dictionary of Contemporary English* defines it as "a planned way of doing something".

The two definitions are applicable to teaching as an activity. In this unit, teaching methodologies will be taken to refer to those techniques and strategies used by teachers in their efforts to facilitate student learning.

Teaching and Curriculum Implementation

In the preceding units, you learned that teaching is the activity that translates curriculum goals and objectives into experiences that students acquire during their interaction with the teacher. All the resources the government and individuals allocate to education should be effectively and efficiently exploited during this interaction.

The question you might ask is, "Do students or learners acquire all the experiences and knowledge that the subject content is expected to generate during the interaction?" The answer to this question is most likely "Yes", but it could also be "No", depending on the methodology the teacher uses to achieve lesson objectives. Some methodologies may not be appropriate for certain subjects and certain lesson situations. The methodologies teachers commonly use are:

- lecturing,
- demonstration,
- illustrating,
- experimentation,
- inquiry,
- role playing,
- song and dance,
- observation,

- dramatisation, and
- projects and research.

Learning experiences can take place when one or a combination of these methods are employed by a teacher during a teaching and learning interaction.

Lesson Implementation

There is no teaching methodology that, on its own, makes students learn. Methodologies are only approaches that teachers use to capture students' interest and motivate them to learn the information provided.

According to Beach and Reinhartz, the teaching from which students learn the most is one in which the teacher does the following:

- Provides opportunities for students to participate actively and successfully.
- Evaluates and provides feedback on students' progress during instruction.
- Organises materials and students.
- Maximises time for teaching.
- Manages student behaviours.
- Teaches for cognitive, affective and/or psychomotor learning.
- Uses effective communication skills.

Beach and Reinhartz state that teaching and learning are effective when:

- The teacher presents clear lesson goals and objectives to students.
- The classroom environment is businesslike in nature.
- The subject matter being taught is effectively covered.
- The teacher is flexible in his or her teaching methods, with extra materials, displays and/or resource materials in the classroom.
- The teacher has vigour, energy and is involved with the students.
- The teacher provides students with positive and negative feedback.
- The teacher asks students questions at different levels and adjusts them appropriately as the lesson proceeds.
- The teacher is able to conduct the class without the lesson being interrupted.
- The teacher sets and articulates the learning goals, assesses student progress and makes class presentations, illustrating how to do assigned work.
- The teacher allocates adequate time to cover the material being taught, yet remains flexible enough to allow for the unexpected.
- The teacher maintains a balance between the level of difficulty of the topic being taught and the pace of the lesson.

Conditions for Successful Lesson Delivery

We have discussed the teaching methodologies and what teachers should do during the delivery process. Now you may want to pose this question: What conditions make effective teaching possible? Provide an answer for yourself. Then, consider the following:

- *Conducive teaching and learning environment.* The place where teaching and learning interaction takes place must motivate both the teacher and the learner. A depressing environment creates tension and impedes maximum participation.
- *Availability of appropriate resources.* Resources to teach the specific subject area must be made available to the teacher in sufficient quantities so that all students have an opportunity to use them.
- *Support from supervisors.* Teachers are motivated by support and encouragement from their supervisors. Occasional visits to the classrooms and the provision of positive feedback encourage teachers to perform even better.
- *Teacher's personality.* Since teachers are the most critical factor in the teaching and learning process, their personal attributes are central to the learning activity. For teachers to capture the attention of all students, they must have the following attributes:
- *Cleanliness and smartness.* Teachers must be appropriately dressed and presentable. Students should want to emulate them.
- *Good health.* A sickly teacher definitely demotivates students. It is likely that such a teacher spends most of the time away from the station or classroom. If the teacher is not present on a regular basis, learning activities are frequently disrupted, and the students are unlikely to establish a meaningful rapport with the teacher.
- *Knowledgeability*. Teachers must be appropriately qualified to teach the subject matter and be thoroughly conversant with the content of the subject being taught. They should know much more than their students.
- *Gender sensitivity*. The teacher must be aware of gender issues and use a gender-neutral approach.
- *Respect*. The teacher must respect the opinions and intellectual capabilities of all of the students.

MONITORING THE SCHOOL CURRICULUM

As you will appreciate, it is important to check on the successes and progress made in the learning and teaching process and to provide professional guidance where possible. This unit discusses the monitoring of the school curriculum to facilitate learning and teacher development.

Monitoring

As a teacher, you have monitored your students and you have been monitored by your superiors. In everyday use, the term 'monitor' means to check, to follow, to keep an eye on and to supervise. In this unit, monitoring the curriculum is defined as a process of helping teachers to improve the learning opportunities for the learners. Monitoring in the educational environment:

- is a process and not an event,
- aims at improving the teacher's skills,
- should result in improved opportunities for the learner, and
- considers all that is involved in the improvement of learning.

The Importance of Monitoring the School Curriculum

The importance of monitoring the school curriculum cannot be over-emphasised. In the school system, monitoring is done to:

- *help the learners*. Learners will learn if they:
- maximise the gain from the learning experiences offered to them,
- sharpen their learning and technical skills,
- develop knowledge and positive attitudes,
- understand the content being taught to them,
- interact with learning materials meaningfully, and
- develop socially.
- *help the teachers.* Teachers need to:
- sharpen their teaching skills,
- improve their delivery methodologies,
- develop their leadership skills and qualities,
- improve their relationships among themselves and with learners and supervisors,
- upgrade themselves professionally and academically,
- improve their communication skills,
- be creative and innovative, and
- ensure goal achievement.
- *help the supervisors*, such as heads of departments, heads of schools and their deputies, inspectors and education officers. These supervisors need to:
- improve their leadership, communication, observation, professional and technical skills,
- upgrade themselves professionally and academically,
- develop their interpersonal skills,
- be creative and innovative,
- check on standards, and
- check on goal achievement.
- *assess learning materials* to ensure they:
- are user-friendly and relevant to the situation,
- are adequate and appropriate to the educational level, and

- are available.
- *assess the teaching methods* to ensure they:
- meet the level of the learners,
- are interactive in nature, and
- are varied and motivating to the learners.
- *assess the curriculum* in order to:
- improve the relevancy and flexibility of content, and
- determine if instructional objectives are achievable.

By monitoring the school system and all its components, it is possible to determine what is and what is not working and to suggest appropriate improvements. However, if the outcomes of the monitoring process are not taken seriously, then no change will occur. This would not help students. All efforts must be taken to facilitate student learning.

Aspects to Be Monitored

This section outlines the monitoring of the school timetable, resource allocation, schemes of work, teaching methods, learning activities and evaluation.

The School Timetable

If the school timetable is available, it should be checked for the following:

- the length of the school day
- the activities to be conducted
- the resources available, both human and material
- the number of subjects offered in the school
- the prescribed period for each subject
- the availability of the timetable.

Generally, timetables are monitored by inspectors and education officers during their routine visits to the schools. If they find anything that needs improvement, the administrators should help the school personnel to improve the timetable.

Resource Allocation

A school needs guidance and checking on how finances are collected and used. Financial management should be monitored closely to ensure that monies received are accounted for. If school personnel lack financial and administrative skills, appropriate training should be provided. The quantity and quality of books should also be checked. Frequently, the checking is performed by education advisors and inspectors when they visit schools. The heads of schools can also check the books given to different departments in their schools. There should be an adequate number of books, and they should be distributed fairly. A head of a school may buy a set of books for a class, but there may not be a book for every student. This is not a satisfactory situation. Each learner should have his or her own text. If textbooks are kept in a departmental office and are never used, this is a waste of resources. Qualifications and training levels of teachers should be checked. The most skilled teachers should be assigned to lower and upper classes in order to give the young students a good foundation and to ensure the learners in upper classes are prepared for employment or additional education.

Scheming and Planning

The subject specialists, including the department heads and inspectors, need to check the level of content schemed and planned, the appropriateness of methods and materials used and the timing of the activities. The organisation of content is checked also for coherence, sequencing, specificity of objectives and suitability of learning activities. These specialists look at the scheme-books and lesson plans. Using their experience, they can guide the teacher on how to produce the best schemes of work and lesson plans. Heads of schools can also supervise schemes and lesson plans.

Lesson Delivery and Teaching Methods

Teaching does not always lead to learning. Smith defines teaching as "a system of action intended to induce learning". For learning to take place, the teacher must use appropriate and interactive methods. The improvement of teaching methodologies is the responsibility of the supervisors, including the head of department, deputy head, head of school and the education officer or inspector at either the district or provincial level. These supervisors need to observe the teacher in the classroom and note strengths and areas requiring improvement. The teacher and the supervisor will then discuss the progress of the lesson. For maximum benefit to the teacher, the supervisor and the teacher should work together so that they contribute to each other's development.

Learning Activities

The teacher should make sure that each learner has done what he or she is supposed to do. The learning activities should be monitored in order to ensure that each experience has had the intended effect. The teacher is the person responsible for assessing and evaluating students' learning on a regular basis. The teacher should give exercises and tests that are corrected or marked immediately and returned to the learner. This interaction establishes what has been learned and what still needs to be taught or reviewed.

Evaluation

Evaluation methods should be checked to assess their suitability and appropriateness. Their purpose must be clear to the learner, the teacher and society, if the evaluation is to be valid and reliable.

SCHOOL CURRICULUM EVALUATION

This final part describes how the school curriculum can be evaluated. Every teacher should be familiar with the concepts of assessment and evaluation and be able to apply them appropriately. By working through this unit, you will enrich your knowledge and skills as a competent and effective teacher.

Definitions

As in other units, it is necessary that the concepts we are discussing be defined and put into context. This will help you to understand and apply the concepts in your own context. Definitions will be given for 'school curriculum evaluation' and 'assessment'.

School Curriculum Evaluation

This refers to the efforts a school may make to determine the extent to which it achieves the objectives of the syllabuses it teaches. The evaluation may involve all subjects or may be directed at certain subject areas only as the need may arise. It focuses on whether the national and school curriculum objectives are being translated into learning experiences during the teacher-student classroom interaction.

Assessment

In assessment, students are required to perform some act such as conduct experiments, draw pictures, perform and so forth. Assessment determines the students' knowledge and skills output.

Why Evaluate the School Curriculum?

The school is the 'pot' in which the curriculum objectives of a nation or a community are processed. All that takes place in a school has some impact on the society in which students live and will work. It is therefore necessary to investigate whether the resources allocated by the central government for educational purposes are being used to achieve the intended outcomes. In addition to governments, other stakeholders who invest considerably in education at the school level also need to know whether children actually learn during their stay at the school. The only way to objectively discover what occurs at a school is to evaluate its objectives, content, processes and outputs. In other words, the school is evaluated in order to determine how it is succeeding at educating students. In order to determine how a school performs in its endeavours, it is necessary to compare it with schools of its own status in terms of human and material resource allocation.

What Is Evaluated?

According to Gatawa, the following should be used as the basis for establishing the criteria for evaluating school curriculum.

- objectives
- content as outlined in the syllabuses
- materials
- process or methodology used by teachers and administrators.

The following questions must be raised when evaluating objectives:

- Are they worthwhile?
- How do specified objectives compare with possible objectives?
- Can they be achieved?
- Can they be accepted by teachers?
- What are the expected outcomes?

With regards to content, Gatawa says evaluation should focus on:

- its suitability, and
- its correlation with the specified objectives.

Materials are evaluated in order to determine whether they are:

- simple to use,
- easy to produce, and
- cost-effective.

The instructional methodology and administrative processes must be evaluated to determine whether they are consistent with the objectives or if the processes employed assist and support the teachers.

Who Evaluates the Curriculum?

The curriculum can be evaluated by a hired professional evaluator, a consultant or qualified personnel from the Ministry of Education. Whether it is a consultant or Ministry personnel, the evaluator should be:

- an educator;
- competent in statistics, methods of observation, constructing questionnaires and conducting interviews;
- confident, precise and able to communicate effectively; and
- able to create a conducive working atmosphere with assistants.

If a curriculum evaluation is to be successful at the school level, it must receive the support of the community, management, staff and students of the school.

Forms of Evaluation

There are two forms of evaluation:

- formative evaluation
- summative evaluation.

With regards to the evaluation of the school curriculum, formative evaluation is the process of looking for strengths and weaknesses in the content, materials and methodology as the evaluation process unfolds. Weaknesses are attended to before the whole process is completed.

Summative evaluation is conducted at the end of an activity. Its purpose is to ensure that the necessary processes have been carried out and that the objectives of the curriculum are being met.

CURRICULUM IMPLEMENTATION

CONCEPTUAL MATTERS

General curriculum *research* is nowadays in German speaking countries a fringe activity. After a boom in interest in the 1970s to which IPN has made trend-setting contributions we see very little recent publication activity in general curriculum research. Consequently, there is also very little specific investigation of curriculum implementation activities. It seems that the study of the processes of curriculum implementation has virtually dissolved to become one element of the more general field of innovation research and theory. And it surfaces from time to time when researchers venture to become practical with their innovative concepts, such as constructivist learning environments or quality evaluation in schools and find out that there are many obstacles placed on the path from concept to reality under practical circumstances.

Let me start with some *conceptual clarifications*. I understand innovation to be a social activity which aims at changes in four dimensions: *social practices*, the *beliefs and understandings* underpinning these social practices, its *material aspects*, and the *social and organizational structures* in which these practices are embedded and which themselves are associated with systems of resources, power and sanction/gratification.

An innovation is usually characterized through some materialized plan which describes the intended practices, and the aspired ways of changing them, and argues the theories which justify the rationale. It uses some material, other resources and specific social structures to make people act in another way. Its real test lies in being put into practice. Thus, innovation is a practice to change practices.

Consequently, a new curriculum may be described as an attempt to change teaching and learning practices which will also include the transformation of some of the beliefs and understandings hitherto existent in the setting to be changed. It is usually strong on the material side by providing a written curriculum, text books, recommendations for teaching strategies, working material for students, and probably also new artifacts for learning. It is usually less explicit on the organizational side but may also advocate the use of changed time tabling and new social structures, such as peer group interaction, decision making in the subject group, etc.

To distinguish these dimensions of innovation has two purposes: firstly, it describes innovation as a *multidimensional phenomenon*, and thereby, offers some categories for analysis and construction. Secondly, it draws attention to the empirical finding that concentration on some dimensions and neglect of other ones usually leads to deficient results. There are scores of examples of curriculum reform which concentrated on the material side and the theoretical justification of their approach and assumed that changes in teaching practice and in the beliefs and understandings of practitioners would follow from their material input - which frequently turned out to be incorrect. In summary, those innovations are expected to be more successful which explicitly stimulate development on all four dimensions and do not assume that changes in one dimension will automatically follow from changes on other dimensions.

Let me turn to the term *implementation.* Its history begins with becoming aware that it does not take place. It is not unfair to say that usually most of the attention and energy of early curriculum developers was focussed on the production side of their enterprise, on the materialized "plan" or "product". The idea was: If the product is good and if it is widely enough disseminated, it will be *adopted* by the realm of practice. However, history showed that many – some say: most– curriculum projects of the 60s and 70s have not been put into practice in a way curriculum developers had hoped. And that practitioners were not even always aware that they violated the developers' intentions. For innovating classroom practice, attention must obviously not only be given to the *production phase* of a curriculum, but also to what happens after the production. What processes happen under what circumstances if practitioners are supposed to "adopt" a curriculum?

Fig. A simplified overview of the change process

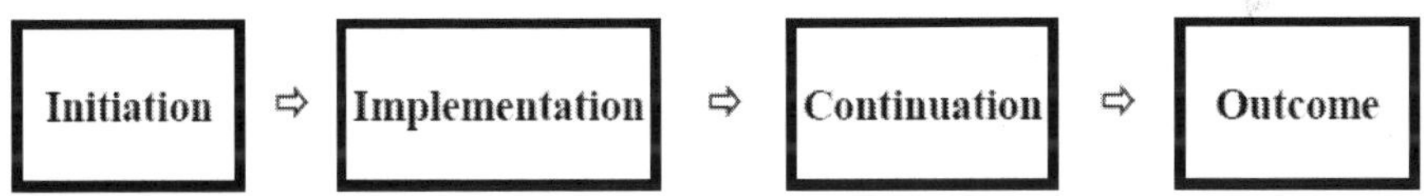

Thus, the term implementation in a broad sense conceptualizes the process through which a proposed concept, model, topic, theory etc. is taken up by some practice. Fullan and Stiegelbauer distinguished three sub-processes in which an innovation is made work in order to produce outcomes. The processes that eventually lead up to and end with the decision to take up a specific innovation proposal have been called *initiation phase*. In the *implementation phase* participants attempt to use the innovation proposal in order to change their practice.

Frequently, extra support for translating the innovatory ideas into reality is offered on a project basis. Thus, while the initiation phase is concerned with the *nominal use* of a curriculum, the implementation phase focuses on the *actual* use. The study of implementation processes is concerned "with the nature and extent of actual change, as well as the factors and processes that influence how and what changes are achieved." Thereby, it aims to find out what type of extra support in the 'project phase' is appropriate to promote actual use of the innovation. In the *continuation phase* the innovation is built into the routine organization, and extra support is withdrawn. Thus, while implementation is concerned with initial use of the innovation under project conditions, continuation deals with mature use under standard conditions.

GENERAL STRATEGIES OF IMPLEMENTATION

How to deal with the "implementation problem", i.e. the problem that so many curricula have not been implemented, or positively: of stimulating a process in which a target group is changing their practices in a way which is considered as improvement? Following Fullan, two *different general approaches* may be contrasted:

The *programmed approach* aims to solve the implementation problem by concentrating on flaws in the *specification of the "product",* e.g.

- gaps in the existing specification of innovations practices;
- failure to articulate the innovation's implication for teachers behavior, and
- theoretical inadequacies with respect to identified means for achieving the intended outcomes of an innovation..

In other words, the specification of the curriculum and of the implementation process is the problem; had they been clearer, problems of implementation would be fewer.

Fig. : Curriculum making in the "programmed approach"

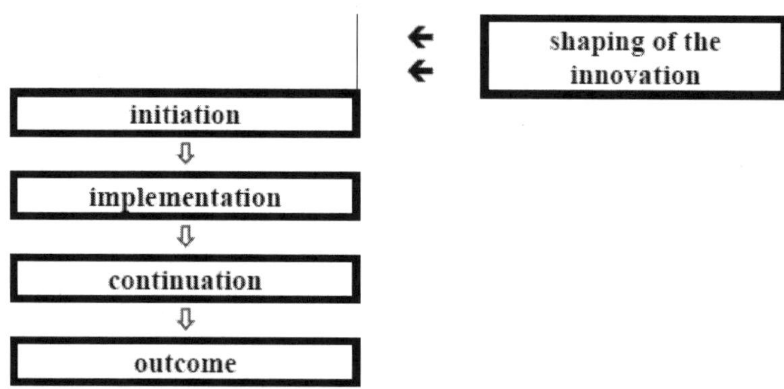

A contrasting conceptualization of the implementation problem is provided by the *adaptive-evolutionary approach* which accepts that the innovation as it has been devised will be modified in the course of its implementation. This is not only seen as just a feature of mundane circumstances wise and realistic persons have to accept but as an essential characteristic of implementation. This resonates a central finding of the Rand Change Agent Study: "The primary feature of effective implementation could be called 'mutual adaptation' in which the project is adapted to its institutional context *and* organizational patterns are adapted to meet the demands of the project."

Particularly with complex innovations, this approach claims that it is conceptually unsound, socially unacceptable, and empirically impossible to solve the implementation problem by programming the persons concerned with putting the innovation into reality through detailed elaborations of the desired practice and step by step specifications for the process of implementation. Rather, innovators to provide their innovation, e.g. a new curriculum, to their audience as "intelligent hypotheses", but invite practitioners to rethink it and further develop it for the specific circumstances they are working in. They expect, even invite negotiation and transaction. They aim to stimulate practitioners to use their practical situational knowledge for implementation and for modifying the original models just as to the demands and resources of the specific locality.

Fig. 3: Curriculum making in the "adaptive-evolutionary approach"

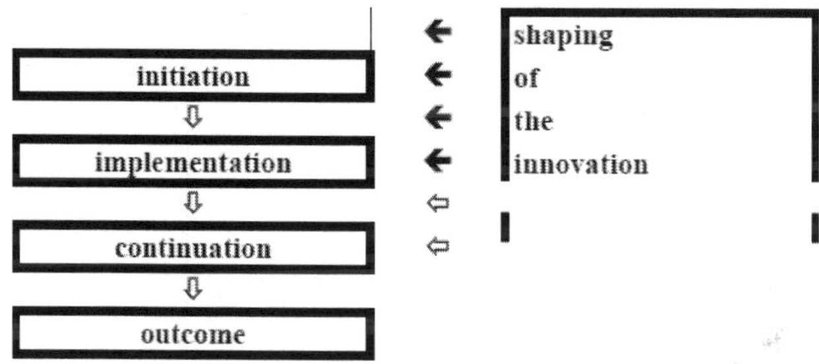

Excursus: Stenhouse's image of the role of teachers in curriculum development

Let me elaborate the arguments which underpin an adaptive-evolutionary approach by reference to Stenhouse's Humanities Curriculum Project which was considered by Goodlad as one of "only a few instances of well-developed curricula that provided students experiential encounters with the problems and issues of their world". Stenhouse argued against the idea to achieve quality changes of educational practice by "programming" teacher behavior. To by-pass collaboration of teachers means to by-pass their rationality and their ingenuity, and this would not solve the implementation problem, but, on the contrary, make it worse. It is the practitioners who must bring a curriculum idea to life in their concrete interaction with specific students under local circumstances.

For Stenhouse, curricula are attempts to communicate - hopefully intelligent – specifications of educational ideas and practices to teachers in order to stimulate their discussion, experimentation and critique. A curriculum is a hypothesis, a starting point for reflection and development done by responsible professionals.

"A curriculum is an attempt to communicate the essential principles and features of an educational proposal in such a form that it is open to critical scrutiny and capable of effective translation into practice.".

Teachers are sometimes sceptical of the innovative products of researchers and curriculum developers. This maybe unpleasant for the developers, however, as Stenhouse argues, teachers' "pragmatic scepticism" should be taken as an impulse of questioning, of wanting to know better, of wanting to develop – in short: as an impulse to research.

If one aims "quality practice" one cannot wish that practitioners take a curriculum proposal literally, that they work towards a one-to-one translation of the curriculum proposal into practice, that they "apply" it the local practice as true as possible to the original intentions, since it is – as knowledge in general – preliminary, hypothetical, incomplete, more or less de-contextualized and worth of being scrutinized and developed. Rather, one must wish that teachers take the specific circumstances of their locality and of their constituencies into account in order to produce and evaluate a local version of the curriculum which is adapted to what is productive and feasible under these specific circumstances.

"The mistake is to see the classroom as a place to apply laboratory findings rather than as a place to refute or confirm them. Curriculum workers need to share the psychologists' curiosity about the process of learning rather than to be dominated by their conclusions."

Thus, the main actors of implementation are the practitioners themselves, because they are responsible for the educational process and they cannot pass on this responsibility to external agencies. External agencies and persons, such as researchers, curriculum developers, in-service trainers may support and stimulate the development of practice; decisions about initiating development and the control over its direction are the realm of practitioners' professional judgment.

For Stenhouse, quality curriculum implementation necessitates curriculum research and evaluation as well as teacher development in the process of implementation and under practitioners' participation. Implementation must attend to specific local conditions and to process experiences of the persons involved in the process of implementation. Curriculum development is not just the production of written goals and materials *before* classroom practice but, at the end, concrete interaction *in* the classroom between learners and teachers aiming to develop situations with high learning potential.

End of excursus

To sum up this comparison of approaches to implementation: While for the programmed approach *curriculum development* takes exclusively place *before* implementation, and implementation is application of pre-specified models, for the adaptive-evolutionary approach the curriculum is also made *during and through* implementation. In the programmed approach an implementation is *evaluated* through the correspondence between the actual use of the innovation and the developers' intentions.

An adaptive-evolutionary approach cannot just test the effects of an innovation against a set of pre-specified objectives, since responsibility for practice will ask for evaluating the overall effects, i.e. including side-effects. Thus, an evaluation must "provide a comprehensive understanding of the complex reality surrounding the programme" in order to "illuminate" the state of the innovation and the options for its further development for the different constituencies involved.

The *programmed approach* has certain strengths: It takes care to communicate its intentions and ways of implementation as clear as possible and, thus, its evaluation criteria are unambiguous. However, it has also some weaknesses, the most important of which are, first, it is only suitable for such innovations which are actually programmable. Many researchers claim that curricula for more complex educational goals are not easily programmable because our knowledge about the conditions of application is not sufficient. Secondly, needs and characteristics of persons and organizations in different regions may vary so much that some leeway is desirable in order to cope with situational implementation problems.

The *adaptive-evolutionary approach* is strong in adapting an innovation to situational characteristics. It also claims that complex changes necessitate relearning and, thus, invites participants to participate actively in the process of implementation which is seen as a prime opportunity for internalizing the main characteristics of the innovation. Its main weaknesses are: first, problems may arise because of ambiguous objectives, variation of ways of implementation, and shifting evaluation criteria.

Secondly, evaluation of success is difficult and may vary between different persons and constituencies because no common criteria are available from the outset.

Similarly, Berman has argued that both approaches have their merits and that the implementation approach should be chosen just as to its fit to the specific implementation situation.

Thus, the programmed approach is appropriate if the amount of change intended is small or orchestrated in a gradual manner, if the curriculum may be specified just as to tested and widely known teaching methods, if the persons concerned by the implementation agree to objectives and methods, if the school is comparatively integrated and its environment comparatively stable. Where these conditions are not met, an adaptive strategy may be more appropriate

Table. Indication for curriculum approaches

	Programmed approach	Adaptive-evolutionary
amount of change	small, step by step	big
curriculum technology	fixed, tested and known methods	adaptive, open methods
attitude of participants	agreement	conflict
integration/ organization	high integration	diversity
stability of environment	stable	unstable

In practice, any practical implementation project will be situated somewhere between the extremes of the dichotomy just introduced. However in my view, it makes sense for curriculum developers to ask themselves what type of solution of the implementation problem they - implicitly or explicitly – favor through their organization of the implementation process, and if this fits to the messages their curriculum implies and to the localities it has to work in.

FACILITATING AND LIMITING FACTORS FOR IMPLEMENTATION

Whatever the general strategy of implementation might be, it makes sense to know more about factors affecting implementation. Although there are a lot of individual and often contradictory research results in different implementation localities, there is, nevertheless, some convergence of research findings about key factors.

Characteristics of the innovation itself

Characteristics of the innovation itself, in our case of the curriculum, affect the process of implementation. It is not surprising that the higher a *need* for the solutions the innovation proposes is, the better the chances for implementation are. Usually, a general feeling of need or the expression of need by some political body or by academia is not enough, rather this need must be perceived by the constituencies directly involved in the implementation. It follows that "careful examination of whether or not address priority needs" lays important groundwork before and during the production phase of a curriculum; and that frequent communication and open discussion of the curriculum's merit for coping with felt need must maintain and develop an awareness of this topic during the implementation process.

However, there are three complications with straightforwardly addressing needs: First, there is a need for the solutions offered by a curriculum must not just be 'one among many others'. Among the "overloaded improvement agendas" of today's schools there is often competition between various innovation proposals which leads not too rarely to vague development agendas within which no critical mass of improvement energy can be accumulated behind any of the projects. "Developing a vision" could be used as an instrument to prioritize among a set of desirables. Secondly and especially in the case of complex changes, both precise needs and solutions offered by the curriculum are not clear from the beginning. Thirdly, need interacts with other factors.

Another crucial factor is the innovation's *clarity.* Curriculum research unearthed examples of educational innovations where practitioners were not clear about what they were expected to do differently – what change meant for them in practice. At least in initial implementation phases teachers relish concreteness and tangibility. They expect that teaching strategies are clearly described and material is well-thought of. The proposal should be clear about ways of doing, but not too linear and restricting in the sense that just one way of doing is advocated and no alternatives are possible. This need for clarity has been interpreted as expression of a feeling of role ambiguity in a situation of uncertainty produced by the new challenges of the innovation on one side and by the partly lacking competencies on the teachers' part. It was also found that a more flexible approach may be appropriate in later phases of implementation when teachers have strengthened their feeling of competence with respect to the innovation.

What does this finding mean for an adaptive-evolutionary approach? Wasn't it saying to be not too clear about ways of teaching to allow teachers' experimentation? In my view "no". Stenhouse advocated the curriculum as an 'intelligent proposal' and he certainly meant by this to be as clear as possible about what the proposal is. But at the same time, he thought, teachers should be encouraged and supported by resources and structure to evaluate this proposal under specific circumstances and to develop it further.

A third factor is *complexity* which reflects the amount of new skills, altered beliefs und different materials etc. required by an innovation. "... simple changes may be easier to carry out, but they may not make much of a difference. Complex changes promise to accomplish more, but they also demand more effort, and failure takes a greater toll. The answer seems to be to break complex changes into components and implement them in a divisible and/or incremental manner.".

A fourth factor lies in the *quality and practicality* of the innovation proposal. Again, it is not the quality a panel of curriculum developers would attribute to the curriculum proposal, but the quality as it is perceived by the relevant actors supposed to implement the curriculum. One might distinguish several aspects of quality in this respect. Firstly, there is *conceptual quality* flowing from plausibility and coherence of the conceptual elements employed.

There is *formal or communicative quality* coming from the language, graphical and social design of the presentation of the innovation before and during the implementation process. And there is *practical or logistic quality* stemming from the availability of materials and other resources, such as, for example, time for development work or the consultation of external experts. As most innovation address 'urgent and ambitious needs', it happens that "decisions are frequently made without the follow-up or preparation time necessary to generate adequate materials".

It must be stressed that "quality" with respect to implementation points to the perceptions of the different stakeholders: Thus, an essential feature of quality is *contextual suitability:* It has been frequently demonstrated that imported programs rarely work equally well in all contexts. Innovation proposals must fit to available funds, specific student characteristics, the communities' language patterns, teachers' abilities, parents' expectations, cultural values and much more.

"Quality" also means that a curriculum can pass the test of *the 'practicality ethic of teachers':* Teachers appreciate these ideas, proposals or teaching methods which have proven to "work" in practice or which promise by their appearance of practicality to do so. Those proposals are considered as 'practical' which "address salient needs, that fit well with the teacher's situation, that are focused and that include concrete how-to-do-possibilities. 'Practical' does not necessarily mean 'easy' but it does mean the presence of next steps."

Local characteristics

A second set of factors focuses on local decision processes and local characteristics of the implementation: First, there is the *regional administration:* The attitude of regional administrators, inspectors and the like towards the local implementation process is essential if change is meant to be serious. Without support of regional administrators change may happen with individual teachers or single schools but it will most likely remain isolated in some innovative pockets without affecting the broader system. Just 'moral support' - in the sense of being given good words without any concrete implementation follow-through - will no be enough. "Teachers and others know enough not to take change seriously unless local administrators demonstrate *through actions* that they should."

There have been too many educational innovations without *adequate follow-through*. In some regions there is a *history of negative experiences* with previous implementation attempts which in itself is an unfavorable condition for change since system members may have built up a cynic or apathetic attitude towards change. Local administrators must show specific forms of *active support* including enduring support for school management and teachers, through realistic time plans and resourcing, and through an adequate information system about the innovation and its implementation. And they must demonstrate *active knowledge and understanding* both of the attempted change and the processes of putting it into reality in order to provide conducive conditions for the implementation.

Another factor are *community characteristics*. Even where communities are "not directly involved in implementation ... they can become activated against certain innovations" if the planning and implementation process does not attend to the political undercurrents in the school's surrounding community. On the other hand, the inclusion of non-professional, such as parents and the public, –

at least in settings where community members are used to influence educational practice - can uncover objections and helps to accommodate to specific circumstances. Then, parents may be "one of the most powerful leverages to better implementation" if they are actively included in the implementation strategy through an adequate information system or realistic offers to participate in key phases of development and implementation.

Finally, *contextual stability* makes a difference. It is much easier to successfully advance an implementation within a stable environment. "Marked social change usually disrupts reform projects that are already on the way."

Organizational characteristics

Actors

Another crucial factor for implementation is the characteristics of the organization which is the venue for implementation, and, in particular, the role of the *management,* i.e. in the case of a school: the principal and the school management team. There is broad research evidence that principals, headpersons and school management teams cannot change schools just on their own, but that they are the single most influential group of persons to make change processes fail. "The principal is the most likely person to be in a position to shape the organizational conditions necessary for success such as the development of shared goals, collaborative work structures and climates, and procedures for monitoring results." Change processes are in need of the management's active support and participation – not necessarily as curriculum experts, but as initiators, as 'change leaders'.

Thus, the school leaders' *level of commitment* is a crucial feature: "The degree to which people are committed to a reform is reflected in the time and energy they devote to its implementation and in the extent to which they remain faithful to their role in the face of opposition and operational difficulties." Commitment is important at all levels of an educational hierarchy but particularly among the personnel at the top, so e.g. among school principals or top administrators of districts or ministers of education. They are in the position to give resources and impose both rewards and penalties, and they provide well-observed images for how seriously the innovation is to be taken.

Firestone and Corbett have identified four *leadership functions* which facilitate educational change:

- *Obtaining resources*
- *Shielding the project from outside interference*
- *Encouraging staff members* and furnishing recognition from peers, experts and supervisors
- *Adapting standard operating procedures* to the needs of the project at an early stage in the reform process and, as Huberman and Miles

suggested, stabilise and codify the new practices in school house operating rules, revised curricula, training programs, evaluation procedures and routine funding. In other words, the earlier – even in the 'project phase' of implementation – the curriculum is partially built into the routine operations of the school, the better.

In reality, headpersons frequently do not play an active role in implementation – not always because they do not like the innovation itself – but sometimes because they find it difficult to transform their traditional, more passive role into a new and more active role as 'facilitator of change'. Thus, some implementation programs provide specific offers for principals and school management, e.g. specific workshops or optional coaching. These are to help them transform and maintain a conducive role among implementation processes which frequently do not pass without some conflict and pressure on the leader's role.

Teachers, their commitment and attitudes, competences, and interaction patterns make up another crucial group of factors for implementation. Both individual and collegial aspects are important. Teachers are a constant factor in the education system and thus have a key role for classroom innovation. If they are not motivated to engage with an innovation, then nothing will happen. In the German discussion, Havelock's position has been criticised in binding curriculum development to the "weakest element of the chain". However, this involves, in my view, overstating Havelock's argument in the way that teachers have to accept *fully* the innovation at any time of the implementation process. Certainly, this cannot be expected. Certainly, every real innovation will involve some aspects which are new for teachers and which will encounter some sceptical reaction. Such discrepancies between claims of the innovation and acceptance of teachers may be important starting points for further development. However, the relationship between "irritation" and "acceptance" must be in such a balance that participants are prepared to embark and continue with the implementation process. Curriculum research shows that it is possible to deal constructively with such discrepancies in implementation processes, but it also shows that it is easier in situations of face-to-face-contact and that, again, it is much more difficult to generalise results of those face-to-face negotiations to a broader group of users.

Participation in decision-making: Traditionally educational innovation has tended to follow a top-down pattern. However, it was frequently shown that including local personnel fosters more effective implementation. "Early participation increases teachers' willingness to continue new practices after the initial incentives have been withdrawn. Engaging teachers in their planning process also helps to equip them with skills required by the innovation and enhances the likelihood that the reform will be adapted to local circumstances." Thus, one of the mottoes of organisational development has been taken up also by implementation projects, i.e. to make persons affected by change to persons involved in change.

Certainly, the *individual teacher's* competencies and attitudes towards change itself and towards the specific innovation intended are important factors contributing to the quality and direction of the change process. Some *schools*, however, have more change-oriented teachers on their staff than others. This is not only due to recruitment but also – as school quality research has shown – an effect of specific school cultures.

Change involves the development of new practices and beliefs, i.e. it involves *learning*. Where these new practices and beliefs are not trivial we must assume that these processes *extend over time* and that they are *fraught with feelings* of being de-skilled, not knowing what to do, lacking instruments, competencies, and resources, etc. Since it is an innovation the learning process will refer to practices already established, i.e. it will involve *re-learning*. Thus, the process of taking up an innovation may also be described in terms of a learning process of individuals, groups, and organizations, and actually implementation projects only can profit from what Mandl has explained as a constructivist view of learning.

Teachers seem to have *changing interests during different phases of implementation*. Initially, concrete proposal and non-paternalistic support seem to be important in order to counteract the feelings of being de-skilled and of time pressure which are connected with the innovation challenge. Later, a more comprehensive view on the substantive and methodical implications of the innovation proposal becomes possible. No wonder if the implementations process is seen as a "dynamic process of appropriating curricular concepts".

Individual teachers' learning is socially situated in a network of co-teachers, managers, administrators, and other relevant participants. It will be easier if it is situated in a such *network which is both sympathetic and competent* with respect to the changes aspired since it will be possible to collegially fill in individual's gaps of motivation and qualification. "New meanings, behaviors, skills, and beliefs depend significantly on whether teachers are working as isolated individuals or are exchanging ideas, support, and positive feelings about their work.

The quality of working relationships among teachers is strongly related to implementation. Collegiality, open communication, trust, support, and help, learning on the job, getting results, and job satisfaction and morale are closely interrelated." Thus, some researchers equal successful implementation with succeeding in building up a *'community of learners'* with respect to the innovation, Such a 'community' invests in different occasions and instruments of collaborating, sharing, and synthesizing individual knowledge and research in order to make full use of the expertise which is 'distributed' within the relevant community and outside of it.

Lave and Wenger have insisted that learning - by virtue of its social situatedness - also involves developing a specific *identity* in and *vis a vis* the respective 'community'. Similarly, to implement an innovation means for the practitioners involved in a long-term commitment to practice the innovation and to give it some centrality in their image of the profession and the organization. Thus, implementation will be connected with some pressure to *transform professional identity*, and it will only be considered successful if this transformation is not just an individual one but is accompanied by other individuals' likewise transformation, or to put it in other words: some by some transformation of the respective community of practice.

Certainly, innovations necessitate also other non-professional participants' learning. In the case of curricular innovations it is obvious that *students' relevant competencies and attitudes* are an important factor in implementation. If the innovative proposal is unclear, against their perceived needs, over- or under-demanding etc. it may lose students' active participation. Also janitors, clerical staff and *other participants* may be affected by the innovation, and in a position to actively support or block implementation.

Organizational characteristics

Compatibility of the goals of the innovation and its implementation with the strategic long-term goals of the organization into which the innovation is to be implemented is crucial, too. The same holds true for situational characteristics: *Organizational structures, instruments and processes* are important factors for implementation. An innovation usually aims at directly transforming some organizational structures and processes and in the process of doing so, also indirectly puts pressure on other organizational structures and processes. The *system of incentives and the career patterns* valid in the organization to be changed must be re-thought in order to be in consonance with the innovation. For curricular innovations the structure of the *existing curriculum and assessment procedures* are particularly relevant: Attempting to change teaching and learning styles while syllabi and assessments remain unaltered will most likely run into difficulties.

Thus, implementation must work towards a fit between the *culture of the organization and both the culture of the innovation proposal and its implementation process.* Intensive collaboration, collegial reflection and sharing of individual knowledge are features which to some extent, run counter to the *culture of traditional schools* which may e.g. characterized by a frame of mind called "autonomy-parity-pattern" by Lortie. This pattern is characterized by two rules which are considered crucial for smooth interaction between teachers: First, no grown-up person should interfere in a teacher's classroom. Secondly, all teachers are to be treated equally, regardless of their actual competencies, energy invested, and qualities displayed. It has been shown that new challenges, such as school development or quality evaluation, tend to interfere with these rules since they usually opt for more coordination and sharpening profiles of the organization. And they are in need of delegation and differential taking up of development roles, and of evaluation which is necessary for rationally steering more autonomous organizations. In a recent study in vocational upper secondary schools we found that the relative weight of teachers who discard "autonomy" and "parity" as guiding principles for collegial life in schools is decisive for successful engagement in school development.

The *culture of learning* valid in an organisation is particularly important because it does not only refer – in the case of curriculum implementation - to central content aspects of the innovation, but also to conditions of learning during the process of implementation. Using Weinert's definition, we see the organizational culture of learning as the totality of forms of learning and styles of teaching which are typical for an organisation at a given time including the anthropological, psychological, societal and educational orientation on which they are based. It is considered conducive for implementation

- if learning is awarded a high profile in the goals, vision, resources, and instruments of an organization
- if there are forums for learning and information exchange in the regular operation of the organisation
- if there are conducive images of learning continuously represented in the organisation by management and other participants; i.e. that the competent learner is valued, not just the full expert who is right in any case.

It follows that innovation also involves or necessitates an innovation of school as an organization, i.e. a process of system change or *organizational learning*. Organizational learning is – as has been frequently described– not a straightforward process because it deals with transforming structures which have been and are continuously partially self-produced and reinforced by the actors in the organization to be changed. Consequently, as suggested, expect some 'resistance' in the course of the implementation process and adverse reaction to innovation does not always aim at the characteristics of the innovation itself but sometimes at the pressure to transform one's way of working and relating to colleagues in schools.

Government and other agencies

Priorities for education which arise from political forces, lobbying of interest groups and public concerns channel resources and gratification, "put pressure on local districts and also provide various incentives for changing in the desired direction." Its instruments are legislation, regional guidelines, incentives, sponsored projects etc. Fullan is critical of government agencies which all too often "have been preoccupied with policy and program adoption, and have vastly underestimated the problems and processes of implementation. The policy maker and the local practitioner inhabit different worlds, each side ignorant of the subjective world of the other."

In fact, the *quality of relationships between central and local actors* is a key issue of implementation. However, all too often it has come "in the form of episodic events rather than processes: for example, submission of requests for money, intermittent progress reports on what is being done, external evaluations, all amounting to paper work, rather than people work."

Through *resource support and training* external agencies can promote curriculum implementation. "... through resource support, standardization, and closer monitoring, state departments of education have sometimes directly influenced implementation of specific objectives, especially when local conditions were favorable. Mostly, however, lack of role clarity, ambiguity about expectations, absence of regular interpersonal communication, ambivalence between authority and support roles of external agencies, and solutions that do not work have combined to frustrate implementation."

PROCESS CHARACTERISTICS OF SUCCESSFUL IMPLEMENTATION

A more holistic and dynamic conceptualization is provided by a formulation of key process characteristics in successful improvement efforts. There is a small number of powerful themes which - in combination - make a difference." What are these themes?

Preparation, initiation and participation

Reform needs some impetus to gets started. Some *preparatory collection and analysis of data* about the state of the system to be innovated will help to focus energy. A *'project architecture'* will have to be built up which includes formal and informal power centers and assigns specific roles to different constituencies involved and which is organizing social places and instruments for participation.

Although *'participation and empowerment'* are key themes of the whole implementation process, that does not mean that widespread involvement at initial stages is "either feasible or effective". To introduce an innovation at the same time to the whole target group may not be the wisest strategy. "It is more likely the case that small groups of people begin and, if successful, build momentum. Active initiation, starting small and thinking big, bias for action, and learning by doing are all aspects of making change more manageable, by getting the process under way in a desirable direction."

Vision building

If an organization or a project has a vision, it permeates the organization with value and purpose which give direction and driving power for development.

Louis and Miles vision has two aspects, an image of the organization to be changed, what it could or should look like, and an image of the change process, for the strategy for getting there. "While virtually everyone agrees that vision is crucial, the practice of vision building is not well understood." Most literature talks about what should or could be, however, there are only a few more thorough empirical studies of actual processes of vision building in education.

Evolutionary Development

"For major change, highly specified planning is unwise. 'Have a plan, but learn by doing.'". Successful schools, e.g. in the Louis and Miles study, "adapted their plans as they went along to improve the fit between the change and conditions in the school to take advantage of unexpected developments and opportunities." The art of implementation lies in blending top-down initiatives and bottom-up participation. Obviously, some pragmatic flexibility is needed "that permits a reform program to accommodate unexpected, uncontrollable events while still attempting to preserve the main trust of the plan."

Initiative-taking and empowerment

In Louis and Miles' study, "leaders in successful schools supported and stimulated initiative-taking by others; set up cross-hierarchical steering groups consisting of teachers, administrators, and sometimes parents and students; and delegated authority and resources to the steering group, while maintaining active involvement with the groups."

For organizational leaders it is obviously essential to get people to act and interact in purposeful directions, and if they do so, also to support them, to give them resources and to delegate power - without themselves fully pulling out of the process. Collaborative work cultures which may develop out of these networks of interaction provide support for the individuals, but also continuous motivation and pressure to go ahead.

Pressure and support

Innovation research teaches us that it is not as simply as 'pressure' equals bad and 'support' is good. The reason is that in organizations there are "many forces maintaining the status quo. When change occurs it is because some pressure has built up that leads to action." 'Pressure' is not to be equated with brute power and oppression, and in fact, such type of 'pressure' would rarely work effectively. Various arrangements of interaction between the implementers, such as meetings, collaborative working groups, presentation meetings etc., serve "to integrate both pressure and support. One of the reasons that peer coaching works so effectively is that it combines pressure and support in a seamless way." As I said: 'pressure' is not simply bad and 'support' is good. Rather it seems that one without the other is bad for implementation.

"Pressure without support leads to resistance and alienation; support without pressure leads to drift or waste of resources." An elaboration of this idea has been proposed by Strittmatter. He argues that in order to sustain change processes in schools there must be both motives of ability, necessity and volition. They are in a multiplicative relationship: If one of these three motivational areas is nil, the sum will be nil, i.e. the overall motivational energy will not be sufficient to sustain an extended change process.

Staff development and resource assistance

Innovation necessitates new expertise. Educational establishments would rarely attempt to acquire this expertise by hiring additional personnel. Thus, innovation involves a process of relearning competencies and attitudes for the existing personnel. Many formats for training staff have been developed, such as e.g. written directions, periodicals, teachers' guidebooks, live or videotaped lectures and demonstrations, in-service workshops, on-site supervision. However, whenever relearning is to mean not only acquisition of new verbal power but of new and stabilised skills and action patterns, then relearning must be based on action and interaction over an extended time span.

Many attempts at change fail because they underestimate the individual and social energy that is necessary for re-learning. Staff development is too often designed as a one-off initiative at too early a stage of the change process. Pre-implementation training may be helpful for orienting people towards new aims and practices, however, support is most crucial when participants actually try to implement new approaches, i.e. *during* implementation, and in particular, during early stages of implementation. "Learning by doing, concrete role models, meetings with resource consultants and other implementers, practice of the behavior, the fits and starts of cumulative, ambivalent, gradual self-confidence are all crucial. Training approaches to implementation are successful when they combine concrete teacher-specific training activities, ongoing continuous assistance and support during the process of implementation, and regular meetings with peers and others."

Monitoring, evaluation and problem-coping

All serious improvement programs will encounter problems. However, it makes a difference whether innovators are prepared to identify them quickly and develop coping measures or whether they avoid to face them. Thus, self-reflection, self-evaluation and monitoring both the outcomes and the process of change is an essential element of every effective implementation strategy. Monitoring does not just fulfil a 'critical function' in identifying problems and failure. It has also a 'constructive' function in multiple respects: Certainly, it is meant to orient adaptation measures. Organized effectively, it may provide some emotional support when implementation problems arise and when participants are in danger of falling into the "implementation dip", into the feeling that situational control is lost among changing circumstances and 'everything is getting worse'. Further, it may give access to good practical ideas which in traditional school cultures too often remain unknown and isolated as individual teachers' knowledge. Thus, monitoring may fuel exchange of implementation experience and collaborative planning of next steps by users and curriculum makers.

Although most innovation researchers would agree to the importance of evaluation and monitoring of progress, it is "probably one of the most difficult and complex strategies for change 'to get right'. ... Accountability and improvement can be effectively interwoven, but it requires great sophistication." Evaluation is very often planned too late. People in initial phases of an innovation are pre-occupied with the "more practical" issues of making the innovation work. As they feel that not everything is working as smoothly as they had hoped, they become more wary of evaluation because they fear that mistakes will become visible. Evaluation also threatens the long-standing culture of autonomy and parity in traditional schools by intruding into the privacy of the classroom and producing information which allows to differentiate between teachers.

However, innovative schools do not only monitor progress, they also act upon the information collected in order to redirect their change process. Louis and Miles found that "unsuccessful sites used shallow coping strategies such as avoidance, denial, procrastination, people-shuffling, while successful sites engaged in deep problem-solving such as redesign, creating new roles, providing additional assistance and time and the like."

Restructuring

"Structure" is meant to "include organizational arrangements, roles, finance, governance, and formal policies which explicitly build on working conditions that support improvement." Our definition emphasized that innovation is always restructuring to some extent. In practice, the need e.g. for revised time tabling, shuffling resources, time for individual and team planning, time for visiting other colleagues or joint teaching, staff development policies and practices, new roles such as mentors and coaches etc. may surface during implementation. Where this task of restructuring is taken up explicitly and pro-actively in the course of the implementation, the chance of producing sustainable results will be higher.

Intensive Communication Und relationships to External Agencies

In the perspective of systems theory organizations are special social systems which are made up of a special form of communication, of decisions. Organizational innovations aims at changing the decisions which are characteristic of the organization. In order to achieve this, phases of innovation must intensify the richness and variety of communication in an organization. Practically, a pro-active in-house information policy is meant to feed in communication with relevant information, and the establishment of forums of information exchange and collaboration are supposed to intensify innovation-relevant communication. Also cross-departmental communication and exchange with external experts are supported in order to enhance the chance of seeing alternative solutions.

But also clear and pro-active information and communication with the organization's environment and the interested public is important in order to avoid adverse reactions, to make the innovative changes understood, and, at times, to invite alternative perspectives.

CONCLUSION

We have presented descriptions of implementation from three different angles, from the view of two broad 'philosophies' of implementation, from an analytic view on important factors contributing to successful implementation which have identified by innovation research, from the perspective of organizational developers formulating critical themes or process characteristics. Out of the overlaps between these perspectives an image of implementation is emerging which may be characterized by the following elements:

- Implementation involves *changes in behaviors and beliefs* and, thus, involves processes of *learning*: If these new practices and beliefs are not trivial, these processes will *extend over time* and will be *fraught with feelings* of being de-skilled, not knowing what to do, lacking instruments, competencies, and resources, etc.
- Innovation requires both *changes in action and attitude*. Contrary to the usual assumption, "it seems that most people do not discover new understandings until they have delved into something. In many cases, changes in behavior precede rather than follow changes in belief." It follows first, that concrete instructions, materials, examples and coaching or peer interaction which help to develop and modify practices are essential for implementation. Secondly however, changes in belief are not futile. Rather, they are essential to make sense of the new practices, organize them and hold them together in a system of meaning which is a precondition for extended practice and flexible adaptation to varying circumstances.
- Implementation involves *development and evaluation:* To implement these new practices into a fairly complex new environment will not be done by just copying a master-plan or a model from some other place, but will involve some process of selection, construction, problem-solving, interpretation, and (re-)invention which 'situates' and changes the original model. This feature necessitates that the

implementation process and its products is monitored as it proceeds, and that the information produced thereby is used for fine-tuning or re-directing the implementation process.

- Implementation is obviously *complex*: "Even if the need and the idea is right, the sheer complexity of the process of implementation, has, as it were, a sociological mind of its own, which frequently defies management even when all parties have the best of intentions."
- Implementation is an *extended and dynamic process*: Learning extends over time and will change the situation in which it is to be learned. "Deeper meaning and solid change must be borne *over time*. With particular changes, especially complex ones, one must struggle through ambivalence before being sure that the new vision it workable and right ..."
- Factors affecting successful implementation are in a *systemic relationship*: Set of factors "form a system of variables that interact to determine success of failure" "Single-factor theories of change are doomed to failure. ... Effective implementation depends on the combination of all the factors ... "
- More than that, implementation will involve *systemic change* and, thus, necessitate some *organization development*. It follows that implementation will involve *learning processes on different levels*: Individual learning processes will be complemented by group learning and organizational learning which aims for changing relevant structures, processes, and cultures in a way which resonates with the main thrust of the innovation.
- Implementation involves *participation, ownership and development of professional identities*. Innovators will want to stimulate persons involved to more comprehensive participation. This is seen as a necessary precondition for successful innovation which asks for practitioners' commitment and "ownership". Ownership in the sense of clarity, skill and commitment is not acquired easily; it is a progressive process which must be supported by the arrangements of the implementation process.
- As social and cultural learning theories stress learning new practices is interwoven with other actors' learning processes in a social setting, and is connected with processes of identity formation. Thus, implementation will always involve some *transformation of the professional identities* of the persons involved.
- Implementation of complex innovations does *not lend itself to a strict separation of phases of research, development and implementation*: On one hand, issues of implementation must be anticipated in early phases of conceiving an innovation. On the other hand, implementation itself

must be seen as a process of further developing the innovation proposal and of researching its effects and transformations under specific local conditions. In this perspective, implementation is understood as an element of a circular process of conceiving implementing reflecting, and re-conceiving innovations proposals, or of theory building, theory application, and testing of theories. If this argument makes sense, then research in implementation processes would hold more theoretical relevance than usually is attributed to it.

- To tighten the relationship between development, implementation, and research – this is the shared message of Stenhouse's 'teacher as researcher'-model and the idea of 'modus 2-research' which is advocated by Reinmann-Rothmeier and Mandl as a complement to traditional research. They argue that knowledge should increasingly be developed in the context of its use; processes of problem formulation and solving should be based on heterarchic teams of persons from different disciplinary and professional backgrounds in a complex application-oriented environment. Modus 2-research opts against a strict separation between basic and application-oriented research: "Research becomes a cyclical process, in which theories and practical recommendations will be continuously analysed, tested in practice and revised, when necessary"

The complexity of the implementation process makes predictions of success risky. However, it makes it very profitable for curriculum makers to actively engage in this elusive process of supporting implementation. And it also makes it very *"profitable to monitor implementation* with care at each stage of the process, so that remedies may be applied periodically toward coping with unanticipated difficulties."

CURRICULUM ASSESSMENT

Curriculum can be divided into the intended, enacted, assessed, and learned curricula. For K-12 education, the intended curriculum is captured most explicitly in state content standards— statements of what every student must know and be able to do by some specified point in time. The enacted curriculum refers to instruction. The assessed curriculum refers to student achievement tests. States, districts, and the U.S. government test various subjects at various grade levels. Teachers use their own tests to monitor student performance.

In what follows, curriculum assessment is taken to mean measuring the academic content of the intended, enacted, and assessed curricula as well as the content similarities and differences among them. Pedagogy, while important to explain student learning. Further, measuring the learned curriculum is a separate topic in its own right and is not considered here.

Clearly, students can and do learn both more and less than the content of the assessed curriculum.

Knowing the content of the enacted curriculum is important because what students are taught is a powerful predictor of student achievement on a test, and helps explain a portion of the achievement gap between White, Black, and Hispanic students. Knowing the content of the intended curriculum is important because the intended curriculum is the content target for the enacted curriculum. Knowing the content of the assessed curriculum is important because student achievement is measured only for the content assessed. Students may learn important content not on the test and that learning may go unidentified.

There are many important questions for research and practice that can only be answered through curriculum assessment of content. Do teachers teach what is tested? Do teachers teach what is in the textbook? Is the content of the textbook the same as the content of the test? Does the content of what is tested match well the content of the intended curriculum? Is standardsbased reform working? Is the content of the enacted curriculum coming into an increasingly better match with the content of the intended curriculum?

In what follows attention is first given to defining content. Having defined content, attention is given to assessing the content of the intended, enacted, and assessed curricula. Where alternative approaches exist, attention is given to each. Having assessments of the content of the intended, enacted and assessed curricula, consideration is given to defining and measuring alignment among them. Next, evidence of the quality of data from the various procedures is summarized. The chapter closes with a section on potential uses of curriculum assessment data in both education research and practice.

BUT WHAT IS CONTENT?

Is content math, science, English language arts, or social studies? Is knowing just the subject specific enough? What kind of mathematics? Is the content arithmetic, measurement, algebra, geometry, or statistics? Even these are general areas to which entire courses are devoted.

What kind of algebra? Is the content functions, matrices, or linear equations? And what are students supposed to know and be able to do in reference to linear equations? Should they be able to distinguish a linear equation from a non-linear equation? Should they be able to solve a linear equation? Should they be able to use a linear equation to solve a story problem? Clearly, curriculum assessment requires important decisions about what is and is not content as well as how fine grained or precise the distinctions among types of content need to be. To some extent, the best definition of content can be decided on only within the context of a purpose. Even then, determining the best definition requires empirical investigation.

For many in education, academic content is defined as the topics that might or might not be taught, tested or included in content standards. Unfortunately, defining content in terms of topics has proven to be insufficient at least if explaining variance in student achievement is the goal. For example, knowing whether or not a teacher has taught linear equations while providing some useful information, is insufficient. What about linear equations was taught? Were students taught to distinguish a linear equation from a nonlinear equation? Were students taught that a linear equation represents a unique line in a two space and how to graph the line? For every topic, content can further be defined just as to categories of cognitive demand. In mathematics cognitive demand might distinguish memorize; perform procedures; communicate understanding; solve non-routing problems; conjecture, generalize, prove. In English language arts and reading, topics might be phoneme blending or suffixes, prefixes and root words and cognitive demand might be recall, demonstrate/explain, analyze/investigate, evaluate, generate/create.

"Languages" can and have been developed to define the content of academic subjects. The content language for an academic subject should be exhaustive in its inclusion of all possible types of content, and it should be common in the sense that the same language is used across studies and purposes. The terms used in the language to describe types of content should have the same meaning across people and time. The language should be reform-neutral in the sense that the content of any particular curriculum reform can be well described using one common language. In short the language should be capable of describing the content of any intended, enacted or assessed curriculum.

Content languages have been developed to describe the content of mathematics, science, and English language arts. The languages are two-dimensional and can be presented in a rectangular matrix with *topics* as rows and *cognitive demands* as columns. A language might have 60 to 100 topics and 3 to as many as 10 levels of cognitive demand. Content is defined at the intersection of a particular topic and a particular cognitive demand—the cells of the matrix. For example, content might be to use a linear equation to solve a novel problem. When defining content, a number of decisions must be made. What topics and how many topics make up the rows of the matrix? What and how many levels of cognitive demand make up the columns? There is a tension between the desire for fine levels of measurement, on the one hand, and the difficulties involved in making such precise measures on the other. To the extent possible, the words used to describe topics and cognitive demand should be clear and have a single common meaning.

ASSESSING THE INTENDED CURRICULUM

Berger, Desimone, Herman, Garet, & Margolin at the American Institute for Research may have been the first to assess the content of content standards.

The research team used subject experts to code each unit of the standards documents on topics and cognitive demands. For content analysis of content standards, the most successful approach has been to pick the most specific version of the content standards and analyze the content of each objective, paragraph, or phrase. Each specific part of a content standard documented is given a weight of 1.0. At AIR, three raters independently content analyzed each content standard document. When an objective was judged to represent content in multiple cells of the content language, the weight of 1.0 for that objective was spread evenly across the appropriate cells. Data are averaged cell x cell across experts. Proportions are created for each cell by dividing by the sum of the average weights across all cells in the matrix. The cell proportions sum to 1.0 across rows and columns and indicate the extent to which the content represented by a cell is emphasized in the content standards document. The Council of Chief State School Officers—in collaboration with the Wisconsin Center for Education Research and The North Central Regional Education Laboratory—also has been working with a number of different states to complete content analyses of content standards in math, science, and English language arts.

Data representation can proceed in several ways. One of the most powerful displays is in terms of topographical maps that can be created using a variety of charting software, including Excel. On the maps, what ordinarily is thought of as north and south represents topics and east and west represents cognitive demand. Shading represents relative content emphasis and is analogous to attitude on a topographical map. The maps clearly show not only what content is emphasized in the content standards, but what content is not.

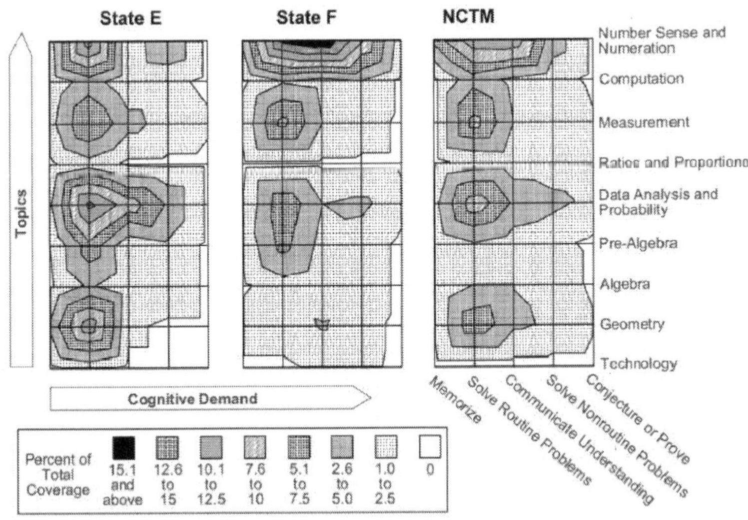

Fig. Seventh-grade standards

Data can be displayed at a coarse-grain size such as in Figure, or one can look more closely at a particular type of content—for example, number sense and numeration—to get a finer grain picture within that area of content.

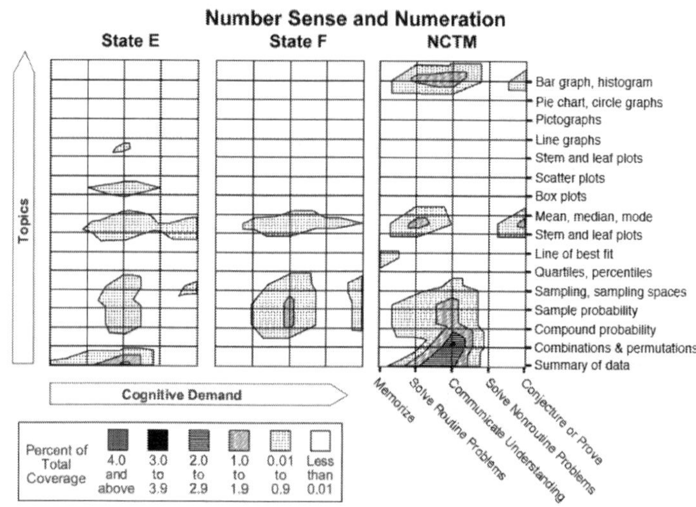

Fig. Seventh-grade standards: Close view.

Visual comparisons can be made by placing topographical maps next to one another. Figure shows that, at the coarse-grain level, not much content is excluded from the standards. There are several similarities across states, but some potentially important differences as well. For example, State E places heavy emphasis on solving routine problems involving data analysis and probability. More differences are revealed by the fine-grained analysis. Here, National Council of Teachers of Mathematics standards are seen as unique in their emphasis on communicating understanding of combinations and permutations.

There is one disturbing property of the maps: topics are interpreted as points on an underlying continuous scale, as are categories of cognitive demand. Of course, there is no underlying continuum for either; each is a nominal scale variable. Thus, while each of the points of intersection between a particular topic or area of topics and a particular cognitive demand is accurately represented in the map, the areas between the points of intersection are meaningless.

The charting software has simply smoothed the data as though there were an underlying continuum. Bar graphs can be also used to present the same data, with a bar at each point of intersection between cognitive demand and topic. In experimenting with this approach, however, the results are busy and difficult to interpret. Communication seems to be easier and more accurate using the topographical maps.

Others have taken similar approaches to assessing the content of the intended curriculum. All have their origins in the work of the Content Determinants Group at the Institute for Research on Teaching at Michigan State University and all are quite similar one to another. Bill Schmidt and his colleagues used similar procedures to content analyze mathematics and science textbooks from several different countries. Textbooks were divided into lessons; lessons were further divided into blocks. Blocks were then content analyzed by independent experts, and averages were taken. Textbook content was interpreted as each country's intended curriculum. The United States was found to have a curriculum that covers more content in less depth than higher achieving countries.

Freeman, Kuhs, Porter, Floden, Schmidt, and Schwille content analyzed elementary school mathematics textbooks and tests. Analyses were limited to the items in the student exercise portions of each lesson. By using a common language to content analyze both tests and textbooks, comparisons were made among the tests, among the textbooks, and between textbooks and tests. Surprisingly, not only was some emphasized content in the textbooks not tested, but some content tested was not covered by the textbooks.

ASSESSING THE ENACTED CURRICULUM

Teachers make content decisions about:

- how much time to spend on a school subject,
- what content to cover within that time,
- which students to teach what content, and
- to what standards of achievement.

In elementary school, for example, is mathematics taught every day, and for how long? By mid-year, one teacher may have spent as much time teaching mathematics as another will have spent by the end of the school year. In high school, students take courses that meet for a specified period of time for a specified number of days. Some high-school teachers initiate instruction immediately at the beginning of each class, while others spend considerable time getting students to sit down and pay attention. Time is only one dimension of content. For example, in first-year algebra, do all teachers teach the same content? For a variety of reasons, the answer is no. Teachers may teach what they believe is most important, what they think the students are ready to learn, or what is most enjoyable and easy to teach. There are many factors that can and do influence teacher decisions about what to teach.

Content can differ from one student to the next, even within a class. In elementary school, instruction is sometimes individualized, with students moving at their own pace through a set of tested objectives. Other times, students are grouped just as to estimates of ability, with different content taught to different groups.

What about standards of achievement? Teachers monitor student achievement and make decisions about pacing based on their assessments of student achievement. Is new content introduced only as old content is mastered, and if so, mastered by all of the students or some fraction of the students? Pacing decisions are important determinants of the content of the enacted curriculum because a slow pace covers less content. Teachers must negotiate between how much content they would like students to learn and how much content students can learn within the constraints of time, pedagogy, and effort.

Assessing the content of the enacted curriculum is substantially more challenging than assessing the content of the intended curriculum. If one is interested in the content of instruction for only a handful of days, then classroom observations using a common content language are a possibility. But generally, interest is in longer periods of time. What is the content of a student's elementary school experience or, at least, what is the content of a student's experience in a particular course or for a particular school year? For longer periods of time such as these, observations are not feasible.

An alternative approach is to use teacher self-report surveys that can be completed daily or retrospectively over longer periods of time. Two competing goods are at play in deciding how frequently to have teachers report on the content of their instruction. The more frequent the reporting, the less burden on a teacher's recall—but the greater the burden on a teacher's time. Teacher logs have been used to study teacher content decisions in mathematics at the elementary school level and to study the degree to which the content of instruction differs among high-school math and science courses with the same name. As for assessing the content of the intended curriculum, assessing the content of the enacted curriculum begins with a definition of content. Surveys are designed to record teacher reports of the content of their instruction, for example indicating what topics they taught, for how much time, and for each topic taught, what level of cognitive demand with what emphasis. These responses can be translated into proportions of content emphasis for each cell in the topics-bycognitive- demand matrix much as described for content analyses of content standards in the previous part on assessing the intended curriculum. Data can be analyzed and displayed as was described for the intended curriculum.

Over time, procedures for teacher logs have become progressively more structured to facilitate ease of data collection and analysis. In one study, teachers were asked each day to identify up to five areas of mathematics content taught that day and with what emphasis. Rather than having teachers describe the content for each student in the class, three target students were selected: one believed to be at the 80th percentile, one at the 50th, and one at the 20th percentile of within-class mathematics aptitude. Teachers were provided a catalog of 288 mathematics topics that might be taught. Logs were collected weekly and edited for ambiguities.

Brian Rowan and his colleagues developed teacher logs for use in studying elementary school reading, writing, and mathematics. Their logs ask teachers to report on what content was covered, what students did, what materials were used, and how the teacher interacted with the student. In Rowan's work less emphasis was put on assessing content and more emphasis was placed on assessing pedagogy. Each log contains 150 questions. A branching strategy is used, with teachers first reporting emphasis placed on each of several curriculum strands. More extensive follow-up questions on pedagogy and content are asked for three focal strands. The Rowan content language does not define content at the intersection of topics and cognitive demand, although a difficulty scale has been formed within strands that may be related to the distinction among levels of cognitive demand.

In the Rowan study, days are sampled with a block of days from the spring, a block from the winter, and a block from the fall for a total of 90 days out of the school year. Students also are sampled. In each class, eight focus students are randomly selected; the teacher completes a log for a different student each day. The motivation for sampling is to ease teacher burden; when sampling is not random, however, bias can result. Teacher logs can provide excellent information on the content of the enacted curriculum, but they are expensive and burdensome. Teachers must be recruited to the task of completing the logs. Given sufficient incentives, a high percentage of target teachers can be recruited. But if the study involves a national probability sample of teachers, recruiting a high percentage of the sampled teachers to the task of completing daily logs may be difficult. An alternative is to use teacher self-report surveys, as in logs, but to ask teachers to report less frequently. End-of-year surveys were used in a study of curriculum reform in high-school mathematics and science. End-of-semester surveys were used in a study of upgrading in high-school mathematics. For these studies, teachers were asked to report on the content of their instruction for an extended period of time—a semester or a school year. Days were not sampled and response burden was substantially less than for daily logs. The trade-off was that by surveying teachers less frequently than daily, the challenge to a teacher to accurately remember and report their content teaching practices was greater.

For assessing the content of the enacted curriculum, direct observation is not feasible except in rare cases where interest is in only a handful of instructional periods. One such case is to validate teacher self report. The only real distinction between logs and surveys is frequency of data collection; all logs are themselves surveys.

ASSESSING THE ASSESSED CURRICULUM

The procedures used to assess the intended curriculum work at least as well for assessing the assessed curriculum. Once again the procedure begins with a common content language. Experts are recruited and trained to use the language and independently perform content analyses. Each item on a test is content analyzed by inferring the content required to correctly answer the item. The main challenge to assessing the content of the assessed curriculum is accurately inferring from reading a test item how students will approach that item. In fact, students may differ one from another in the approach they take to answering an item. For example, in mathematics one student may have seen many problems virtually identical to a story problem on a test. For them, the item represents the cognitive demand of performing procedures. Another student may have little familiarity with story problems of the type represented by the item. For them, the item represents the cognitive demand of solve a novel problem. Experts doing the content analyses must make a judgment as to the most likely approach that students will take to answering the item. Experts make their judgments independently in ways that produce high inter-expert agreement. Still, careful empirical work involving students using think-aloud protocols can be used to investigate the modal student approach and differences among students.

Item score points are evenly distributed across the range of content tested by an item. An average is taken across content analyzers. Using total test score points as the base, proportions of content emphasis are calculated for the cells of the topics-by–cognitive-demand content matrix. Data can be analyzed and displayed in the same way as described when measuring the intended curriculum.

WHAT IS ALIGNMENT AND HOW MIGHT IT BE MEASURED?

Once the enacted, intended, and assessed curricula have been assessed, questions can be asked about the extent to which content is similar across them. To the extent content is the same, they are said to be aligned. For example, one might ask to what extent a student achievement test is aligned with a state's content standards. In fact, the No Child Left Behind Act of 2001 requires that each state align assessments to content standards. If the content assessed is exactly the same as the content represented in the standards, alignment is perfect. There are two ways in which alignment can be less than perfect: Content in the standards may not be assessed, and content assessed may not be in the standards. Figure represents various types of alignment that might be measured.

Curriculum is at the top, with the enacted curriculum below. At the district, state, and national levels there is both the assessed curriculum and the intended curriculum. Within a level of the school hierarchy—at the state level, for example—one can ask questions about horizontal alignment. Is the state test aligned to the state standards? Questions also can be asked about alignment across levels of the school hierarchy. Is the district test aligned to the state test, or are the district standards aligned to the state standards? Vertical alignment can also explain an important aspect of opportunity to learn. The extent to which the content of the enacted curriculum a student experiences is aligned to the content of the test a student takes, the student can be thought of as having had an opportunity to learn.

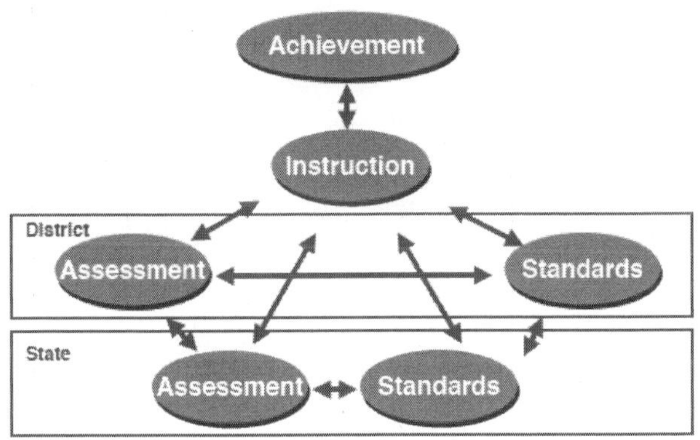

Fig. *Vertical and horizontal alignment*

The learned

Researchers in education have been interested in one type of alignment or another for decades but recently interest has heightened. In part, this increased interest in alignment is due to findings that the content of the enacted curriculum is a strong predictor of gains in student achievement. Further, the U. S. Department of Education has been monitoring compliance of NCLB's requirement that states have assessments aligned to their content standards. States themselves have sought to provide increasingly better information about the degree to which their assessments are aligned to their content standards. Several reviews of different approaches to measuring alignment have appeared.

One method for measuring alignment of assessments to content standards was developed by Norman Webb. His procedure has been used for studies of alignment in language arts, mathematics, social studies, and science at the elementary, middle-, and highschool levels. The procedure involves experts' judgments on four criteria related to content agreement between assessments and standards:

- Categorical congruence,
- Depth of knowledge consistency,
- range of knowledge correspondence, and
- balance of representation. Webb provides no single overall composite measure of degree of alignment.

Webb, categorical congruence is met if there are at least six items measuring the topics represented by a standard. Depth of knowledge consistency asks experts to judge whether items in the assessment are as demanding cognitively as what the students are expected to know and do as stated in the standards. At least half the items corresponding to an objective have to be at or above the level of knowledge of the objective. There are four ordered levels of depth of knowledge. In mathematics, for example, Level 1 is recall, Level 2 is skills/concept, Level 3 is strategic thinking, and Level 4 is extended thinking.

Ordered levels of depth of knowledge assumes that when a student demonstrates achievement on a higher "depth of knowledge" they necessarily have achieved on all lower depths of knowledge. Range of knowledge correspondence is met if at least half the objectives for a standard are measured by at least one assessment item. Balance of representation indicates the degree to which one objective within a standard is given more emphasis on the assessment than another. Webb's index of balance of representation is a function of only those objectives for a standard that had one or more items assessing the objective; the index ranges from 0 to 1.0. Webb's procedures for assessing the alignment of a student achievement test to a state's content standards have been adapted by others. For example, researchers at the Buros Center on Testing used a modified Webb procedure to determine if items from commercially available tests match the Nebraska standards. Their criterion for alignment was a function of not only an item's assessed level of alignment to the standard, but also of agreement among the teachers doing the content analyses. Herman, Webb, and Zuniga convened panels to judge alignment between California's Golden State Examination in high-school mathematics and the University of California statement on competencies in mathematics for high-school graduates applying to the university. They did not use Webb's balance and range criteria, but did add a criterion of *source of challenge* indicating whether an item was difficult not because of its content, but because of some confusing aspect of the item that was irrelevant to the content being assessed.

Karen Wixson used a modified version of the Webb method to assess the alignment of achievement tests in four states to content standards in elementary reading. Wixson and colleagues dropped Webb's categorical congruence criterion and added *coverage* to indicate the extent to which objectives are represented by at least one assessment item. They also added a criterion, *structure of knowledge comparability*, to indicate the extent to which the philosophy of the standards matched the philosophy underlying the assessments.

There are several aspects of Webb's measure of alignment that are important. First, a set of content standards is a given, and Webb measures how a particular assessment aligns to those content standards. Second, for each of the four dimensions of alignment, Webb sets a criterion for how much alignment is enough. Third, alignment is a function of content, and content is defined by topics and cognitive demand. Cognitive demand is considered as an ordinal scale such that if an item has equal or higher cognitive demand than the standard, alignment is judged to be present. In all cases, content standards dictate the level of detail at which topics and cognitive demands are defined. The more general the standards, the less precise the distinction among types of content. Webb's procedures have been used by many states.

Another frequently used measure of the alignment between assessments and content standards was developed by Porter and his colleagues. The procedure begins by completing content analyses of a state's content standards and a state's assessment of student achievement. Again, the basic data are proportions of content emphasis in each cell of the topics-by-cognitive-demand matrix. Alignment is perfect if the proportions for the assessment match cell by cell the proportions for the standards.

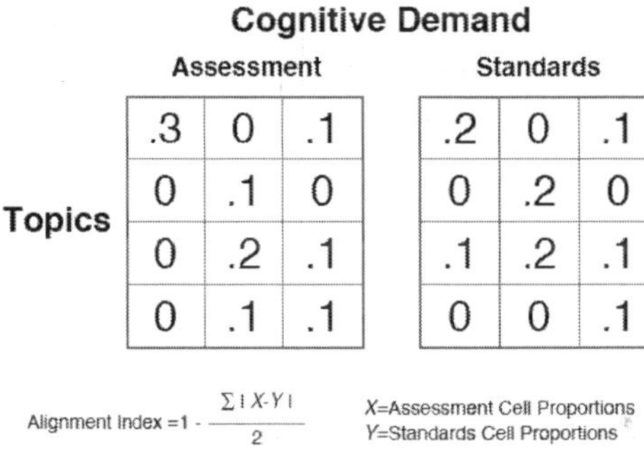

Cognitive Demand

Topics

Assessment

.3	0	.1
0	.1	0
0	.2	.1
0	.1	.1

Standards

.2	0	.1
0	.2	0
.1	.2	.1
0	0	.1

Alignment Index $= 1 - \frac{\Sigma \mid X - Y \mid}{2}$

X=Assessment Cell Proportions
Y=Standards Cell Proportions

Fig. Example matrices to measure alignment

A conceptually straightforward index of alignment is defined

$$\text{Alignment} = 1.0 - \frac{\sum |x - y|}{2}$$

where x = assessment cell proportions and y = standards cell proportions. The index ranges from 0 to 1.0. Starting with matrices of proportions, there are other ways that an alignment index can be calculated. One example is the correlation of proportions of content emphasis across cells between the assessment and the standard. For one data set, Porter found that these two indices of alignment correlate .86. Other quantitative measures of alignment using the basic content-emphasis proportions are possible. The alignment measure offered here has been used to describe alignment in many states in the subjects of mathematic, science, and reading/language arts.

Whichever quantitative index of alignment is used, several important properties exist. First, the basic data are a function of a common content language. Thus, all measures of alignment are a function of the same levels of detail in distinctions among topics and cognitive demand. Second, because measuring alignment begins with content analyses using one common content language, once a state's content standards have been content analyzed, data can be used not only to measure the alignment of one state's standards with that state's test, but with other tests and standards as well. Further, if a state should change its test but not its content standards, then the standards do not need to be reanalyzed—only the new test needs to be analyzed.

Third and perhaps most importantly, the procedure is not limited to measuring the alignment of tests to standards. Anything having content that can be described using the common content language can be aligned with anything else having content that can be described using the common content language. The alignment among content standards across states can be measured. Similarly, alignment across states can be measured for instruction or tests. The procedure is not limited to measures of horizontal alignment; the alignment of instruction to content standards can be measured to assess opportunity to learn. Alignment between instruction and standards can be measured at the individual teacher level, and variance across teachers can be studied. Fourth, the alignment index is symmetric. For example, degree of alignment is a function of both content that is tested but not in the standards, and content that is in the standards but not tested.

What the index does not indicate is how much alignment is enough. Is an alignment of .4 between a state's assessment and its content standards sufficient, or should it be higher? A reasonable but somewhat arbitrary criterion for how much alignment, is enough could be set as Webb has done for each of his four dimensions of alignment but there is no absolute criterion for alignment. Instead, alignment has been judged comparatively. For example, is alignment of a state's test to that state's standards higher than the alignment of the state's test to other state standards? The answer should be yes at least just as to NCLB. When a state's assessment is no more aligned to that state's content standards than it is to other states' content standards, alignment probably needs to be improved. At the same time, alignment of a test with content standards for only one form of the test should not be perfect. One form of a test is a sample of the content in the standards. If the state uses a different form of the test each year, as it should, then content analyses could be conducted across multiple forms of the test. As the number of forms increases, the total number of items increases. At a point when sufficient numbers of items are present so that the sample becomes close to being the population, the test should be perfectly aligned to the content standards. But the specificity of the content standards also limits the degree of alignment. The more vague and general the content standards, the less perfect alignment can be.

Use of a common content language allows for some powerful data displays. For example, if one has content analyzed standards and assessments from each of several states and perhaps national professional standards, the results can be displayed in a standards-by-assessment matrix of alignment values. An example comes from *Moving Standards to the Classroom: The Impact of Goals 2000 Systemic Reform on Instruction*. Table shows the results for four states and the NCTM content standards.

Table

Alignment of Assessments With Standards

Standard	Assessment			
State	B	D	E	F
B	.37	.39	.37	.45
D	.35	.37	.36	.40
E	.36	.33	.43	.31
F	.32	.35	.30	.41
NCTM	.34	.40	.33	.47

Note. Average within-state alignment = .40; average between-state alignment = .39; average state-test-to-NCTM alignment = .39.

The main diagonal of the matrix reports alignment of each state's test with that same state's content standards. Presumably, a state's assessment would be more highly aligned with its own content standards than with other states' content standards. For these states, however, within-state alignment—on average, .4—is no higher than between state alignment. What might account for the result? One possibility is that state standards are not sufficiently specific to allow an assessment to be tightly aligned. Another possibility is that states need to work harder on getting their assessments aligned to their standards. Of course, if all state content standards were perfectly aligned with one another, there could be no difference in the degree of alignment within state versus between state. But the state content standards in Table are far from perfectly aligned.

Achieve Incorporated, founded in 1997 jointly by state governors and chief executive officers of major corporations, also developed a method for measuring alignment between assessments and content standards. The procedures have been used by several states in mathematics and English language arts.

Achieve measures alignment on six dimensions:

- content centrality—assesses the match of an item to a standard using four levels of degree of match;

- performance centrality— matches an item's level of cognitive demand to the standard's level of cognitive demand using four levels to indicate the degree of match;
- source of challenge—assesses whether item difficulty is primarily a function of content or of some aspect of the item that is irrelevant to the content being assessed;
- level of challenge—looks to see if as a set the items matches the span of difficulty in cognitive demand found in the content standards;
- balance—looks at the set of items to judge the balance in content emphasis against the standards; and
- range—looks at the set of items to judge the extent to which the full amount of content in the standards is represented in the assessment by at least one item.

Achieve uses a team of teachers, curriculum specialists, and subject matter experts to do the content analyses. Content analyses are completed by the group rather than by experts individually.

Project 2061 at the American Association for the Advancement of Science has designed procedures to critique textbooks in mathematics and science from the perspective of alignment with selected standards. Again, experts are used to do analyses.

Two independent two-member review teams are created; each team is comprised of one experienced teacher and one education researcher. Rather than average results across the two teams, any differences are reconciled by Project 2061 staff. Training of experts to do the analyses is extensive and involves one full week.

The Project 2061 procedures consider the alignment between content in the textbook and content in the standards. The procedures also consider alignment between the pedagogical strategies of the textbook and those implied in the standards. For instruction, they consider:

- providing a sense of purpose,
- taking account of students' ideas,
- engaging students with phenomena,
- developing the use of scientific ideas,
- promoting student reflection,
- assessing progress, and
- enhancing the learning environment.

The procedure also assesses the content accuracy of the textbooks. Clearly, the 2061 procedures reach well beyond asking about alignment of content between textbooks and content standards. Even when assessing alignment of content, they not only ask about match in terms of topic by cognitive demand, but also in terms of content coherence and accuracy. Under "coherence," for example, they ask about connections among the ideas treated.

QUALITY OF DATA

In curriculum assessment, various approaches have been used to assess the intended, enacted, and assessed curricula and to measure the nature and degree of alignment along them. While somewhat different approaches have been used over the years and by different researchers, there are a number of important common issues concerning the quality of data.

QUALITY OF COMMON LANGUAGE

Several of the procedures start with a common language for describing content. Most of the languages are subject specific, and most consist of defining content at the intersection of topics and cognitive demand. Procedures using a common language are dependent upon the quality of the language on which they are based. Does the language make all of the content distinctions that are useful for the purposes to which the language will be used? Are topics described using terms that have common meaning across users of the language? Is the language exhaustive—in other words, does it include all of the content that might be intended, taught, and/or assessed for a particular academic subject at a particular grade level?

While within a subject and grade level languages have evolved over time, and while there are some differences among languages used by investigators, all of the languages have been created through a careful process of studying national professional content standards, state content standards, textbooks, and tests—and through an iterative process of review and revision by content experts including professors, professional educators, and teachers. Languages have sometimes been simplified in recognition of the burden they might otherwise create for respondents when used in a questionnaire, for observers when used in classroom observations, or for content analyzers when used to describe the content of a document.

Such simplifications come at a price if they result in a language that glosses over important distinctions among types of content that are useful for the purposes to which the language is to be used. There is no way to ensure the perfect language. With each use, content that needs to be added can be identified, and distinctions among topics and/or among levels of cognitive demand can be sharpened or stated in a way that helps ensure a common meaning. At the same time, there is value in having a language that stays fixed over time. Results of one study can be compared more directly to results from another study, and content analyses of standards need not be redone when tests are revised and new studies of alignment are desired.

EXPERTISE OF CONTENT ANALYSTS

Measuring the content of the intended curriculum and/or the assessed curriculum invariably involves using experts to do the content analyses. Even experts need to be trained in the particular procedures; thus, the quality of data is a function of the degree of expertise recruited and the quality of training conducted. To make the research replicable, the recruitment and training of experts needs to be carefully described.

INTER-EXPERT RELIABILITY

Most content analysis procedures use multiple experts who complete the content analyses independently. The resulting data are averaged across experts. Assessing the reliability of the summary data is an important part of the research. Reliability is underestimated by interrater reliability; generalizability theory needs to be used to estimate the reliability of the aggregate data. Even when the content language is defined at the intersection of 70-100 topics by five levels of cognitive demand, reliability of aggregate proportions of content emphasis tend to be quite good, not only for assessments, but even for the more challenging task of analyzing textbooks and content standards. In one study, for example, reliability of aggregate data was .7 across just two raters and .8 across four raters for both tests and content standards. Increasing the number of raters beyond four results in diminishing returns in terms of increased reliability and is probably not warranted. Often in a set of independent raters there is one expert who completes the task in ways that do not agree with the rest of the group. Eliminating the odd expert increases reliability and, hopefully, validity.

Some of the procedures used to measure alignment of a test to a content standard use experts who operate as a group, not as independent individuals. If one group is used, then no estimate of reliability is possible. To estimate reliability would require multiple groups, each operating independently. Generally, such reliability studies have not been conducted, and are needed.

TARGET PERIOD OF TIME WHEN ASSESSING THE ENACTED CURRICULUM

When measuring the enacted curriculum, quality of data issues are more and more complex. One of the decisions that must be made in a study of the content of the enacted curriculum is the time period to be described. While in theory the relevant period of time could be a day, a unit, a semester, a year, or even the elementary school experience, most studies have focused on a school year. Perhaps the focus on a school year is because students often stay with one teacher for a full school year. Perhaps it is because studies of longer periods of time are extraordinarily difficult to conduct. Studies of shorter periods of time are often of substantially less value if one is interested in understanding gains in student achievement.

When a full school year is the focus, the task is to measure all of the content taught during that school year. Observing many classrooms every day for a school year is expensive. If one could take a representative sample of days, that would make observations more manageable. But how many days should be sampled, and should the sampling be random or systematic? Some research exists on the number of days that need to be sampled for classroom observations to yield reliable and valid results. These studies have tended to focus on pedagogical practices that are used on many, if not most, days. Samples of 8 to 12 days are acceptable.

The rarer the event, the larger the sample of days necessary. When measuring content at the fine-grain level of topics by cognitive demand, much of the content is fairly rare in the sense of being taught on many, if not most, days. In elementary school, for example, geometry might be taught every day but only for two weeks. Thus, samples of days need to be large and representative, beyond what would be possible for classroom observations.

STUDENTS TO BE STUDIED WHEN ASSESSING THE ENACTED CURRICULUM

Another sampling issue concerns students within a classroom. Are all students taught the same content or are different students taught different content? The amount of content variability across students within a class is an empirical question. Different approaches have been taken to assess within-class variability; one is to have teachers describe the content of instruction for each of several target students each day. Another approach has been to have a teacher describe the content of instruction for a different target student each day. The latter approach is less burdensome, but confounds day with student.

FREQUENCY OF DATA COLLECTION WHEN ASSESSING THE ENACTED CURRICULUM

Teachers may be surveyed daily, once a week, once a month, once a semester, or once a year. An end-of-year survey requires a teacher to remember the content for the entire school year. A daily log asks the teacher to remember the content for that particular day. Certainly the quality of data from daily logs is better than the quality of data from end-of-year surveys, everything else being equal. Keeping everything else equal requires that logs be kept every day for the period of time under investigation. If logs are kept for a sample of days, then studies must be conducted to show that the sample results are accurate descriptions of the full year results.

Some studies have been conducted to address the issue of how well end-of-year survey data agrees with data collected through daily logs aggregated across the full school year. In turn, daily logs have been compared to data from classroom observations for selected days during which both data exist. Agreement between observations and logs was high, with correlations of .6 to .8. Agreement was lowest for cognitive demand, but in that study there were nine levels of cognitive demand rather than the more typical five. Agreement between daily logs aggregated to the full school year and end-of-year surveys was similar, with correlations generally in the range of .6 to .8. Agreement between logs and end-of-year surveys were lower for content rarely taught and content that was not the focus of the course under investigation.

THE POSSIBILITY OF BIAS WHEN ASSESSING THE ENACTED CURRICULUM

There is, of course, possibility for observer bias or respondent bias. When observers are used, they should be carefully trained to complete their observations in a way that is common across observers and valid to the content language being used. If the research involves treatments, the observer should be blind as to who receives treatment and who does not.

When surveys—including logs—are conducted, anonymity should be insured. It is important for teachers to understand that there are no high stakes consequences for them or their students in relation to their responses. Generally, surveys should ask questions that clearly indicate what is wanted in behavioral terms, not evaluative. How much and what type of content was taught should be asked, not whether the content taught what was intended, was good, or was aligned with the state content standards. To the extent possible, the survey should make clear the nature of the distinctions respondents are to make. For cognitive demand, it is useful to provide elaboration of each level of cognitive demand. In mathematics, for example, the cognitive demand "perform procedures, solve routine problems" can be elaborated as "do computations, make observations, take measurements, compare, and develop fluency." Unfortunately, such elaborations are only helpful when they do not greatly increase response burden.

A number of investigations of the validity of survey data for reporting instructional practice have been completed. Most of this work has been done in mathematics. The findings are that survey data are excellent for describing quantity—what content is taught, and for how long—but not good for describing quality.

COMPLETENESS OF THE DATA SET WHEN ASSESSING THE ENACTED CURRICULUM

Another dimension of the quality of measures of the enacted curriculum concerns the completeness of the data set. If surveys are used, what is the response rate? For those who respond, how complete are their responses across all of the questions asked? Generally, if surveys are carefully conducted, incentives provided, and follow-ups rigorously pursued, response rates can exceed 75%. If the survey is well formatted and not too long, most respondents complete all of the questions.

GAINS IN STUDENT ACHIEVEMENT AS A CRITERION FOR VALIDITY

One criterion for judging the quality of the data for measures of the enacted curriculum is to use the data to predict gains in student achievement. If prediction is good, then the quality of the enacted curriculum data must be good as well. If the quality of prediction is not good, then interpretation of the results is ambiguous.

Perhaps the delivery of the content was so poor that even though the content was taught, it was not learned. Generally, however, studies that have used measures of the content of the enacted curriculum to predict gains in student achievement have found strong correlations. For example, Gamoran et al. found that end-of-semester surveys aggregated to the school year were good predictors of gains in student achievement for first-year high-school mathematics. Importantly, when the data were collapsed to measure just cognitive demand or just topics, correlations dropped to near zero. At least, this study strongly suggests that simplifying a content language to either just cognitive demand or just topic would be a huge mistake if one is interested in collecting data that predict gains in student achievement.

What Are the Uses of Curriculum Assessment Data?

Some uses of curriculum assessment data were mentioned at the beginning of the stage. Now, with a better understanding of the types of measures and data available, more thorough attention can be given to uses, not only in research but in the practice of education as well.

THE INTENDED CURRICULUM

Bill Schmidt and his colleagues used data from content analyses of textbooks to describe the intended curriculum for countries participating in the Third International Mathematics and Science Study. They found that textbooks in the United States cover many more topics in less depth than those in higher achieving countries.

With the current emphasis on state content standards, one could use content analyses to better understand what content is to be taught and what content is not to be taught. Content standards are linear— primarily text—and are not particularly analytic. Content analyses make the content messages of content standards clearer and easier to understand. Content analysis results could be used to better communicate the intentions of content standards to teachers. One finding has been that the standards are very broad and general. Perhaps the content languages could be used to build better and more focused content standards. A committee of experts might be convened, given the content language, and asked to reach consensus on what content is to be taught and what content is not to be taught. To force focus, experts might be given an upper bound on the number of topics by cognitive demand that can be included in the content standards for a given subject at a given grade.

THE ENACTED CURRICULUM

The earliest work on assessing the enacted curriculum was done to create a dependent variable for use in research on teachers' content decisions. Rowan and his colleagues use measures of the enacted curriculum as an intervening variable in their research on the effects on achievement of models of comprehensive whole school reform. Measures of the enacted curriculum can also be used to investigate the quality of implementation of a new curriculum. When states increased the number of math and science credits required for high-school graduation, some hypothesized that the influx of new and weaker students in courses would result in the watering down of course content. A study was conducted to see if the enacted curriculum in courses experiencing a large influx of new students was different from courses where there was not such a large influx. The answer was generally no.

THE ASSESSED CURRICULUM

When student achievement tests are constructed, items are written against test specifications detailing the content to be tested. The items on the test are to serve as a representative sample of the domain of content. Content standards specify the domain. Test construction requires careful attention to building test forms that are well aligned to the content standards. Where tests are used for student accountability the law requires that students have an adequate opportunity to learn the content tested; the enacted curriculum must be aligned to the assessed curriculum.

MEASURES OF ALIGNMENT

As was stated earlier, the No Child Left Behind Act requires states receiving Title I funds to align their student achievement tests with their content standards. Alignment of instruction to textbooks can be used to study the effect of textbooks on the content of instruction. Alignment of instruction to assessments can be used to study the effects of assessments on the content of instruction. Alignment of instruction to content standards can be used to assess the effects of standards-based reform. If standards based reform is successful, then over time instruction should become increasingly more aligned with content standards.

The alignment of instruction to assessments can be used as a control variable in research on teacher pedagogical practices. Clearly, what is taught is an important determinant of student achievement, but so are the pedagogical strategies describing how the content is taught. By using the alignment of the content of instruction to the assessment as a control variable, research on pedagogical practices has greater precision. Alignment can also be used to study the coherence of a state or district's policy system. Policies include content standards, assessments, professional development, and curriculum materials. Alignment results can be displayed in a policy-by-policy content matrix. The greater the coherence of the policy system, the larger the alignment values in the off-diagonal elements.

Where alignment is low, adjustments can be made. The above are just a few of the potentially many uses of curriculum assessment data. You may think of others. Perhaps your own research will use curriculum assessment data in new and powerful ways that shed light on the effects of education policies and practices and how they might be strengthened.

TECHNOLOGY PLANNING

WHY PLAN

As we meet with teachers and administrators across the country and in our service area, it becomes very clear that while most educators understand that they need a plan, it is the rare district that appreciates the necessity of a *strategic* plan. A strategic plan contains a vision for technology's place in the classroom and is accompanied by a series of goals and objectives, an action plan, and a timeline. Within this strategic framework, there are broad outlines and details for all of the steps involved in technology implementation—the building of the infrastructure (hardware and software), adoption of student and teacher technology competencies, professional development strategies, purchasing, funding, scheduling, support, and evaluation. The value of a strategic plan is that it creates the big picture and also provides the framework for the myriad individual strategies and actions that must take place to bring everything together successfully.

While planning is a key to successful technology implementation and integration, planning for technology is not an end in itself. It is a process that strategically moves from vision to reality—from planning into practice.

With multiple technology funding opportunities available from state departments of education, the federal government, and many private sources, school districts are usually required to submit their technology plans in order to access the funds. Even if a school or school district doesn't search out external funding for its technology program, having a well-designed technology plan is quickly becoming an integral part of comprehensive educational planning. It is not surprising that funders have established such a requirement or that districts require a plan for technology integration. However, we often wonder whether the words in these plans connect with teachers and students and result in generating strategies with a positive impact on teaching and learning. With this in mind, we have two goals to accomplish in this publication. First, we want to assist readers in making their district or school technology plan a *strategic* educational plan. Second, we want to describe the variety of actions that teachers and others involved in the process can take to implement the goals and objectives of the plan.

Desired Outcomes

In addition to the aforementioned motivators for planning, making things turn out right is also a powerful motivator. But what do we mean by "right"? Our experience indicates that "right" is the desired outcome for an individual, group, or institution. Following are some desired outcomes that planners strive to achieve:

- Technology is an integral part of a comprehensive plan for improving student learning.
- Teachers are sufficiently comfortable with learning and using technology tools, and they use these tools as a natural and welcome extension of their teaching.
- Teachers use technology fluidly and almost transparently to accomplish curriculum goals.
- Technology is well-supported both in terms of fiscal resources (money allocated to buy materials and equipment) and human resources (people allocated to support users and equipment).
- The school community is confident that funds (and other resources) they allocate for technology are responsibly used to the maximum benefit of students.
- Parents and others in the school community are satisfied that students are learning information-age skills but do not believe that technology is the focus of instruction.
- The school community is confident that a path has been set which accounts for constantly changing technology as well as student needs.

THE PLANNING PROCESS

You may have experience in project planning and implementation that you can use for technology planning. Your experience might come from planning and carrying out educational programs, sports events, family vacations, parties, art exhibits, and so on. Maybe you have even built a house or boat! While the scale of the project and the results of those activities might have been different, the processes for accomplishing them are basically the same as those applied to technology planning.

For comparison, let's use the analogy of building a new house and compare it to the technology-planning process. While you may not have had either of these experiences, just imagine along with us. Keep in mind that these are not necessarily sequential steps, and they may occur in any order. Furthermore, while carrying out the process you may find that some of these components need to be reviewed when new information emerges and takes on new importance.

Just like building a house, technology planning and integration are both complex processes that require time and take place *over time.* This point is often lost on technology planners who would like to believe that they can simply write a plan and then implement it quickly and easily. You cannot build a house without taking the time to plan and taking the time to build properly. It doesn't just happen as you go along! Furthermore, in the same way that building a house requires more than just a lot of materials, technology planning is not simply about hardware, software, cables, and connections. It's also about managing people and resources for accomplishing what you have set out to do. In essence, there are two key points of technology planning—time and strategic action:

- Time. Describing what you want to accomplish in your technology plan is not enough. You must also indicate when you need to perform specific tasks. In short, a strategic plan is about taking certain actions just as to a time schedule to accomplish or achieve your ultimate vision of technology's place in your teaching and learning environment.
- Strategic Action. In practice, strategic planning is a series of linked and interwoven action steps. These actions include planning to plan, gathering information, identifying resources, managing resources, providing professional development, purchasing materials, writing curriculum, and evaluating progress, as well as many others. All of these actions are designed to achieve particular goals, and each goal is designed to support the overall *vision* of the plan. In general, you need to plan with your results in mind.

Guiding Structure:

- A New House
- Be aware of deed restrictions in the area where you want to build your house.
- Technology Planning:
- Be cognizant of state and district guidelines.

Stakeholders:

- A New House:
- Identify all those who will be living or staying in your house.
- Technology Planning:
- Identify all those who will be using your technology (students, teachers, parents, businesses, community).

Preparation:

- A New House:
- Plan to plan.

- Gather information: look at other houses and house plans.
- Consult with a builder or architect.
- Research the features you want to include in your house.
- Draw upon your own experiences.
- Talk to others who have built a house.
- Identify resources available and how much they will cost.
- Technology Planning:
- Plan to plan.
- Start to accumulate information on the pieces of the plan.
- Solicit the help of outside experts.
- Research the ways that technology enhances teaching and learning.
- Draw upon your own experiences.
- Consult with others who have experience with technology integration.
- Visit other schools and school districts.
- Identify resources and how much they will cost.

Time:

- A New House:
- Start with the end in mind and work backwards. If that is not practical, readjust your expectations and timeline accordingly.
- Technology Planning:
- Start with the end in mind and work backwards. If that is not practical, readjust your expectations and timeline accordingly.

Vision:

- A New House:
- Your dream home
- Technology Planning:
- Your school or district's concept of how technology can successfully support teaching and learning

Goals:

- A New House:
- Beauty
- Comfort
- Location
- Resource efficiency
- Technology Planning:
- Technology is adequately supported as a tool for teaching and learning.
- There is a continuing flow of resources to support technology integration.

Activities:

- A New House:
- Deciding on the final plan and design
- Hiring a builder

- Acquiring the financing
- Selecting interior and exterior materials
- Designing special features
- Building the house
- Approval and final walk through
- Technology Planning:
- Planning to plan
- Creating the committee
- Gathering planning resources
- Writing the plan
- Implementing the plan
- Evaluating

Ongoing:

- A New House:
- Repairs and improvements
- Technology Planning:
- Repairs and improvements

BUILDING A FRAMEWORK

The Big Picture

This picture of your overall plan is a helpful tool for reminding your committee members and other stakeholders that every action must relate to your vision. It also serves to remind you that it is the vision, not the technology infrastructure that guides your plan.

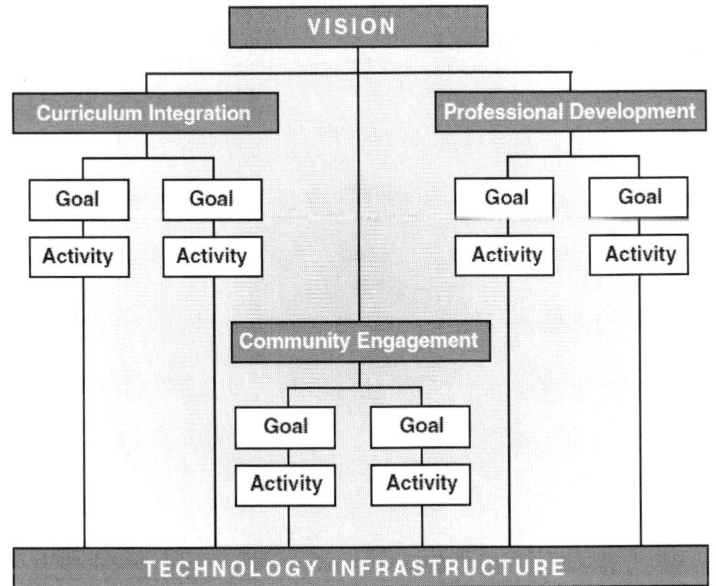

The diagram represents the interrelationship of the three key elements of a strategic educational technology plan. The goal groups shown in the diagram—*Curriculum Integration, Professional Development,* and *Community Engagement*—are the broad areas that your plan should include. Your plan may have some variation, and you may choose to have more or different major areas. Having a framework enables you to maintain a direct relationship of goals to your overall vision.

Every activity—regardless of exactly how many you might have—must link to a goal. Furthermore, each goal has to link directly to your plan's vision. *Technology Infrastructure*—wires, software, hardware—is subordinate to vision, goals, and activities. In other words, your plan is not about infrastructure. Rather, your plan should focus on vision, goals, and the activities that will support them.

PLANNING TO PLAN

Components of the Planning Process

As you begin the planning process, think about three important components: the technology planning committee, research and information that will be resources for the committee, and time.

The Committee

- Teachers. The committee should include teachers from a range of grade levels and subjects representative of your school or district composition. Include non-teaching staff as well.
- Administrators. The presence of a few administrators on your committee helps to establish accountability and ensure that your efforts are on track with school, district, and state guidelines/objectives. To help keep the big picture, try to include district-level curriculum and professional development coordinators.
- Parents. Parents can be your most valuable allies.
- Board members. These are particularly important if your plan will need to be approved or funded by the local school board.
- Students. After all, they are the ultimate stakeholders!
- Community representatives. Remember your community consists of more than school staff, parents, and students.
- Process People. People who understand the planning process and are organized.
- Committee chairperson. Someone to keep everyone on track and on task.
- Writer/editor. Someone to polish your finished product and to ensure readability.

- Administrative assistant. There's a lot of paperwork to attend to, and someone needs to be responsible for taking meeting notes.

Research and Information

- Planning guidebooks and toolkits
- State and/or district guidelines
- Copies of state/district curriculum frameworks
- Sample plans from other districts—preferably from within your own state
- Visits to other schools/districts to see how they have implemented technology as a tool for teaching and learning
- Examples of lesson plans/units demonstrating how technology can be integrated within the existing curriculum
- Workshops, courses, institutes, and other staff development that relates to technology integration, strategic planning, and/or state guidelines for technology plans

Time

A minimum of four months from start to finish, with a clear understanding that the process is quite likely to take longer. Based on our experience, most districts may need closer to half a school year to complete the plan.

Forming Your Technology Planning Committee

Stakeholders are people who have a keen interest in technology planning because it will impact their work or interests. Stakeholders are also those who have expertise that is important for the planning, implementation, and integration processes.

To write your school technology plan, you need a committee composed of educational-technology stakeholders *who will actively work* to help write the school's plan. Keep in mind:

- Your committee members should represent all aspects of your school community. This means teachers (from a variety of grades and/or subject areas), administrators, parents, community members (e.g., business people), and perhaps students. Community Engagement, for possible community members who can contribute to your planning committee.
- While working by committee may be burdensome, resist the temptation to form a committee of only one or two people. On the other hand, avoid committees that are too large and unmanageable.
- Since the planning process contains many different tasks, you will need members with a variety of skills: curriculum design, professional development, technology infrastructure expertise, and experience with budgetary matters, administrative policy, and process tasks.

- Committee members need to understand that planning, implementation, and integration are ongoing processes, not short-term commitments. The committee members should be willing to assist in your school's technology implementation efforts long after the actual plan is written.
- You can use the following worksheet when forming your planning committee.

Planning a Timeline

Following is a broad timeline of what you will need to do for planning, when, and how long it will take. We have to note that this eighteen-week timeline is considerably more optimistic than what most districts are able to accomplish. Weeks in which there are no named activities allow time for completing the work necessary to move the plan to the next step. While it is highly likely that certain steps will take *longer* to complete, it is very unlikely that steps can be completed in less time than is shown.

Components of a Good Technology Plan

There is no single best model for an effective technology plan. You will find a number of templates, checklists, and frameworks to help guide your work. Our experience indicates the best plan is one that suits local priorities, is closely linked to its district's instructional goals, and is developed by a broadly representative planning group. As with any educational innovation, it can take as long as five years for improvements (including technology implementation) to impact student achievement measures. Therefore, most technology plans are designed with goals and objectives that extend over a five-year period. Included are the activities that will take place within that time and the sources of funding that will support that plan.

We have selected several key items that you will want to include in your technology plan, along with applicable goals and objectives. We direct you to the sections in this book where you can get more information regarding these various items.

A vision statement

An effective technology plan begins with a vision statement that focuses on learning goals and outcomes. This stage includes steps and activities that you and your planning team can use to create that vision statement.

An assessment of current technology use in your district

Where you are and where you want to be. This information provides a baseline for planning and implementation. We have included some survey forms in this stage for carrying out this assessment.

Curriculum integration

Curriculum integration involves curriculum goalsetting, infrastructure planning, and professional development planning. These may be stated broadly, or you may prefer to list specific outcomes by grade level.

An evaluation plan

Once you start to implement the technology, how will you evaluate its effectiveness? You will want to assess all elements of your technology initiative—from teachers' instructional use to the effectiveness of local policies regarding access, training, and support.

Equitable—and practical—access for teachers and students

What is your strategy for providing technology access to teachers and students? Do you have provisions for an Acceptable Use Policy, especially for the Internet?

Professional development

Teacher training is one of the most important elements in a successful technology effort. If teachers do not have the understanding or the skills to use technology, then technology integration will have little impact. How do you plan to deliver the necessary professional development? Suggestions for developing a staff development curriculum are also included.

Community engagement

Community engagement should not be an afterthought to technology planning. In fact, it is a crucial component to success. You should recognize that your community includes everyone in your school district—board members, administrators, teachers, support personnel, and students, as well as parents, business leaders, and others who are directly or indirectly associated with your schools.

Infrastructure

Infrastructure is a complex area of technology planning; here we break it into four main categories.

Specifications for hardware and software acquisitions

The software (instructional materials and applications) that best suits your school or district's instructional needs should determine hardware (equipment) purchases. Compatibility and ease of use are also important considerations. Focusing on cutting-edge or specialty items can be a waste of resources, unless they address a specific need. This is an area in which an external consultant can be invaluable. As suggested, help you create a set of realistic goals and objectives.

- *Networking and multimedia access.* Items in this category may include wiring and cabling, provisions for a local area network, Internet services, and access to cable or satellite television. This is another area where an external consultant can be of great help.
- *Facilities modification and other infrastructure supports.* If you are building a new facility, plan to include access to telecommunications and networks. Or, if you have older facilities, consider the need to add electrical outlets or telephone lines, or to adapt heating, cooling, and ventilation systems. You may also need to add or remove carpeting, alter acoustics, or repair a leaky roof.
- *Safety and security measures.* This may include not only concerns about physical safety and protecting equipment and supplies, but also provisions for assuring the security of student records, teachers' files, and so forth.
- *System maintenance, troubleshooting, and technical support.* This is another critical but often-neglected topic.

Assessment of your infrastructure

Technology systems and software will become outdated and equipment will wear out. While you don't need to keep up with every technological innovation, your technology planning process should include provisions for regular review.

Budget summary and funding strategies

Funding your technology plan is an important piece of your total plan.

Timeline

You will need to develop several timelines for carrying out different parts of your technology plan. Don't forget to include those timelines in your technology plan, too. We have incorporated timelines in this stage and in various other survey and assessment forms throughout this book.

Sample Technology Plan Outline

The following sample outline of an educational technology plan is intended to show the various sections and flow of a typical plan. You need first to check with your state or district technology administration to determine if there is a particular format that your plan must follow. Often it is acceptable to have more than the state requires, but it is never acceptable to leave out a state-required section. As long as your planning committee follows state and local guidelines, they might decide to vary the actual order of sections, or even add sections.

Sample Technology Plan Outline

I. Executive summary/Introduction

II. Our school's vision for educational technology

A. Why are we interested in using technology?
B. How will technology impact teaching and learning in our school?
III. Current status of educational technology in our school
IV. Planning focus areas
A. Curriculum integration
1. Overview of our curriculum integration strategy
2. Goals and objectives
B. Staff development
1. Overview of our staff development strategy
2. Goals and objectives
C. Community engagement
1. Overview of our community engagement strategy
2. Goals and objectives
D. Infrastructure
1. Overview of our infrastructure strategy
2. Goals and objectives
V. Technology infrastructure design
VI. Equitable and practical access for teachers and students
VII. Action plan by year (for five years)
A. Curriculum integration
B. Staff development
C. Community engagement
D. Infrastructure
VIII. Roles and responsibilities
IX. Budget summary/Funding strategies
X. Evaluation
XI. Appendices—Committee membership, Inventories, Survey data, Glossary, Bibliography

Technology Needs Survey

The *Technology Needs Survey,* developed for the SEIR?TEC intensive site schools is designed to determine teacher needs and attitudes related to instructional technology. You may find that some of these questions do not apply to your situation; in that case, you would want to customize it for your own needs before administering it to your district's staff.

Administering this survey *early* in your planning process can help you accumulate valuable data on the current status of technology implementation and integration in your school or district. You will need a comprehensive picture of how teachers currently think about and use technology in their teaching. After you gather this information, you can use it as valuable *baseline data* to measure your progress in future planning years. Administering this survey again after a year or two will inform you of changes or additional activities you need to undertake. If you have already begun implementing technology in your school or district, this survey may be useful for measuring the progress you've made. Whether you use the SEIR?TEC survey, or create your own, these are the areas of information that should prove useful:

- What types of activities do teachers use with educational technologies and how often do they use those activities?
- Do teachers have access to a computer for their own use, or do they routinely use a personally owned computer to prepare materials for use in their classrooms?
- What ideas does the staff have about what is needed to make technology more useful?
- What student benefits have the staff members observed in relation to the use of technology in the school/classroom?
- What new software or hardware do teachers frequently request for use in classrooms?
- What are examples of special work or projects teachers and students have done with technology?
- Which courses or subjects most often use technology?
- Who supervises and assists students in the use of computers?
- Who assists and supports technology problems within schools on a daily basis?
- Who handles major technology problems that have come up regarding the use of technology in the school/classroom?
- What is the type and frequency of participation in educational technology professional development in the previous two years? What effect has it had on instructional practices?
- What hardware and software are available in the school or classroom? Don't overlook existing networks, TVs, VCRs, Channel 1, laser-disc players, scanners, digital cameras, access to the Internet, and so on.
- What are the levels of technology experience of teachers and other staff?
- What new professional development do teachers and staff members frequently request?

Technology Inventory Worksheet

Before you create a want list, be sure to inventory what you already have on hand.

You might be surprised at what currently exists in your district. Often teachers or principals have gained access to some computer technology through special projects or other funding. Sometimes a teacher or administrator who is no longer with the district may have purchased technology that now sits unused and forgotten.

IDENTIFYING CORE VALUES AND CREATING A VISION STATEMENT

A well-defined vision statement is the cornerstone of any good plan. Before the planning committee starts drafting goals and objectives, it should first define or describe its vision for technology. This vision should reflect your district's core values as they relate to educational improvement and the role that technology will play in helping support those values. We suggest that you conduct brainstorming sessions such as those to develop your vision statement and identify your core values.

Brainstorm to develop a vision

Introduce the activity with the following:

- The overall goal of a strategic educational technology plan is to lay out an operational plan for using technology to enhance teaching and learning. It is expected that the process for implementing technology will not be instantaneous or finite. Rather, technology integration is an ongoing process, throughout which we should be able to look back and see definite changes and growth. If the plan has been successful, the changes and growth will have followed the basic structure—the goals, objectives, and timelines—of the technology plan. As a technology planning committee, your task is to write that plan.
- To help us develop a picture of what our district will look like as this technology plan is implemented, imagine one of our schools five years from now. Specifically, think about a student who is attending that school. As you imagine a day in that student's life, identify the ways that technology touches the student's experience in the school.

Brainstorm images that help you see technology being used to:

- Support new ways of teaching and learning
- Expand learning beyond the walls of the traditional classroom
- Support teachers in their instructional tasks and professional learning
- Bring the school closer to its parent community
- Make more efficient use of teacher and administrator time and resources

Write these ideas on a flip chart and refer to them later when you create your vision statement.

Identify core values

The *Core Values Worksheet* activity is useful for helping your committee identify core values that support your common vision. In the *Core Values Worksheet* you are asked to describe why you believe that technology is a necessary tool for teaching and learning in this district. The worksheet also asks you to describe in broad terms your core educational values and the ways in which technology will impact student learning and to discuss your commitment to making sure that students, teachers, administrators, and your entire educational community have access to technology tools.

Use this tool to catalog the core values of your district or school—paying particular attention to how these values relate to technology's role within the teaching and learning environment. Make sure that your vision statement reflects these core values. Each person on your planning team should complete the worksheet individually, and then a facilitator should work with the entire group to reach consensus on the core values for your campus or district. Once expanded upon, these reasons can form the basis of the vision statement of your technology plan.

Create the vision statement

Once you have completed the brainstorming activity and have identified core values, your school technology planning committee can begin to work on your vision statement. You may use the statements from the brainstorming and core values activities to stimulate conversation and spur additional thoughts about why your school needs to integrate technology in its teaching and learning environments. The vision statement should result in a single, concise paragraph that summarizes your answers to the questions "Why is technology important to the students and teachers in our school?" and "Why do you believe that technology is a necessary tool for teaching and learning in this district?" As you start work on your vision statement, it may be useful to examine vision statements of other schools and districts. As you will see, there are many different interpretations of what constitutes an appropriate vision statement. One thing that is consistent across all of these statements is that their bottom line is an expression of how technology will be used to impact student learning and achievement.

We have included portions of the vision statements from plans of several of the SEIR?TEC intensive sites and other schools with which we have worked. You may wonder why you cannot just adopt a vision statement that someone else has generated. The point is that the vision statement should reflect your own situation, values, and context. For many it may be the process of jointly *creating* the vision that makes it a useful guiding light to your own plan. The vision setting process can help get your committee all on the same page, which will certainly be invaluable in fulfilling that vision down the line.

We suggest that you postpone reading the examples that follow until the latter part of your vision-creation process, and do so as a reality check. You will notice that some of these schools have lengthy vision statements; be aware, however, that the value of a vision statement is not determined by its length. And, most importantly, remember that your vision statement will be unique to your own school or district.

Sample Vision Statements

Lakeside School District:

- Our Vision for Educational Technology
- It is the vision of the Lakeside School District that all students and faculty be provided with the latest technology tools and training so that they can function in society and be competitive in the global market. We envision that students will develop the necessary skills to be productive members of society. Technology will support this development by refining their critical thinking skills, enabling effective communication, and fostering creativity.
- Lakeside School District is committed to providing ongoing and continuous training to all of its teachers in the use of and integration of technology tools. To ensure equity of learning, these tools will be made available to all students in support of their varied learning styles and needs by providing faculty access to state of the art information and resources.
- To achieve our vision, the Lakeside School District will enlist the active engagement of our parents and community and offer the technological resources of the schools.

Lincoln High School:

- Vision for Educational Technology: Technology offers students an avenue to succeed as citizens in a global society in which information is growing at an incredible rate. Technology can improve communication, enhance thinking skills, make instruction more efficient and effective, and develop life skills critical to success. Lincoln High School will incorporate technology as a means of integrating curriculum across subject areas. Students and educators will be guaranteed opportunities to use technology as an integral part of education. In support of this vision, Lincoln High School offers its Strategic Educational Technology Plan.

Ricardo Richards Elementary School:

- Vision: As an educational institution, Ricardo Richards School is committed to ensuring that all students and staff acquire the knowledge, skills, and attitudes necessary to be lifelong learners.

Rosemary Middle School:

- Our Vision for Technology Integration: Students, parents, and educators will use communication and information technologies to enhance and expand the traditional role of education in the Andrews community. We believe the basic goal of education has not changed, that is, to prepare our students for life-long learning and success in a changing society. However, the tools and instructional methods to achieve these goals have advanced dramatically. Technologies such as computers, networks, and widearea communications offer tremendous opportunities to students and educators as a way to improve life within our community and a link to the world outside of Andrews. Rosemary Middle School has the responsibility for developing curriculum and applying instructional methods enriched with technology and in ensuring that our students and teachers are proficient users of these new technologies. This technology integration plan will outline our strategies for turning this vision into reality.

Groton Public Schools:

- A Vision for Technology: We envision using technology to further a learning community where:
- Students are engaged in a challenging curriculum that is focused on inquiry based, hands-on learning. Students are comfortable using technology. Students take responsibility for their own educational success.
- Teachers use technology to support all learning across the curriculum. They function as coaches, mentors, advocates, and managers of information. Through ongoing, comprehensive professional development, all teachers acquire the knowledge and skills to integrate technology into a challenging and interdisciplinary curriculum that addresses students' specific needs, developmental levels, and learning styles.
- Administrative functions, including those performed by instructional staff, are fully automated, thereby allowing more of the school system's energy and resources to be focused on student education.
- The schools become an environment where all students and staff have ready access to a full range of current technology, software tools, and applications. The schools have knowledgeable staff and external resources (such as parents, community members, business, higher education, and network resources) to further the curriculum goals.

Creating Goal Statements

Once you have created your vision statement and your planning team has a focus for its direction, it's time to create goal statements.

What Is a Goal Statement?

Goal statements are the specific pieces of the plan that support your vision. For technology planning, appropriate goal statements should be created for these three broad areas:

- Curriculum integration
- Professional development
- Community engagement

Other areas are possible if they fit your situation. Also, remember that you *must* abide by the structure set for technology plans by your state department of education. If this structure requests a particular focus area, then you must create goals for that area. Goal statements describe what you want to accomplish. While your vision statement might not change over a period of time, your goals might change. School districts may have similar vision statements but the goals that support their vision may be quite different. Goal statements, however, do not describe *how* a goal will be reached. *How* things will get done is described in an *action plan.* Tools and formats for creating action plans follow the sample goals.

Sample Goals

Curriculum Integration

In general, most technology plans have three basic goals related to technology integration:

- A goal that describes technology as supporting the core curriculum and/or state curriculum frameworks. Most districts choose to support this goal with one sample activity illustrating how technology would be used within each core curriculum area.
- A goal that describes technology as supporting learning and thinking skills for all students, such as inquiry, critical thinking, problem solving, and creativity. Most districts support this goal with three activities, that is, one activity illustrating how technology would be used at elementary-, middle-, and high-school levels to support these skills. Plans might also specify technology and learning activities for special populations, such as students with disabilities or those who speak English as a second language.
- A goal that describes technology expertise as a critical skill that prepares students for a technological future. This goal touches on how and why students become effective and efficient users of technology. Most districts develop several activities that support this goal.

Following are some sample goals:

- Our students will learn to solve problems cooperatively through teamwork, assisted by appropriate technologies.
- Our students will develop an appreciation for and the ability to use technology in problem-solving situations.
- Our students will have opportunities to work with voice, video, and data technology in an atmosphere conducive to their varied learning styles.
- Our students will have equitable access to computers and other technology tools where instructional needs are best served.

- Our students will be provided with a range of experiences designed to develop the technological skills necessary to function responsibly in life situations marked by rapid technological change.

Professional Development

Professional development is the training and development needed by teachers and administrators to use technology tools within teaching and learning environments. Be sure to include goals that relate to learning new, technologysupported pedagogical approaches as well as the mechanics of hardware, software, and network operations. Teachers not only need to know how to use technology effectively, they also need to understand reasons for using technology. Your professional development goals should address both the how and the why of teaching and learning with technology. Some examples follow:

- Our teachers, administrators, and staff will participate in professional development as necessary to make them proficient technical users of the district-wide network, its resources (such as e-mail and online information collections), and other technology devices and resources.
- Our teachers will participate in professional development as necessary to develop pedagogical techniques and strategies to facilitate learner-centered, project-based curricula that integrate the use of technology tools.
- Our teachers and staff will be provided with adequate time to take advantage of professional development opportunities related to learning technology skills and strategies.
- Our teachers will be provided with time, incentives, and opportunities to share their individual technology skills and expertise with other teachers in their schools and around the district.

Community Engagement

Schools and their communities are mutually dependent. All too often, schools forget that they can both obtain tremendous resources from their communities *and* put back as much as they gain.

Your plan's community engagement goals should express this give-and-take. These goals are designed to address the many ways that your schools can draw support from your community of stakeholders and at the same time serve as rich resources to a diverse community. Here are some examples:

- Our ongoing technology planning process will address the needs and concerns of a wide range of school and community stakeholders, including teachers, administrators, school staff, parents, students, local business and industry, and community service providers.

- As suggested, operate and maintain our technology infrastructure in partnership with the local community.
- As suggested, create information on our wide area network that is useful and relevant to a diverse range of users, both within and outside the schoolsystem network.
- As suggested, provide opportunities for teachers, students, administrators, and community members to use technology resources at school and in other locations throughout our community.

TAKING ACTION

Creating an Action Plan

Once you have stated your goals, the next step is to determine how you are going to achieve them. For that purpose, you need to have an action plan. Creating individual action plans for each goal can become quite complicated, since you need to determine *what* it is exactly that you need to do to support that goal, *who* will be responsible for carrying it out, *when* an activity needs to be completed, *what* resources are required, and *where* the activity will take place.

Furthermore, some activities will depend on the completion of another activity. It may be helpful to create a flowchart or diagram to show how all of the action plans relate to each other, to each of the goals, and to the vision statement. Many tools are available for accomplishing this task. Check the *Technology Planning Resources* section in this stage for different templates, rubrics, or matrices that you can use for this process.

Defining Activities for Your Action Plan

Appropriate activities within your action plan should allow you to answer YES to each of the following questions:

- Does this activity *directly relate* to at least one of your goals? Remember that you should not have goals that do not support your vision, and you should not have activities that do not support goals.
- Is this activity *critically important* to accomplish or fulfill the goal it supports? If you do not perform this activity, would you be unable to accomplish your goal? It is important to choose activities which have a clear relationship to the goal and which create sustained and measurable impact in terms of the goal.
- Is the activity do-able? Do you have the resources—financial, human, and time—to accomplish this activity by the end of the time period you have specified? Have you accounted for all of the resources—time, hardware/software, staff development, funding—that you need to accomplish this activity?

- What impact will the activity have on related activities in years to come? Is there anything about this activity that would prevent you from performing other related activities beyond year one of your plan? For example, is this activity so expensive that you would deplete all of the funds that might be designated for such activities? Is it an activity that needs to be ongoing?
- Does this activity build upon other activities and initiatives undertaken within the district? Certain activities—particularly those related to professional development, curriculum revision, and infrastructure development—should be linked to district initiatives much broader than those discussed directly in this technology plan. Examples might include building renovations, district reform plans, and professional development plans. It is to your benefit to be aware of and to build upon those other district initiatives.
- Is this a *measurable* activity? How will you evaluate this activity? Are there data you can identify and collect which will allow you to document your progress and/or success in accomplishing the activity? A handy way of summing up these rules is to apply the SMART test. That is, are your activities:
- Specific?
- Measurable?
- Attainable?
- Relevant?
- Time-Bound?

Aligning Your Technology Plan

For example, does your vision talk about curriculum? If so (and it *should*), what plan goals relate to that part of your vision and what action plan steps relate to fulfilling those goals? Is there overlap or duplication between efforts? Can some areas be consolidated or linked together? What efforts depend on other efforts? Have you forgotten something? By using such a tool, you can often spot inconsistencies between various elements of your plan and know where the plan needs more work. This framework is also useful for updating your plan periodically.

INTEGRATING TECHNOLOGY INTO THE CURRICULUM

WHAT DO WE MEAN BY INTEGRATION

One thing that we have found to be consistent as we work in schools around the nation and in the SEIR¨TEC region is that there are many different definitions of the term technology *integration.* So, we offer our definition of the term. To us, integration is *the use of technology by students and teachers to enhance teaching and learning and to support existing curricular goals and objectives.* In other words, we are not talking about computer classes or some other sort of stand-alone technology curriculum that focuses on teaching students about technology. By and large, we are thinking about regular classroom teachers using the different technologies to support the learning of all students within and across curriculum areas. We are always careful to remember that technology is not a cure-all, and sometimes the best teaching tool is not a technology tool. Technology benefits skilled teachers and engaged students but does not by itself *create* either. As with any teaching tool, technology must be understood within the broad context of curriculum and pedagogy.

At the same time, technology tools come with their own particular challenges and benefits. We work toward a vision in which all teachers use technology fluently and seamlessly to support student-focused learning rather than teacher-driven instruction. At present, however, teacher use is typically neither fluent nor seamless. Indeed, the attention paid to technology planning and use often serves to highlight other educational problems such as teachers with weak pedagogical skills and insufficient understanding of the curriculum; a lack of staff development and other support for teachers; and conflicts between educational expectations and the effort required to meet those expectations. The bottom line is that many teachers find it difficult to integrate technology because it usually means changing the way they teach. And, it doesn't help matters when policymakers measure the success of technology initiatives in terms of student scores on standardized tests.

Fortunately, there are a number of research studies that give evidence that effective teaching and learning with technology can improve student outcomes. For example, research conducted through the Apple Classrooms of Tomorrow (ACOT) indicates that students who use technology extensively as part of their daily school experience exhibit the following behaviors and characteristics:

- Explore and represent information dynamically and in many forms.
- Become socially aware and more confident.
- Communicate effectively about complex processes.
- Use technology routinely and appropriately.
- Become independent learners and self-starters.
- Know their areas of expertise and share that expertise spontaneously.
- Work well collaboratively.
- Develop a positive orientation to the future.

Our experience suggests that when teachers realize that technology can improve student learning, they are willing and eager to begin integrating it into the ongoing educational program.

Once teachers realize the potential for improving learning through the effective use of technology, and as they strive to become competent or even proficient technology users, they begin to change the way they teach. The ACOT studies revealed that teachers go through stages as they learn to infuse technology into teaching and learning. As teachers move through the phases and learn to fluidly integrate technology into the curriculum, they usually find it hard to understand how they could have taught without it.

ACOT Stages of Technology Integration

Stage	Example of What Teachers Do
Entry	Learn the basics of using the new technology.
Adoption	Use new technology to support traditional instruction.
Adaptation	Integrate new technology into traditional classroom practice. Here they ften focus on increased student productivity and engagement by using word processors, spreadsheets, and graphics tools.
Appropriation	Focus on cooperative, project-based, and interdisciplinary work—incorporating the technology as needed and as one of many tools.
Invention	Discover new uses for technology tools (for example, developing spreadsheet macros for teaching algebra or designing projects that combine multiple technologies).

As teachers integrate technology into teaching and learning, shifts occur in classrooms. In essence, traditional teacher-focused instruction changes to studentoriented knowledge construction, as the following chart from ACOT's research shows:

	Traditional Instruction	Extended (Knowledge Construction)
Activity	Teacher-centered and didactic	Learner-centered and interactive
Teacher role	Fact teller and expert	Collaborator and sometimes learner
Student role	Listener and learner	Collaborator and sometimes expert
Learning Emphasis	Facts and replication	Relationships and inquiry
Concept of knowledge	Accumulation	Transformation
Demonstration of success	Quantity	Quality
Assessment	Norm-referenced and multiple guess	Criterion-referenced and performance portfolios
Technology use	Seat work	Communication, collaboration, information access, and expression

Technology allows students to become active learners and to develop their problem solving, critical-thinking, and creativity skills. Technology offers students and teachers rapid and broad access to information and resources.

Tools such as the Internet provide the means for students and teachers to engage in inquiry-based learning and to interact with a world of collaborators, information providers, and fellow learners.

Computer-based simulations can engage students in open-ended explorations of *what if?* scenarios that would be impossible to recreate in the physical (as opposed to virtual) universe.

Common information-technology tools, such as spreadsheets and databases, allow the rapid and flexible manipulation of information, enabling students (and teachers) to analyze data and to form insights from a number of different perspectives and in sync with an individual's own particular patterns of mind. Also, the use of technology tools such as word processors and multimedia presentation managers help students improve communication skills and assume responsibility for the quality of their products of learning. True, all of this *could* be done without technology, but if the tools are there, and are undeniably used in the world outside of school, why *wouldn't* teachers and students want to use them?

PUTTING THE TOOLS TO WORK

Technology Standards for Students

Many districts struggle with the issue of teacher and student technology competencies or standards. Overall, competencies or standards mean those things that teachers and students should *know about* technology and be able to *do with* technology. In many cases, a district may need or want to adopt standards that have been established at the state or national level. Some states, such as Florida, have standards for academic subjects and indicate specific technology uses that help students reach the standards.

Since we live in a time when standards, frameworks, and benchmarks are becoming increasingly prominent, it makes sense that some sort of competency or standard would be desirable for teacher and student technology use. The bottom line on adopting technology standards is that it must be done as part of the district technology planning process.

Teacher competencies are intimately related to the professional development goals and are in turn tied to the curriculum integration goals. Likewise, the student standards are parallel to the curriculum integration goals and are highly dependent upon the teacher professional development goals and, therefore, teacher competencies.

Competencies, goals, and standards are linked in a cycle. And as we know, this cycle is driven by your district's *vision* for how technology will be used to support teachers, students, and the entire educational community. With this cycle in mind, it is clear that you cannot adopt or develop competencies and standards without the context of the other elements.

As a committee of stakeholders develops your plan, they need to review and consider competencies for teachers and standards for students. If your standards are ever going to be met by your teachers and students, then they must be rooted in *your* reality. We suggest the following process steps for developing teacher competencies and student technology standards:

- Engage your committee of stakeholders in a discussion about the need for competencies and standards and how these relate to other elements of the technology plan.
- Be sure that your committee has a common definition of key concepts such as technology integration. This ensures that your entire committee can have a common goal. Review your plan's vision statement to refresh your committee's understanding of the big picture for technology in your district
- Begin work on the curriculum integration portion of your plan. This helps ensure that the curriculum will drive your process of determining what students should be able to do with technology (the student standards) and what teachers need to know in order to support student use (the teacher competencies).
- Review your state's requirements regarding student standards and teacher competencies, the professional literature on standards and competencies, and examples of other districts' work in this area. Note that we suggest taking this step later in the process rather than at the beginning. This helps avert the natural desire simply to appropriate existing work without first grounding it in your school's reality.
- As you adopt or develop competencies and standards, ask yourself if what you are developing is (1) *do-able* by teachers and students with the existing or projected resources; (2) *flexible* enough to account for changing technology; and (3) *exemplary* rather than mandatory. That is, do you provide examples of what you expect to observe, or do you just give orders with little guidance?

Establishing student standards is a bit more complex than establishing teacher standards. Part of this complexity comes from the issues surrounding any standards for student learning. Unfortunately, much of the discussion we hear in the districts struggling with this issue relates to defining what sorts of *mechanical* skills students are expected to have in order to operate various devices. What is often lost in this discussion is any reflection about *why* students might use computers, software, the Internet, and so on. Once again, educators need to think about the more important issue of helping students learn which tools are best used for a particular learning task.

The best student-technology standards—and we believe that the term *standard* is more appropriate here than *competency*—focus on ensuring that students be exposed to a wide range of situations in which technology is used as a part of an active, engaged learning experience. Naturally, this can be achieved only when technology use is thoroughly integrated throughout the curriculum rather than allowed to stand as a single curriculum subject. Students are not in school to learn technology, particularly at the elementaryand middle-school levels. Just as with teachers, total mastery of a particular software package or hardware device is only really instructive as a pathway to understanding the broader place of information technology as a tool for exploration and learning.

When viewed this way, student technology standards are very closely related to the *curriculum integration* goals of the district's strategic educational technology plan. If students are in school to master the curriculum, then the goals for their use of technology should be to help them do the same.

One thing to be very wary of is the urge to teach the standard, a practice that some districts fall into after they adopt student-technology standards. This seems to happen most often when standards are construed to be very specific skills or technology-related facts that students are expected to master by particular grade levels.

Often, districts with these types of student standards feel that they have to involve their students in specific technology classes where particular applications and operation skills (e.g., keyboarding) are taught. While this *may* lead to mastery of the skills specified in the standards, it also has the effect of pulling technology use entirely out of the regular classroom and its learning activities. For many students, this diminishes technology to the level of any other class and thereby negates many or most of its educational advantages related to inspiration, creativity, and engagement.

There are several ways to avoid isolating technology as a subject matter in itself. The first consideration is to create student technology standards that relate entirely to using technology within the curriculum. Therefore, your standards will connect technology use to actual curriculum-related projects or activities.

Rather than the simple requirement "Use the World Wide Web," an appropriately focused standard would be to require that students use the World Wide Web as part of a research project that is part of an integrated language arts and social studies unit. Use your district's curriculum and its objectives for creating student technology standards.

A major weakness in the writing of student standards is the fact that few technology planners are sufficiently familiar with their district's curriculum goals and objectives. As a result, technology specialists write the technology plan and tie student standards to what they themselves know best—technology. We cannot overemphasize the importance of this issue. Student technology competencies cannot and should not be separated from curriculum goals and objectives. They are also woven into teachers' professional development, and specifically into professional development that helps teachers understand the role of technology within their classrooms and curriculum.

With all of this in mind, we offer the following guidelines for adopting student technology standards for your district. Teacher-technology standards and competencies are addressed in the next stage, which focuses on professional development.

- Make sure that the same people who are writing your plan's curriculum integration goals are also working on student standards. Student standards are about how students will use technology within the curriculum. This should be consistent with integration goals.
- Avoid the urge to focus narrowly on using specific technology tools. Instead, think categorically about technology use. For example, it is better to talk about the fact that students will need to learn how to use word processors within the writing process than it is to talk about mastering a specific word processing program on a specific machine in a specific class. Keep in mind that your plan should last a number of years. If you upgrade your software or hardware, will this negate your standard?
- Think about *who* will be responsible for ensuring that students meet the standards. If the answer to this is the classroom teacher—as we advise—then make sure that you have given adequate thought and resources to how teachers will be prepared to assist all of their students in meeting the standard.
- Ask yourself, "Is the standard reasonable and achievable?" Is it reasonable to expect that classroom teachers with no technology training can provide students with opportunities to use technology tools in their learning activities? Is it reasonable to expect that a single *computer teacher* in the school will be able to *train* every student in a particular software application described in a particular student standard?
- Create student standards that evolve and escalate over time. This strategy allows you to correlate student standards to professional development for teachers and the growing technology infrastructure.

Examples of Student Competencies

- The National Educational Technology Standards (NETS) for Students project is a collaborative national effort to set student technology standards. Several nationally known nonprofits and technology manufacturers sponsor this work.
- A related approach to developing student standards involves assessing student technology skills and assigning various levels to the skill

groupings. This is the approach taken by the Bellingham (Washington) school district. The various assessments Bellingham uses form the basis for determining what skills training a given student requires.

Integrating Technology into the Curriculum

Finding the Right Tool for the Task—Four Categories of Technology Use

Information technology such as computers, software applications, video, audio/visual multimedia, and telecommunications can be integrated into virtually any classroom situation. The key is to focus on what you are trying to accomplish within your curriculum (i.e., your learning goals and objectives), and then to identify an appropriate technology tool that will help you accomplish your goal. This is not as simple as it sounds.

We believe that one path towards simplification lies in the identification of different categories of technology that can be broadly said to support different classroom strategies. Educational researchers, and in particular Barbara Means in her landmark work on technology's role in school reform, have identified four categories of software applications. While by no means exclusive, this categorical identification helps illustrate the point that not every strategy can be supported by any or every technology. More specifically, you need a variety of tools to accomplish the variety of objectives associated with a given curriculum.

No single piece of software or hardware can be expected to address all of your classroom needs. Sorting educational technology by *category of use* is a step towards learning how to apply the right technology tool towards a given task. We don't maintain that this is the *only* way to separate the types, but it is comprehensive and one which we have found to work with many teachers.

In fact there are many titles which would be equally valid examples for most of these categories, and our citations below do not imply recommendations or endorsements.

Tutorial Uses of Technology

Tutorial technologies are those that support the transmission of information from source to student. The technology itself might be a software application that presents questions, allows time for answer, and offers corrections or rewards for the right or wrong response. Often, tutorial technologies present their lessons accompanied by a variety of multimedia. Tutorial technologies are useful for the development and reinforcement of basic skills. Thus, it is not surprising that tutorial technologies are often found in lower grades (and in remedial programs at higher grades) and are used to support skills such as spelling, grammar, vocabulary development, and basic-function mathematics.

Examples:

- Drill and practice games such as the MathBlaster series, Grammar Games, and SpellIt
- Integrated Learning Systems (in their most common use, one student per computer)
- Computer-based training and testing

Application Uses of Technology

Application technologies include such tools as word processors, spreadsheet programs, databases, and other data collection/manipulation/ analysis programs. The operative term is *tool,* since applications such as those above have no content in and of themselves. For example, a word processor may be used at all grade levels and in every subject. The application use of technology is an interim, or process, step towards achieving an instructional goal.

Examples:

- Integrated packages such as AppleWorks and Microsoft Office and their word processors
- Excel and other spreadsheet programs
- TimeLiner (as an information organization and presentation tool)
- HyperStudio, KidPix Studio Deluxe, PowerPoint, and other multimedia packages
- Multimedia encyclopedias such as Microsoft Encarta and Grolier's
- World Wide Web and student research

Exploratory Uses of Technology

Exploratory technology combines some content with a particular delivery strategy to encourage students to explore a subject and construct their own knowledge. The majority of exploratory technology applications are open-ended and can produce a variety of narrative outcomes. The primary goal when using an exploratory technology is not to get the right answer but rather to use the technology to engage with a subject and derive meaning from that engagement. Exploratory technologies are often used to facilitate student cooperation, critical thinking, and group problem-solving.

Examples:

- Simulations such as SimCity and Sim Earth
- Life and physical science simulations
- Simulated journeys, such as Oregon Trail
- Role-playing, group problem solving packages, such as The Great Ocean Rescue, Decisions Decisions, and Rainforest Researchers
- Multimedia encyclopedias, such as Encarta and Grolier's
- World Wide Web searching and student research

Communication Uses of Technology

Communications technology describes those uses of telecommunications that support teaching and learning. Communications technology can be used in any of the three modes/categories (tutorial, application, and exploratory). Often, communications technology is used in an exploratory mode to facilitate student collaboration and research across great distance. As with the application category, communications technology is a tool which in itself is content- neutral. On the other hand, the use of this tool can enable the teaching of certain content and the fulfillment of certain learning goals that would otherwise be more difficult if not impossible.

Examples:

- E-mail (student-to-student, student-to-professional, etc.)
- Collaborative, online projects, such as The Journey North or those found at EnviroNet
- Teleconferencing
- World Wide Web searching and student research
- Student publishing on the World Wide Web

Software Applications Commonly Used in Curriculum Units

Applications technology describes software programs that in themselves have no subject-matter content. These programs are tools in the classic sense. Therefore, not surprisingly, the software application tools used in education are the same tools used in other settings such as business. Spreadsheets, database programs, word processors, and presentation authoring tools are commonly used by all personal computer users and are readily available for many teachers and students. Applications tools are often bundled together by a manufacturer or distributor and arrive as part of a new computer purchase. These bundles are often referred to as *integrated software* or *application suites* and are sold under brand names such as Microsoft Office, Microsoft Works, or AppleWorks. The programs that comprise the bundle are determined by the manufacturer. Nevertheless, the basic idea behind bundled applications is the same. Central to the concept of integrated-software bundles is the idea of a menu interface that is common among the elements of a bundle (i.e., the word processor, spreadsheet, and other programs have the same menus and icons). This simplifies learning the different commands that work across the programs, and it allows the user to move data easily among different application tools.

Spreadsheets

Examples: Microsoft Excel, AppleWorks

A spreadsheet is a program that organizes cells of numerical data into tables of rows and columns much as one would find in an accounting ledger. Through the use of equations (written in a simple programming language unique to the particular spreadsheet program in use), the spreadsheet program is able to perform basic mathematical functions across the rows and columns. For example, it is possible to total a column of numbers, divide that total by cells within the column, and report the resulting average elsewhere on the spreadsheet. Most spreadsheet programs provide a capacity for graphing data. Graphs can range from simple X-Y line graphs to more complex three-dimensional representations.

Spreadsheets are excellent tools for collecting and analyzing data and thus work well in curriculum units that call for students to address both interdisciplinary content and process/information analysis tasks. Students can design spreadsheet layouts, collect the data to fill in the various rows and columns, and then write equations to analyze the data they have collected. In this way, a spreadsheet becomes a vehicle for learning about and representing both simple and complex relationships between numbers and pieces of information.

While the use of spreadsheets is common in mathematics and science curricula, they can be used whenever data collection and analysis are required. Many teachers use spreadsheets in social studies curricula where students might collect numerical information and organize it chronologically. Projects on genealogy and immigration make particularly good use of spreadsheets.

Database Management Programs

Examples: Microsoft Access, FileMaker Pro

A database-management program is used to create, organize, and manipulate information in databases. Databases work much like spreadsheets, although they are often used where textual information is more important than numerical data. Databases are primarily used for creating records of collected information. Most database-management programs allow for some degree of numerical analysis of the collected information (e.g., counting, grouping, sorting by rank order, etc.).

Databases are often used in interdisciplinary curriculum units. They become a vehicle for information collection and organization. The manipulation of information within a database calls for mathematics and critical-thinking skills. These skills are further enhanced when a student designs a database using a databasemanagement program.

Word Processing Programs

Examples: Microsoft Word, AppleWorks

Most teachers are familiar with word processing programs as tools for producing lesson plans, student/parent communications, and personal correspondence. Students make use of word processors in similar ways. Certainly, research papers, projects, and other written communications can be accomplished with the use of a word processor. Aside from simply making student work appear neater, word processors have pedagogical importance in that they have been found to encourage students to write more, with greater ease in editing and revising their work.

Thus, word processors are powerful tools in developing writing, critical-thinking, and research skills. Furthermore, the word processor as a technologybased tool encourages and motivates certain students who have difficulty with the manual task of handwriting. Finally, many students take greater pride in work that has been produced with a word processor, and this motivates them to continue writing and performing the other learning tasks associated with their writing.

Word processors are not just used within language arts curricula. Students often use these tools to produce work related to any subject area, and this work often becomes the source document for importing data into databases, spreadsheets, and presentation programs.

In this way, the word processor is often the cornerstone application within integrated application suites such as Microsoft Office, Microsoft Works, or AppleWorks.

Presentation Tools

Examples: Microsoft PowerPoint, Hyperstudio

Presentation tools allow students and teachers to take text, numerical data, graphs, sounds, and visual images and organize this information into multimedia presentations.

While it is possible to use multiple media (e.g., sounds and images) within a presentation, it is also possible to create a text-only presentation. It is important to remember that although most presentation tools support the creation of very sophisticated products, the degree of sophistication and complexity is very much under the control of the author.

Almost any student project can result in a presentation. Presentations can be made before an entire class or be designed for individual viewing. Multimedia presentation tools can be integrated into any lesson or unit that would otherwise result in a paper-and-paste-project product. While a presentation tool such as PowerPoint is simply software, this software usually requires the use of particular hardware to acquire digital images/sound, including digital cameras or scanners, and to display the resulting multimedia presentations. Quite often, the material that makes its way into presentations is imported from other software applications such as word processors and spreadsheets that create tables and graphs.

Additional Information

We presented software tools teachers can use to support learning in different content areas.

The next question that many teachers would have relates to finding specific curriculum-unit ideas for teaching and learning in the one-computer classroom. In fact, this is where the *real* fun lies.

Available Technology Inventory Worksheet

Do you have technology resources such as those listed here to use in curriculum- based projects? When considering the way in which technology can enrich your curriculum, it is first necessary to inventory your available technology so that you will know what is possible in terms of access for you and your students.

In other words, "available" refers to a particular device or software program that is actually accessible to you. This is differentiated from existing technology to which you have no ready access.

Steps Toward Infusing Technology into an Existing Curriculum Unit/ Activity

Many teachers find it useful to explore the process of technology integration by modifying an existing curriculum unit to make use of technology tools. In this way, the teacher is not so much creating new curriculum activities as using technology to improve the delivery of the current curriculum.

- Examine the unit/activity. Think about how technology can be added to this unit to support and improve student learning.
- Combine technology with traditional resources: Use electronic resources along with traditional print-based materials.
- *Example:* Use CD-ROM encyclopedias, atlases, or web sites for research.
- Substitute or add a technology element to an existing project.
- *Example:* Instead of creating graphs using pen and pencil, use a graphing program to display information.
- Adjust or expand a project to reach higher student expectations.
- *Example:* Have students use multimedia presentations to get across ideas and increase enthusiasm.
- Use the appropriate tool at the appropriate time.
- *Example:* Use e-mail when introducing the concept of friendly letters. Introduce presentation software when needed for public speaking.
- Critically evaluate the quality and quantity of your instructional materials. Recognize essential activities that support critical learning objectives and eliminate the nonessential.

- *Example:* Eliminate an assignment on a topic already presented.
- Recognize that technology use takes time. Rearrange and prioritize unit activities and assign a time frame that reflect changes in the time it takes to perform certain activities.
- *Example:* Shorten, eliminate, or rearrange tasks.
- Rewrite the lesson unit. If necessary, revise your goals to reflect changes due to technology infusion.
- A lesson planning template, such as the one that follows, helps you focus on what changes are brought to your activity through the infusion of technology.
- *Example:* What technology tools and resources will you use in the unit?
- In what ways does technology add value to the curriculum activity? Think about why the use of technology improves student learning in this redesigned unit.
- *Example:* Use of a technology tool (e.g., a spreadsheet program) allows students to manipulate data and produce graphs more easily.
- Prepare your unit/activity materials. Develop instructional materials, handouts, and assessments. Create a schedule that allows students maximum use of technology.
- You will need instructional materials that take into account the new tools used by students.
- *Example:* Create step-by-step instructions for using technology with which students may not already be familiar.
- Create new assessment materials, such as rubrics, that assess both content learning *and* technology skills.
- *Example:* When students create an electronic presentation (e.g., Hyperstudio stack) for a research project, the assessment should be on the quality of their research and the quality of their presentation.

Classroom Observation Worksheet

As a technology planner you will want to know what kind of technology teachers are using and how they are using it in their classrooms. If teachers in your school or district do not yet use technology, we recommend that you locate a school that does and plan a visit to that school.

Take time to observe teachers and students interacting with the technology during an actual classroom session. Follow up that observation with an interview with the teacher you observed.

Also, interview other educational professionals in various schools to gather their thoughts and recommendations regarding technology use in the classroom.

Technology Integration Progress Gauge

SEIR¨TEC developed another useful tool for planners to determine a school's or district's current status in five areas or domains impacting technology integration. The five domains are:

- Student Engagement,
- Teacher Engagement,
- Availability and Accessibility of Appropriate Resources,
- Organizational Support, and
- Community Involvement.

11

Textiles, Clothing and Laundry

TEXTILE MAINTENANCE

The maintenance of a textile product after purchase is of prime interest to the consumer and to commercial fabric care operations. The major factor to be considered is cleaning and soil removal of the textile during continued use. In order to have a fuller understanding of the cleaning process, one must examine the nature of textile soils, detergency, and soil removal, and the wet or dry cleaning processes used.

TEXTILE SOILS

Soils come from a number of sources in the environment that textile structures are subjected to during wear and use. These soils include:

- solid particulate matter (clays, minerals, soot),
- oil-borne soils (fats, greases, etc.), and
- water-borne soils (water-soluble salts, etc.).

Solid particulate matter such as clays, metal oxides, and soot is often mixed with water- and oil-borne soils but can also soil a textile alone through application in the dry state. When applied from the dry state, these solid soils can often be removed by mechanical action such as brushing and shaking. Clays in general are complex inorganic silicates with color derived from the structure of the silicate. Oil-borne soils are organic hydrocarbons or related derivatives which are soluble in oils.

The aliphatic and aromatic hydrocarbons and fatty acid esters of glycerol are the most predominant oil-borne soils. Less polar hydrocarbons such as mineral oil are more easily removed from textile substrates than are the more polar glycerol esters of fatty acids. Carbon-based matter such as soot is not completely soluble in most hydrocarbon solvents or oils but must be considered an oil-borne soil. These soils can be removed by solvent (dry) cleaning or through emulsification and removal in laundering systems. Water-borne soils are usually water-soluble inorganic and organic salts or natural proteins and starches and can be readily removed by water-based laundering systems. Soils from foods can be oil- and/or water-borne soils, depending on the composition of the particular food.

DETERGENCY AND SURFACTANTS

Detergency and Soil Removal

Detergency is a term used to specify the ability of an agent to lift and remove soil from a substrate and to suspend the soil within the cleaning media. Agents which aid directly in soil removal are called detergents or surface active agents (surfactants). Since the term detergent ha s come to mean complex laundry formulates containing several components, the soil lifting components of such formulations will be referred to as surfactants here to avoid confusion. Surfactants are compounds containing a heophi1ic (oil-searching) hydrocarbon tai 1 and a hydrophilic (water-seeking) polar head that can effectively aid in wetting of a soiled textile surface, in penetration and removal of the soil from the surface, and in suspension of the soil in the liquid medium. Surfactants are materials which effectively make the transition between the relatively nonpolar hydrocarbon soil and the polar cleaning medium such as water. The hydrocarbon tail of the surfactant associates with the surface of the oily soil, whereas the polar head of the surfactant associates with the aqueous medium, thus making a transition from the oily soil to the aqueous media. When oily soil is lifted from a fiber by the surfactant the oi1y soil-detergent combination is suspended as small particles in the medium through micelle formation. The low-energy micelle formed must be sufficiently stable to permit its removal in the laundering process. Mineral soils, being partially hydrophilic in nature, undergo a more complex process in soil removal. The soil mixes with the surfactant to form a 1iquid crystal. Additional surfactant forms a complex micelle which includes myelinic tubes to provide sufficient surface area to remove and stabilize the solubilized soil.

Surfactants

Surfactants are divided into five major classes: soaps, anionic, nonionic, cationic, and amphitricha surfactants. Each contains a hydrocarbon tail and a polar head.

Soap

Soap has been known since antiquity as a surfactant for removal of soil from textiles. Soap is readily made by basic hydrolysis (saponification) of animal fats (fatty esters of glycerol). Soap is the resultant sodium salt of the fatty acids, with the composition depending on the source of fatty acid esters. Soap suffers from one major deficiency as a surfactant: in hard water containing calcium and magnesium cations, the sodium ion in soap is replaced by these multivalent ions to form insoluble salts which cannot act effectively as surfactants.

Anionic Surfactants

Anionic surfactants by definition contain an anion (negative ion) as the hydrophilic head of the detergent and are usually sodium, potassium, or ammonium salts of organic sulfonates or sulfates such as alkylbenzene sulfonates or alkyl sulfates. Anionic surfactants are effective in removal and suspension of oily soil and remain soluble in the presence of calcium and magnesium ions.

For this reason, they are preferred over soap and are the most used surfactant in laundry formulations. The alkylbenzene sulfonates and particularly sodium dodecylbenzene sulfonate are used in such formulations. In the 1950s, foaming problems in water supplies were attributed to these surfactants due to their low degree of biodegradability. Studies at that time showed that branching of the alkyl group substituted on the benzene ring was responsible for this problem.

Reaction conditions for formulation of these surfactants were changed so that the more biodegradable linear alkyl derivative was produced, thereby correcting the problem. Since anionic surfactants tend to foam readily, they are seldom used textile processing.

Nonionic Surfactants

The nonionic surfactants contain a polar head which provides sufficient hydrophilicity to give detergent activity. Polymers of ethylene oxide (called polyethylene glycols or polyethoxyethanols) commonly are used as the polar head attached as the the alkylbenzene or alkyl moiety to form the nonionic surfactant.

The hydrophilicity of the ethoxy repeating unit comes from the hydrogen bonding capability of the ether oxygen with water . The nonionic surfactants are used in conjunction with anionic surfactants in some laundry formulations and as wetting agents in many textile dyeing and finishing wet processes.

Cationic Surfactants

Cationic surfactants possess a positive cation and are usually quaternary amine salts. Owing to their high cost, they are less important than anionic and nonionic surfactants in detergent formulations. They are mainly used as fiber wetting agents and as bacteriostats and fabric softeners in selected applications.

Amphoteric Surfactants

Surfactants that have both positively and negatively charged hydrophilic groups within the molecule are referred to as amphoteric surfactants. The detergency of these surfactants varies with pH, and they show bacteriostatic activity at appropriate pH. Amphoteric surfactants are effective leveling agents and aid in controlled diffusion of dyes and finishes onto the fiber.

LAUNDERING AND LAUNDRY FORMULATIONS

Laundering

Laundering is essentially a wet cleaning process s in water solvent in the presence of a detergent formulation. The physical parameters, agitation and temperature affect the ea se and effectiveness of soil removal. Agitation permits the aqueous surfactant solution to flow through the textile structure, conveying the surfactant to the soil, and aids in removal of emulsified soil from the fabric. As the laundering temperature increases, the surface activity of the surfactant solution increases, which in turn increases the ease and rate of soil removal. Although higher temperatures markedly improve soil removal, the maximum temperature that can be used may be tempered by a number of factors, including the stability of the textile and its washfastness. The nature of the impurities in the water has a major effect on soil removal from a textile. If the water is hard and contains significant amounts of calcium and magnesium salts as carbonates, sulfates, or chlorides, these salt ions will interfere with the soil lifting action of the surfactant unless appropriate water softening agents are added. Dissolved iron salts or the presence of clays, silts, and other colorants can interfere with cleaning, also .

Laundry Formulation

Laundry powder formulations or synthetic detergents (often called syndets) are complex mixtures of surfactant and other materials including many of the following (average range of composition in syndets in parentheses):

- surfactant (10-30%),
- builders and chelating agents (5%-40%),
- anti-soi1redeposition agents (0.5%-2%),
- corrosion inhibitors (5%-10%),
- foam stabilizers and antifoaming agents (0%-5%),
- electrolytes and fillers (5%-40%),
- oxygen bleaches (0%-25%),
- fluorescent brighteners and colorants (0.1%-1%),
- bacteriostats (0%-2%),
- perfumes (0%-1%), and
- moisture (0-10%).

The composition of the detergent formulation will change with the manufacturer and intended use. The liquid detergents are aqueous solutions of similar composition to detergent powders with the fo1lowing exceptions:

- the anionic surfactants present will tend to be the more soluble miscible potassium, ammonium, or alcohol amine salts;
- the nature of added foam stabilizers will differ, and
- the amount of builder present will be lower.

A series of specialized product formulations, including enzymes, bleaches and brighteners, water softeners, etc., also are on the market as auxiliary cleaning agents.

Builders

Builders are salts added to a detergent composition to improve the effectiveness of the surfactant present through complexation or precipitation of calcium and magnesium and other multivalent salts. The builders act through complexation (chelation) with these cations to form a stable complex or through reaction with the cations to form an insoluble salt that precipitates from the wash bath. Complexing builders include the sodium polyphosphates (trisodium tripolyphosphate and tetrasodium pyrophosphate), amine carboxylates, citrates, carboxylate polymers, and zeolite ion exchange resins. These builders all complex with calcium and magnesium ions to form water-soluble complexes (chelates) or suspensions that do not interfere with the action of the surfactant. The polyphosphate builders are the most effective builders but have come under increasing pressure over the last decade due to their role as biological nutrients and contributors to algae growth.

The percentage of polyphosphates used in detergent formulations has declined in recent years, but substitutes that are as effective have been difficult to find at a comparable cost. Nitrilotriacetic acid was introduced in the late 1960s as a builder, but adverse factors, including its possible activity as a carcinogen, caused it to be withdrawn from the market. Precipitating builders include sodium bicarbonate and sodium carbonate, sodium sesquicarbonate (a mixture of the two), and the borate salts.

These builders provide basicity and react with calcium and magnesium ions to form the insoluble carbonates or borates. These builders are not as effective as chelating builders. After repeated washes they leave deposits of carbonates mixed with soil on the textile being cleaned. They also may decrease the water absorbency of the textile with time.

Anti-Soil-Redeposition Agents

Soil removal is a dynamic process in which suspended soil may be redeposited on the textile as well as removed during the laundering process. Addition of agents with appropriate soilrepelling functional groups inhibits such redeposition. Carboxymethyl cellulose is an inexpensive negatively charged water-miscible polymer that forms a thin deposit or coating on the textile and repels the charged soildetergent micelle. Other polar or charged water-miscible polymers such as polyvinylpyroll idone are particularly useful on synthetics as effective anti-soil-redeposition agents and can be incorporated with carboxymethylcellulose to improve the overall effectiveness of anti-soil-redeposition particularly on synthetic-natural fiber blends.

Corrosion Inhibitors

The basicity and reactivity of ingredients found in laundry formulations lead to attack and corrosion of various metal parts in laundry equipment . To minimize this effect, the sodium silicates are added to the detergent formulation.

Foam Modifiers

Excess foaming during laundering can occur readily due to agitation and can lower the overall effectiveness of soil removal. On the other hand, the consumer views moderate and stable foam formation during laundering as an indication of detergency and soil removal. Two approaches have been used to provide products which meet both of these concerns. Antifoaming agents such as long-chain aliphatic alcohols, emulsified terpenes (naturally occurring alcohols), and organosilicones are used in conjunction with foaming surfactants to lower and moderate foam formation. The second approach has been the use of detergentlike derivatives that modify and stabilize foaming in conjunction with surfactant. These foam modifiers include monoalkylolamine adducts of fatty acids and their polyethylene oxide derivatives.

Electrolytes and Fillers

Inorganic salts such as sodium sulfate are added to laundry formations to bring them up to uniform cleaning strength and to provide appropriate measurable quantities for addition in laundering by the consumer. These materials may be considered fillers but also are electrolytes in solution that serve to enhance to some degree the migration and action of the surfactant as well as improve the physical characteristics of the product.

Bleaches and Fluorescent Brighteners

Oxygen bleaches such as sodium perborate are often added to enhance the whitening power of the formulation through destruction of color centers remaining on the fabric. Fluorescent brighteners are added to nearly all synthetic fibers in manufacture to cover yellow coloration through blue fluorescence of these colorless dyes in the light. Fluorescent brighteners added to laundry formulations are mixtures of brighteners which have affinity for all fiber types commonly found in a wash load. Bleaches and brighteners also can be purchased and used separately to enhance whitening of the textile substrate.

Germicides

Biologically active germicides are added to some syndets and are particularly important in low-temperature laundering, where biological agents are not destroyed by heat. The germicides include cationic surfactants and phenol derivatives as well as natural products such as contained in pine oil. Chlorine bleaches al so act as germicides in laundering.

Perfume

Perfumes are added to laundry formulations to mask odors of other ingredients and to convey a pleasant odor which may be suggestive of a natural fragrance or of a clean wash. The perfume has essentially nothing to do with effective soil removal but adds to product aesthetics and aids in consumer acceptance of the product.

Fabric Softener

Fabric softeners are product compositions containing a cationic or nonionic surfactant or alkoxyalkylamide, and they may be applied during the laundering rinse cycle or transferred to the textile during drying from an inert cellulosic or polyurethane substrate.

Liquid softener compositions usually contain:

- alcohol (0%-2%) (to increase solubility of the softeners),
- softeners (2-8%),
- surfactant (0-2%),
- electrolytes (0%-0.25%),
- fluorescent brighteners (0%-0.32%),
- germicides (0%-2%),
- colorants (0%-0.2%), and
- perfumes (0%-2%).

The rest is water. Fabric softener components used in dryers are less complex, containing softener with a carrier and perfume in an inert substrate.

Starches

Starches used to give a textile stiffness and body are usually added during the rinse or applied as a spray after washing. Starches include naturally derived starch, starch derivatives, and acrylic polymer emulsions.

Enzymes

In the late 1960s enzyme presoaks and laundry products containing enzymes were introduced. The proteolytic enzymes contained within the products must have a presoak period to be effective. They act as catalysts is speeding the hydrolytic attack of protein and carbohydrate components in soils, breaking them down into more easily removed de composition products. Since oily soils are not readily attacked by the enzymes, their use and effectiveness is limited.

DRYCLEANING

Drycleaning is not carried out under dry conditions at all but rather uses a solvent other than water in the cleaning method. The cleaning is carried out in petroleum hydrocarbon (Stoddard solvent), in a chlorinated solvent (tetrachloroethylene and trichloroethylene), or in a fluorohalocarbon (Freon). Although the solvents will effectively remove saturated or oily soils, the solvent is charged with water plus surfactant to aid in soil emulsification of the more hydrophilic soils. Tetrachloroethylene is the predominant solvent used in drycleaning in the United States. The drycleaning process involves prespotting by an appropriate method to clean any badly soiled areas on the textile. The textile is immersed in the cleaning fluid, and the fluid is circulated through the textile and then filtered through activated charcoal and diatomaceous earth to remove impurities. After a certain period of continued use, the drycleaning solvent is redistilled to remove residual oils and so forth and then recharged with water and detergent. Drycleaning solvents cause less fiber swelling and deformation and have less tendency to remove dye from the textile. Less agitation is involved than in laundering, and drycleaning is therefore preferred for textiles in which water-induced dimensional change will occur. Care must be taken in drycleaning some textiles, since damage may occur due to attack of the fiber, of finishes on the fiber, or of one or more components in the fiber structure.

LAUNDRY

Whether you wash your clothes at home or send them to a laundry, you expect them to come out clean and crisp, looking and feeling as they did when they were new. The dirt, oils, perspiration, and stains should all have vanished, leaving the fabrics and their colors completely intact. Moreover, the clothes should retain their shapes, sizes, structures, and surface textures. With so many expectations, it's no wonder that the word "miracle" appears so frequently in advertisements for laundry detergents.

Achieving these many goals is something of a balancing act. The chemicals that contaminate clothes aren't always so different from those that give them their structures and colors. Trying to remove one chemical while leaving the other isn't easy and washday in the nineteenth century was hardly a treat for the garments being cleaned. However, in recent years laundering has developed from a simple art to an advanced technology. The miracles promised by the detergent commercials are almost reality. In this section, we'll examine physical and chemical mechanisms that make those miracles possible.

Questions to Think About: How do soaps and detergents help to clean clothes? What is the difference between a soap and a detergent? What is hard water and how do you "soften" it? Why does soap form soap scum in hard water? How do detergents keep soil from redepositing on the clothes? Is dry cleaning really "dry"? Why do some clothes wrinkle and shrink when you wash them in water but not when you dry clean them? How does bleach remove stains? Why do fabric softeners increase the volume and fluffiness of towels? Why do fabric softeners reduce static cling? How do "brighteners" make clothes appear whiter than white? Experiments to Do: You don't have to do laundry to know that soaps and detergents help to remove oil and grease from just about anything. Spread a little oil on a rag or your hand and try to wash it off with water. You'll find that the oil is difficult to remove with water because it doesn't dissolve in water—oil and water don't mix.

But if you add a little soap or detergent to the water and try washing again, you'll find that the oil is carried away in the water. The soap or detergent molecules surround tiny droplets of oil and allow the water to remove them. Soaps and detergents are remarkable materials. They are "at home" in both water and oil and they assist water in handling oil. That simple fact is the basis for laundering and the central issue in this section.

SOAP

One of the most difficult problems in laundering clothes is how to remove all of the different soils in a single operation. Some soils consist of polar molecules, those that have electric charges or electrically charged regions, while others consist of nonpolar molecules, those that are effectively neutral throughout. These two types of soils are so different from one another that a liquid that dissolves one is unlikely to dissolve the other. To make things worse, there are also soils that don't dissolve well in anything, or at least not in anything that you could imagine putting on your clothes. Getting all of these soils out of the clothes without harming the clothes is what laundry is all about.

Polar soil molecules include salts from perspiration and ground dirt. These salts generally dissolve in water, where they become ions that are carried away in shells of water molecules. Because they are basically at home in water, these polar soils are described as hydrophilic (water loving). Because carbohydrates such as sugar have electrically charged regions and form hydrogen bonds with water, they dissolve easily in water and are thus also hydrophilic.

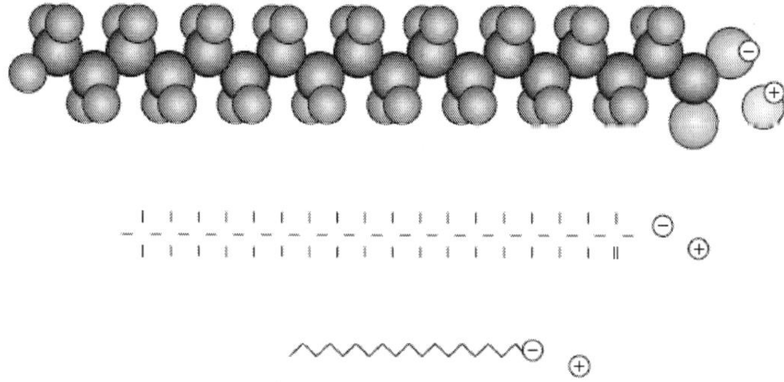

Fig. Soap is a peculiar salt. Its negative ion consists of a long hydrophobic (water avoiding) hydrocarbon chain attached to a hydrophilic (water loving) carboxylate group. A nearby positive ion, usually sodium (Na), balances the negative charge of the carboxylate group. A soap molecule can be represented as (*a*) balls, (*b*) letters, or (*c*) a zigzag hydrocarbon chain with charges attached to it.

Nonpolar soil molecules include oils, fats, and waxes from skin, foods, and plants. These oily molecules tend to dissolve in nonpolar solvents such as gasoline or kerosene. Because they can't form hydrogen bond with water molecules, they don't bind well with water and are essentially insoluble in it. These nonpolar soils are described as hydrophobic (water avoiding).

You could launder your clothes by first washing them in water to dissolve and remove hydrophilic soils and then laundering them in gasoline to dissolve and remove hydrophobic soils. But this would take a long time and would be very hard on the fabric. After the process was over, your clothes would have aged considerably, yet some of the soils would still remain. Cleaning clothes requires something more than water and gasoline. That's why we use soaps, detergents, bleaches, and brighteners in our laundry.

Soap is a peculiar type of salt. Like all salts, soap contains a mixture of positively and negatively charged ions. There is nothing special about the positive ions, which are usually just sodium or potassium atoms that are missing an electron. What makes soap so unusual and so effective at cleaning is its negative ions. The negative ions in soap have the negative charge located at one end of a very long molecule. The other end of the molecule is an uncharged hydrocarbon chain such as those encountered in oil molecules. The negative soap ion is so long that its two ends operate independently. Its charged end is polar and hydrophilic. Water molecules cling to this end's electric charge and try to carry it into solution. But the soap ion's hydrocarbon end is nonpolar and hydrophobic. This end of the soap molecule is expelled from water but binds nicely to oil molecules. The one half of a soap ion is at home in water and the other half is at home in oil. The hydrophilic end is attracted to water while the hydrophobic oil end is attracted to oil. This split affinity causes soap ions to accumulate at interfaces between water and oil. The negative ions spontaneously orient themselves at such an interface with their electrically charged ends in the water and their hydrocarbon ends in the oil. The positive ions hover around in the water near the interface to keep everything electrically neutral.

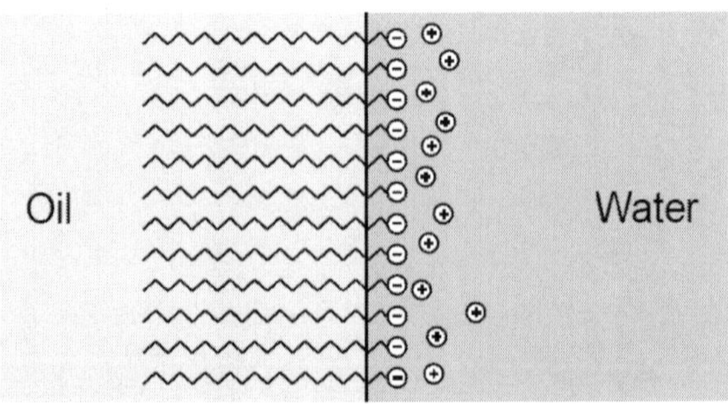

Fig. Soap negative ions move spontaneously to interfaces between water and oil. Their hydrophobic ends project into the oil and their hydrophilic ends project into the water.

This tendency for soap ions to order themselves at interfaces is an example of *self-organizing behavior*. While mixtures of table salt and water are random and homogeneous, mixtures of soap and water are not. Even when there's no oil present, soap ions migrate to water's surface because individual soap ions don't mix freely with the water. Since water molecules don't bond well to the nonpolar hydrocarbon chains, the water molecules push the soap ions to the water's surface.

A tiny amount of soap added to a bowl of water soon creates an ultra-thin layer of soap ions on the surface of the water—a layer that's only a single molecule thick. The soap ions arrange themselves with their polar ends in the water and their nonpolar ends in the air. The uppermost water molecules in the bowl are then able to hydrogen bond to the soap ions above them and don't pull together as strongly as they would if they had only air above them. Thus the water molecules contribute little to the liquid's surface tension.

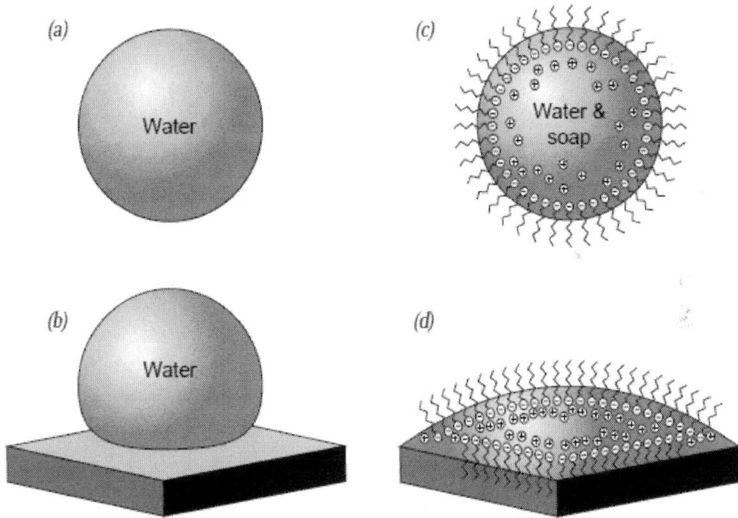

Fig. (*a*) Surface tension in pure water causes its droplets to be spherical. (*b*) These water droplets remain almost spherical on many surfaces. (*c*) Soap ions coat the outside of a water droplet and dramatically reduce the surface tension. (*d*) The soapy droplet is able to spread out more easily and wets many surfaces completely.

The hydrocarbon chains of the soap ions now form the uppermost layer in the liquid. With nothing above them to stick to, these chains pull together and create surface tension. However they attract one another with van der Waals forces, not hydrogen bonds, and create a surface tension only about 30% that of water molecules. The soap's presence in the water significantly reduces its surface tension. This reduced surface tension is soap's first contribution to the laundering process. Pure water keeps to itself, beading up on any surface that doesn't bind strongly to water molecules. Surface tension makes falling water droplets spherical and they remain almost spherical on oily, hydrophobic surfaces. But adding just a tiny bit of soap to the water reduces each droplet's surface tension and allows it to wet the surface. A soapy droplet spreads outward because van der Waals forces attracting the droplet to the surface are strong enough to stretch it out into a flat puddle.

In effect, soapy water is "wetter" than pure water. Soapy water doesn't bead up on fabrics; it soaks right in. When you are cleaning clothes and want the water to wet every fiber in the fabric, you add soap to the water. Because soap helps water to wet surfaces, it's a wetting agent. It's also a surfactant or *surfaceactive agent* because of its tendency to modify the properties of surfaces or interfaces. There are other kinds of surfactants, but soaps and soap-like materials are the most important group.

However, not all soap molecules make it to the water's surface. If you put lots of soap in the water, or the surface is far away, the soap ions assemble themselves into spherical structures called micelles and remain inside the water. In these micelles, all of the soap ions are oriented with their charged, polar ends pointing outward and their uncharged, nonpolar ends pointing inward. The water molecules stick to the micelles' polar outsides and carry the micelles about. As usual, the positive soap ions hover about nearby to keep everything electrically neutral.

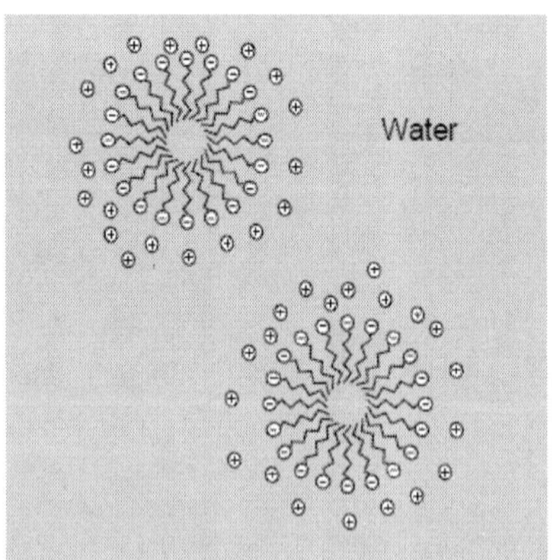

Fig. 17.2.4 - In water, negative soap ions form spherical micelles. The hydrophobic chains form the centers of these micelles and tend to accumulate oily soil molecules.

These micelles are soap's second contribution to the laundering process. They tend to trap and collect oily soil molecules. The inside of a micelle is a nonpolar environment and ideal for oil molecules. When an oil molecule bumps into a micelle, the water pushes it into the center of the micelle and there it remains.The micelles in soapy water move randomly, collecting any oil molecules they encounter in their travels. With a little thermal or mechanical agitation, micelles can even pluck oil molecules from the surfaces of fabrics. Naturally, this is helpful when you are doing laundry. Little by little, the oily soils in the clothes become trapped in micelles in the water.

Soap also helps to remove insoluble debris from clothes. Micelles form around dust particles and help the water to carry these particles away. Since most dust particles don't dissolve in any liquids, soap micelles are essential to their removal from clothing.

Since soap micelles are composed of negatively charged soap ions, they are negatively charged objects and tend to repel one another in the water. They remain separate and mobile and are easily washed down the drain along with their contents. In fact, most fabrics also become negatively charged in water. Their fibers include weakly attached hydrogen atoms that are carried away as positive ions by the water. The fibers are left with negative charges and they tend to repel the negatively charged soap micelles. This repulsion prevents soils from redepositing on the clothes.

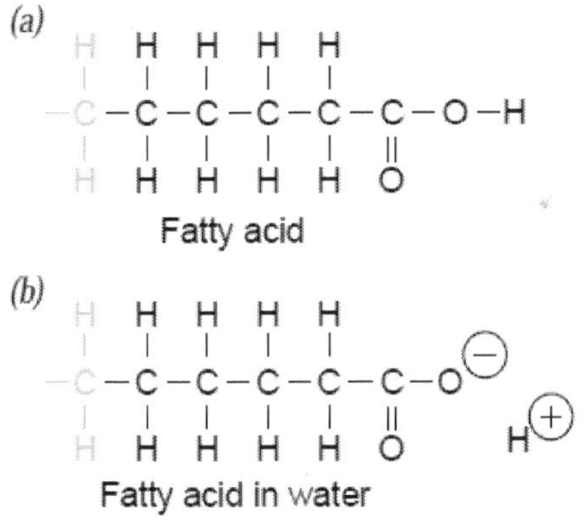

(a) Fatty acid

(b) Fatty acid in water

Fig. 17.2.5 - (*a*) A fatty acid is a long hydrocarbon chain ending in a car boxylate group. (*b*) In water, the carboxylate group's hydrogen atom is carried away by water molecules as a positive ion, leaving the rest of the molecule negatively charged.

This arrangement, soap micelles in water, is a stable emulsion. Unlike a simple mixture of oil and water, it doesn't separate when you let it sit. A surfactant that helps to form and stabilize emulsions is called an emulsifier. Emulsifiers are particularly important in food preparation, where egg yolks, lecithin, and various gums are used to make mayonnaise, chocolate, and other foods smooth and creamy. Soap is clearly useful in laundering clothes, but where does it come from and what is its structure? Soap is made from naturally occurring oils and fats. Each molecule of oil or fat consists of three fatty acid molecules bound to a glycerin molecule. A fatty acid molecule resembles a paraffin or olefin molecule, with its long chain of carbon atoms surrounded by hydrogen atoms. But the fatty acid molecule has a special arrangement of carbon, oxygen, and hydrogen atoms, a *carboxylate group*, at one end that makes it an organic acid.

An acid is a molecule that can easily lose a positively charged hydrogen ion when it is mixed with water. One of the hydrogen atoms at the special end of the fatty acid falls off easily because the adjacent oxygen atom has largely removed its electron. Oxygen and hydrogen form a covalent bond, with a pair of electrons between them, but the oxygen atom attracts the pair of electrons more strongly than the hydrogen atom does. As a result, the hydrogen atom's nucleus is relatively exposed and is easily carried away by passing water molecules. This loss leaves a negatively charged fatty acid ion.

In an oil or fat, these three fatty acid molecules are not ionized. Instead, they have reacted with a glycerin molecule like three large ships docking at a small port. The glycerin molecule has a chain of three carbon atoms and each of these carbon atoms plays host to one of the fatty acids. The resulting structure is called a triglyceride. Assembled in this manner, the triglyceride is nonpolar and virtually insoluble in water. It looks and feels like petroleum oil because both have the same long hydrocarbon chains. However triglycerides are digestible while petroleum oils are not.

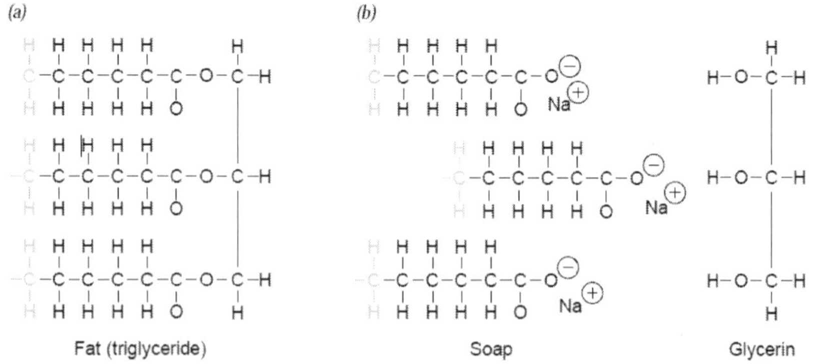

(a) (b)

Fat (triglyceride) Soap Glycerin

Fig (*a*) A fat molecule or triglyceride consists of three fatty acids bonded to a glycerin molecule. When the triglyceride reacts with sodium hydroxide (lye), the fatty acids break free of the glycerin and produce a mixture of soap and glycerin (*b*).

Triglycerides composed entirely of paraffin-like fatty acids are called saturated fats because they have only single covalent bonds and as many hydrogen atoms as possible. Such molecules experiences strong van der Waals forces, forming fats that remain solid at relatively high temperatures. These fats are found in animals and tropical plants such as palms and coconuts.

Triglycerides containing olefin-like fatty acids are called unsaturated fats because they have double bonds that reduce their hydrogen atoms count. Double bonds stiffen the hydrocarbon chains and prevent them from bonding as strongly to one another. Oils contain these molecules melt at relatively low temperatures and are found in fish and temperate plants such as soybeans and corn. Unfortunately, people find the less healthy saturated fats more tasty and satisfying than the unsaturated fats. Converting unsaturated fats to saturated fats, a process called hydrogenation, is commonly used to stiffen oils for use in foods such as margarine and candy

Soap enters into this picture when triglycerides react with sodium hydroxide (lye). Sodium hydroxide is a salt consisting of positive sodium ions and negative hydroxyl ions (a hydrogen and an oxygen atom together) and it rapidly dissolves into independent ions when you put it in water. When you mix fat, water, and lye together, the hydroxyl ions from the lye attack the fat molecules and remove the fatty acids from the glycerin as negative ions. Soon the water is filled with glycerin molecules, negative fatty acid ions, and positive sodium ions. When the reaction is complete and most of the water is removed, the result is soap. The glycerin may or may not be removed. The hardness of the soap depends on the fats from which it was made. Saturated fats produce hard bar soaps while unsaturated fats produce soft liquid soaps. Soft hand soaps often include the glycerin. While most modern soaps are made with lye and are thus sodium salts, earlier soaps where made with potassium hydroxide obtained from wood ash and lime and were potassium salts.

WATER SOFTENING

Unfortunately, laundering clothes isn't quite this easy. While soap is wonderful at removing oils and fats from fabric, it has problems in hard water. Hard water is any water with more than about 120 milligrams of positively charged calcium and magnesium ions per liter. These two metal ions, and a few others, bind with the negative soap ions and form insoluble soap scums that deposit themselves on sinks, showers, bathtubs, washing machines, and clothing. If you try to launder clothes with soap in hard water, you are in for a messy surprise.

The problem occurs because calcium and magnesium ions behave differently from the ions of sodium and potassium normally found in soap. Sodium and potassium atoms each have one more electron than they need to complete an electronic shell—a quantum physical structure that is particularly stable. That extra electron is relatively easily removed, creating a positively charged ion that is easily drawn into solution in water. Water is so strongly attracted to sodium ions that almost every sodium salt in existence dissolves in water. Sodium's fantastic solubility explains why there is so much sodium in seawater. Potassium ions are almost as soluble as sodium ions. Salts consisting of sodium or potassium positive ions and soap negative ions are extremely soluble in water.

But calcium and magnesium atoms have two more electrons than they need to complete an electronic shell. They give up those two electrons somewhat reluctantly to form positively charged ions and aren't particularly soluble in water. While some calcium and magnesium salts are modestly soluble in water, calcium and magnesium soap salts are not.

When you put soap in hard water, the positive calcium and magnesium ions in the water combine with the negative soap ions and quickly form insoluble salts. These salts are pasty solids that cling to everything. If you want to do laundry in a place where the water contains substantial amounts of dissolved minerals, you must either remove the calcium and magnesium ions from the water or replace the soap with something else. Actually, you often do both.

Removing the calcium and magnesium ions is the first option. This step is called *water softening* and is done routinely in most industrial laundries long before the water enters the washing equipment. There are several different ways to soften water, but the most interesting scheme and the one used most often in houses is called ion exchange. The water passes through an ion exchange material that replaces the calcium and magnesium ions with sodium ions.

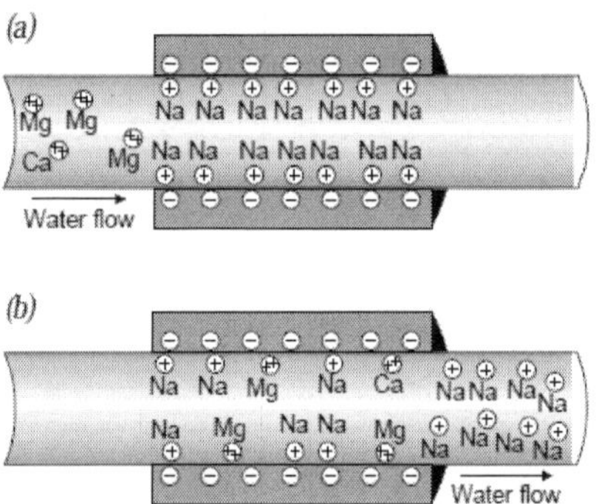

Fig. 17.2.7 - (*a*) A fresh ion exchange water softener contains sodium ions, located near negatively charged sites in a resin or zeolite ceramic. (*b*) As water containing magnesium (Mg) and calcium (Ca) ions passes through the softener, the sodium ions are released and the magnesium and calcium ions remain behind.

The ion exchange material is a special ceramic (zeolite) or plastic resin with many negatively charged regions in its porous structure. To keep the material electrically neutral, a positive ion is located near each negative region. The negative regions are part of the material, so they can't go anywhere, but the positive ions are mobile.

When the ion exchange material is fresh, nearly all of the positive ions inside it are sodium ions. As hard water flows through the material, the sodium ions are gradually replaced by calcium and magnesium ions. Since the sodium ions are more soluble in water than the calcium and magnesium ions, the sodium ions tend to enter the water and the calcium and magnesium ions tend to leave it. Each calcium or magnesium ion that sticks to the ion exchange material releases two sodium ions, which leave the water softener in the water itself. While the water leaving an ion exchange water softener still contains dissolved ions, they are sodium ions rather than calcium or magnesium ions. The sodium ions cause no trouble when laundering clothes or washing your skin, but people who are on low sodium diets should avoid softened water. Moreover, you shouldn't use softened water in a steam iron.

When all of the sodium ions in the ion exchange material have been replaced by calcium or magnesium ions, the water softener stops softening the water. To regenerate the ion exchange material, you must flush it with very concentrated salt water. The many sodium ions in the salt water dislodge most of the calcium and magnesium ions and return the ion exchange material to its original condition—it is once more full of sodium ions and ready to soften water.

Because many homes don't have water softeners, most laundry soaps soften the water themselves. They contain chemicals called builders that bind to the calcium and magnesium ions and keeping them away from the soap ions. The most effective of these builders is sodium tripolyphosphate and, at one time, most household detergents contained large amounts of it. However, phosphates encourage the growth of algae, threatening the ecologies of rivers, lakes, and bays, and have been banned from detergents in many regions. Builders such as sodium carbonate, citric acid, and sodium citrate are now often used instead.

Another building technique used in some products is to incorporate small zeolite ceramic particles directly in the detergent. These builder particles exchange sodium ions for calcium and magnesium ions and soften the water directly in the washer. They fall to the bottom of the washer and are rinsed away.

DETERGENTS

But water softening is only half the solution. Because it's hard to eliminate all of the calcium and magnesium from water, the manufacturers also eliminate the soap from the laundry powder. That's right—most laundry detergents aren't soap at all. Instead, they are synthetic detergents that are structurally related to natural soap but aren't quite the same. Actually, soap is a type of detergent. Detergents are a broad class of molecules that stabilize mixtures of oil and water. There are many other kinds of molecules that can perform this task and thus many types of detergents.

The most common laundry detergents are the linear alkylbenzenesulfonates. These petroleum products are sodium salts, just like most soaps, but the structures of the negative ions are different. Recall that a negative soap ion is a long hydrocarbon chain attached to a negatively charged carboxylate group.

The detergent ion is also a long hydrocarbon chain, attached to an aromatic or benzene ring, attached to a negatively charged sulfonate group. The sulfonate group involves one sulfur atom and three oxygen atoms.

The two important parts of the detergent molecule are the charged head and the long nonpolar tail. The charged end is a *sulfonate group* in which a sulfur atom attaches to four other atoms: a carbon atom and three oxygen atoms. This arrangement is roughly tetrahedral in shape. But sulfur normally attaches to only two atoms, so how is this arrangement possible?

First, the sulfur atom forms normal covalent bonds with the carbon atom and with one of the oxygen atoms. That oxygen atom has an extra electron, making it a negatively charged ion that can only form a single covalent bond.

Second, the sulfur atom allows each of the two other oxygen atoms to share a pair of its electrons. Because these shared electrons can travel between both atoms, their wavelengths increase and their kinetic energies decrease. In this manner, the oxygen atoms become attached to the sulfur atom. The overall result is a negatively charged structure that's easily carried about by water molecules.

The detergent molecule's long nonpolar tail is essentially an unbranched paraffin chain, also referred to as a *linear alkyl group*. This chain provides the oily tail of the detergent molecule. While early alkylbenzenesulfonate detergents included branched paraffin chains, these proved to be less biodegradable than the linear versions. Bacteria can metabolize long linear chains because those chains are common in animals and plants, but branched chains are rare in nature and bacteria are unprepared for them. To keep detergent foam out of streams and lakes, manufacturers have learned to produce purely linear detergent molecules.

The last piece of the detergent molecule is the aromatic or benzene ring. This ring is a vestige of the manufacturing process. It's much easier to attached the linear alkyl tail and the sulfonate head separately to an aromatic ring than it is to attach them directly to one another. Unfortunately, the ring actually reduces the biodegradability of the molecule somewhat. There are other detergents, such as linear alcohol sulfates and linear alcohol ethoxysulfates, in which the aromatic ring is replaced by an oxygen atom or a string of oxygen and carbon atoms. The most common linear alcohol sulfate is sodium lauryl sulfate, with 14 carbon atoms in its hydrophobic chain. Sodium laureth sulfate is a common linear alcohol ethoxysulfate, also with 14 carbon atoms in its chain. These detergents are derived from tropical oils and often used in shampoos and dishwashing liquids.

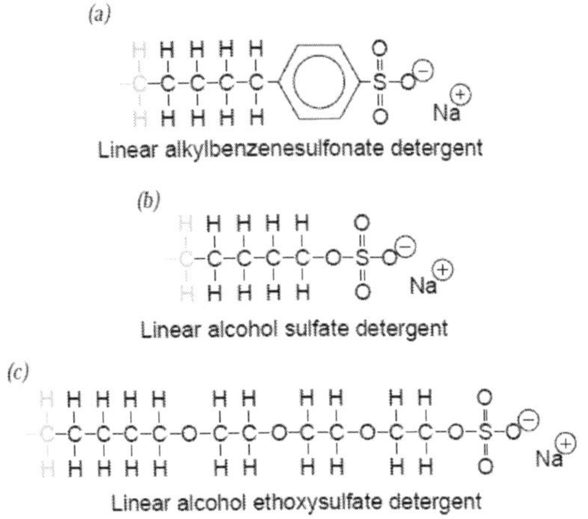

(a) Linear alkylbenzenesulfonate detergent

(b) Linear alcohol sulfate detergent

(c) Linear alcohol ethoxysulfate detergent

Fig. 17.2.8 - (*a*) The most common laundry detergent has an aromatic or benzene ring connecting a long hydrophobic hydrocarbon chain to a hydrophilic sulfonate group. Common shampoo detergents connect the chain to the sulfonate with either (*b*) an oxygen atom or (*c*) a string of oxygen and carbon atoms.

Since calcium and magnesium ions don't cause these sulfonate or sulfate detergents to form insoluble detergent scums, why do laundry detergents still worry about softening the water? Unfortunately, calcium and magnesium ions interfere with the micelles, making it difficult for them to extract soil from fabric and keep it suspended in water.

Because each calcium or magnesium ion has twice the positive charge of a sodium or potassium ion, these highly charged ions approach the micelles closely and partially neutralize their surfaces. Since these neutralized micelles don't repel one another or the fabric well, they do a poor job of cleaning clothes. That's why laundries and laundry detergent still work to remove the calcium and magnesium ions.

Before leaving detergents, it's worth noting that not all detergents are negative ions (anions). It's also possible to construct detergent molecules that are positive ions (cations) and even ones that aren't ions at all. However, cationic detergents and surfactants aren't used in laundry detergents because they tend to stick to fabric—we'll discuss their use as fabric softeners later on. But nonionic detergents are often used to launder clothes.

The only requirement for a detergent is that its molecules stabilize a mixture of oil and water. Nonionic surfactant molecules don't have an electric charge, but they do have a hydrophilic end and a hydrophobic end. Like most detergents, the hydrophobic end is just a long hydrocarbon chain. But the hydrophilic end is also a long chain, consisting of oxygen and carbon molecules attached one after the next and decorated with hydrogen atoms. The oxygen atoms in this special chain form hydrogen bonds with water molecules, giving that end of the molecule its hydrophilic character. These nonionic molecules form micelles and are very effective at removing grease.

Nonionic surfactants are unaffected by hard water and are actually better than anionic detergents at removing some soils—they are particularly good at removing skin oils from synthetic fabrics. However, they aren't salts and exist either as liquids or waxy solids. As a result, nonionic surfactants are difficult to formulate into powdered detergents but are common in liquid detergents.

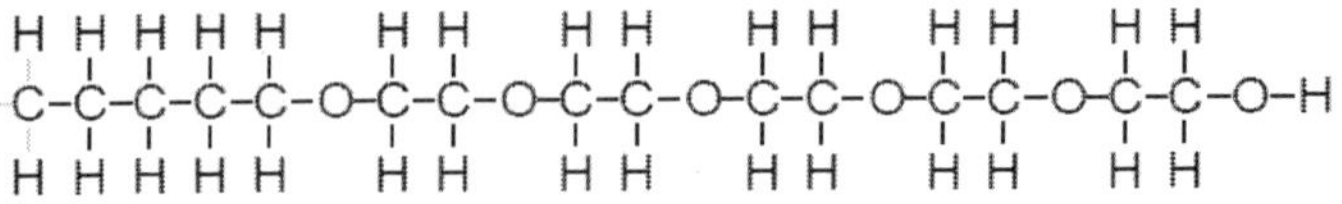

```
H H H H H   H H   H H   H H   H H   H H
| | | | |   | |   | |   | |   | |   | |
C-C-C-C-C-O-C-C-O-C-C-O-C-C-O-C-C-O-C-C-O-H
| | | | |   | |   | |   | |   | |   | |
H H H H H   H H   H H   H H   H H   H H
```

Nonionic surfactant

Fig. Nonionic surfactants have a hydrophobic hydrocarbon chain (on the left) attached to a hydrophilic chain containing oxygen atoms (on the right).

BLEACHES AND ENZYMES

Not all soils can be removed from fabrics with detergent and water. Molecules that form covalent bonds with the fabric create stains that can only be eliminated with bleaches or enzymes. Bleaches act to destroy the coloration of stain molecules or to cut them free from the fabric. Enzymes act to dice up large stain molecules into smaller fragments that can be washed away. With a little luck, these steps can be taken without destroying the fabric or its color.

Unlike soaps and detergents, bleaches react chemically with the soil molecules. They are particularly aggressive at converting double bonds to single bonds by attaching oxygen and chlorine molecules to the two atoms involved. Double bonds often give organic molecules their colors so this sort of rearrangement tends to make them colorless.

Just as atoms absorb and emit photons of light that are characteristic of their electronic states, so molecules absorb and emit photons that are characteristic of their electronic states. Each electron in a molecule is sensitive to passing electromagnetic radiation and responds to photons that can transfer it to some unoccupied state with more energy. If the electron finds such a photon, it may undergo a radiative transition to the excited electronic state and absorb the photon. The electron will eventually return to its original state, converting the extra energy into thermal energy, but the photon will be gone forever. If a particular molecule contains electrons that can absorb photons of visible light in this manner, it will appear colored.

In most single covalent bonds, the two electrons are bound so tightly between the two nuclei that any transition to a new electronic state requires more energy than a photon of visible light can provide. Only ultraviolet light can cause radiative transitions in these electrons. Molecules based entirely on single covalent bonds are normally unaffected by visible light and are thus colorless.

However, the outer electrons in a double covalent bond aren't so tightly bound and can be transferred to other electronic states relatively easily—a photon of visible light may well be able to cause the transfer. A double bond that absorbs blue photons from passing light appears yellow. One that absorbs red photons appears cyan. The usual rules of subtractive color apply.

Just how much energy it takes to cause this transfer depends on the chemical nature and environment of the double bond. Most important are the two atoms joined by the double bond. In addition to double bonds involving a pair of carbon atoms, there are also carbon-oxygen, carbon-nitrogen, nitrogen-oxygen, and nitrogen-nitrogen double bonds. These double bonds are often colored, particularly the latter two. Groups of atoms that give rise to color in molecules are called chromophores.

(a)

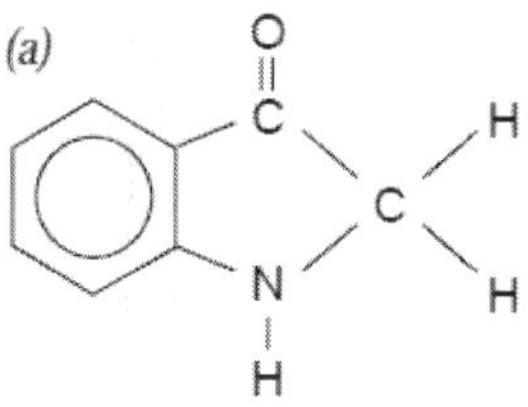

Indoxyl

(b)

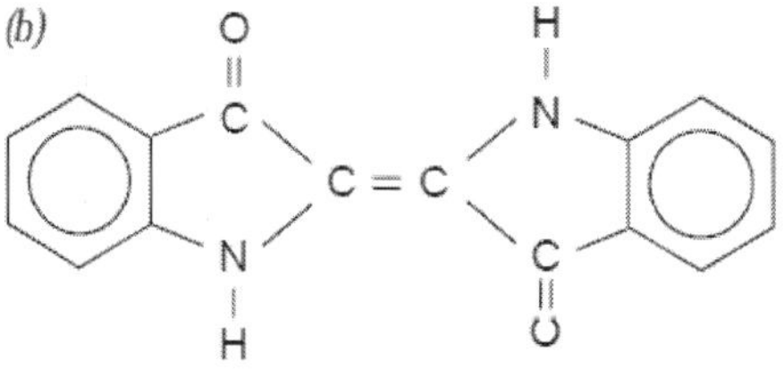

Indigo

Fig.(*a*) Indoxyl is a colorless, water-soluble chemical obtained from a fermented plant extract. When indoxyl is exposed to oxygen in the air, it reacts pairwise to form water-insoluble indigo (*b*), the blue dye used in blue jeans. The double bonded carbon atoms at the center of this molecule are the chromophore and the rest of the molecule determines the precise color of the dye. Bleaches and ultraviolet light can destroy the double bond, giving blue jeans a faded look.

However the exact color of a double bond is determined by the detailed structure of the molecule around it. Since all of the electrons in that molecule affect one another through electrostatic forces and the Pauli exclusion principle, the whole molecular structure contributes to the color of the electrons in the double bond itself. A subtle change in a molecule's structure may change its color from red to orange. That's how organic dye manufacturers construct rich pallets of colors from a small number of different chromophores.

Colored molecules are wonderful if you are an artist, but you don't want extraneous ones attached to your clothes. That's where bleach comes in. Bleach attacks double bonds, destroying the chromophores in the stain molecules. The molecules may remain on the fabric but they no longer absorb visible light.

The two major classes of bleaches are chlorine bleaches and oxygen bleaches. The chlorine bleaches tend to put chlorine and oxygen atoms on the two atoms involved in a double bond. The double bond vanishes as one of its atom binds to a chlorine atom and its other atom binds to the oxygen atom of a hydroxyl group (OH).

Unfortunately, chlorine bleaches are so effective at attacking chemicals that they damage the clothes, too. Sometimes they destroy the chromophores in dye molecules, turning colored fabric white. Other times they modify the dye molecules and change the fabric's color. But chlorine bleaches also damage natural fibers themselves, breaking up their molecules and weakening the fabric. While chlorine bleach may succeed in cutting stain molecules free from your clothing, it may also cut holes in the clothing itself.

Oxygen bleaches used hydrogen peroxide to attack double bonds. A hydrogen peroxide molecule is a water molecule with an extra oxygen atom inserted between the oxygen atom and one of the hydrogen atoms. This molecule decomposes in water and its fragments, either ions or free radicals, attack double bonds. Once again, they destroy chromophores and decolorize stains.

Hydrogen peroxide is less reactive than chlorine bleach and causes less fabric damage. It's also less damaging to commercial dye molecules than chlorine bleach. However, since hydrogen peroxide is often used to bleach hair, oxygen bleaches can obviously destroy the colors in some natural fibers.

Hydrogen peroxide itself is rather unstable and is often generated right in the washer by the decomposition of another molecule, sodium perborate. This decomposition occurs only above about 50 °C, so bleaching must be done in hot water. Some laundry detergents contain activators that help sodium perborate decompose in cooler water but it still works best in hot water.

Enzymes are biological catalysts. Your body uses a great many different enzymes to catalyze various chemical reactions that would otherwise rarely occur at body temperature or that might proceed along the wrong paths without help. Enzymes help to construct molecules, to take them apart, or to rearrange their components.

The enzymes used most often in detergents are those that degrade proteins. Protein molecules cling tightly to fabrics, are insoluble in water, and prevent detergents from penetrating to the fibers. They act as binders for other molecules, creating stains that are hard to remove. Familiar proteinaceous stains include blood, milk, eggs, and gravy. The most effective way to remove these stains is by taking the protein molecules apart. This decomposition is done by *proteolytic enzymes*—enzymes that catalyze reactions between water and protein. In these reactions, protein molecules are broken up and water molecule fragments cap the severed ends. In time, proteolytic enzymes can dice up long protein molecules into their constituent parts: *amino acids* and short sequences of amino acids called *peptides*. The stain falls apart and is carried away by the water and detergents. Meat tenderizers operate in a similar fashion, using papain—a proteolytic enzyme extracted from unripe papaya—to degrade protein in meat before cooking.

However, proteolytic enzymes may have an effect on the people who use them. You certainly don't want the protein in your body decomposed while you do laundry or while you wear freshly laundered clothes. Although studies seem to indicate that the enzymes in household detergents pose no serious health threat, they're used sparingly in detergents to avoid any possible adverse effects.

BRIGHTENERS AND FABRIC SOFTENERS

Not all laundry chemicals disappear down the drain when the wash is done. Brighteners and fabric softeners do their jobs by remaining on the clothes long after they leave the drier. Brighteners affect the appearances of the clothes while fabric softeners affect their feels.

With age, white fabrics such as cotton tend to absorb more and more blue light and begin to look yellow. Cleaning and bleaching do little to reduce this effect. In fact, bleached fabric molecules tend to appear slightly yellow themselves. The old fashioned solution to the yellowing problems was to adding *bluing* to the wash. This blue dye absorbed red and green light, balancing the blue absorption of the fabric itself so that the fabric appeared colorless. To mask the yellowing of age, bluing darkened the whole fabric to a light gray—the amount of light reflected by the fabric was noticeably less than that striking it.

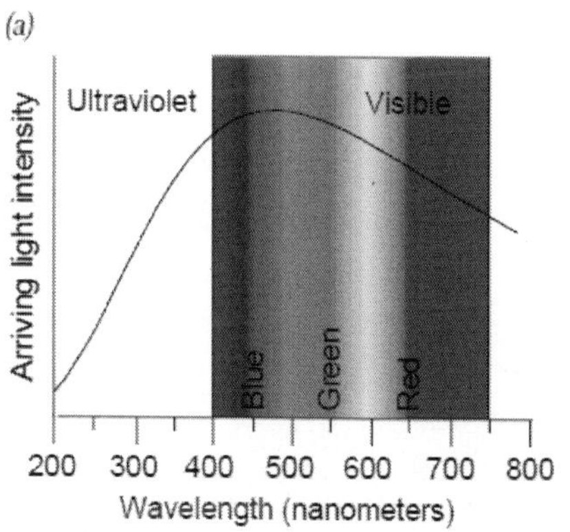

(b)

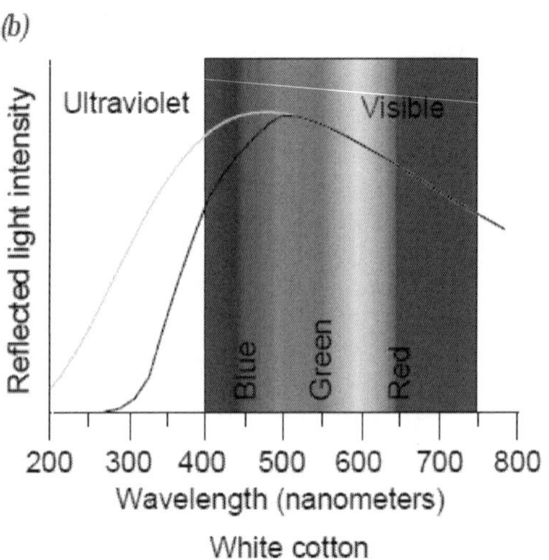

(c)

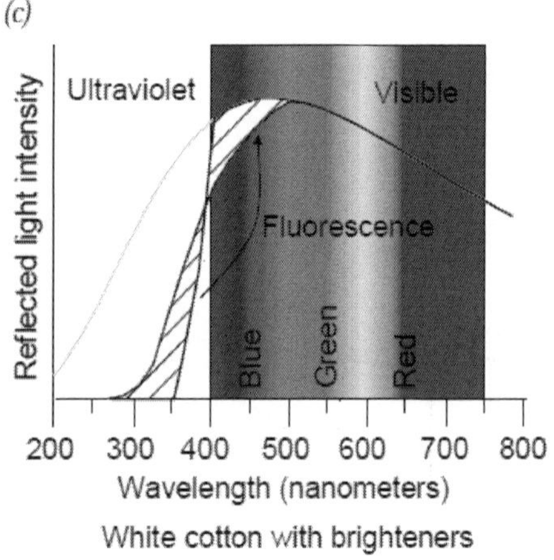

Fig. When white cotton cloth is exposed to sunlight (*a*), it reflects a little less blue light than it should (*b*) and appears slightly yellow. This yellowness increases with age. But when fluorescent brighteners are added to the cotton (*c*), they convert ultraviolet light into blue light and make the cloth appear dazzlingly white.

Instead of using bluing, virtually all modern laundry detergents add chemicals that optically brighten the fabric. These brighteners are actually fluorescent dyes, designed to absorb ultraviolet light and emit bluish-white visible light. Instead of absorbing red and green light to balance the white appearance of a fabric, the brighteners reintroduce the missing blue light. They work best in sunlight, which is rich in ultraviolet light. A brightener molecule absorbs a photon of ultraviolet light and reemits it as a photon of blue light. The energy not reemerging from the molecule in the second photon is converted through vibrations into internal energy in the clothes.

When clothes are washed in these fluorescent dyes, the dye molecules stick to the fabric to create brightened fabric. We can't see the ultraviolet light that the brightened fabric absorbs but we can see the bluish light that it emits. With the missing blue light restored by this fluorescence processes, the brightened fabric appears dazzlingly white. In fact, it may emit more blue light than it is exposed to, making it effectively "whiter than white." In a room illuminated only by ultraviolet light, the brighteners give clothes an eerie violet glow.

Fabric softeners are also chemicals that remain on fabrics after laundering. They are primarily cationic surfactants called *quaternary ammonium compounds*. These compounds are based on the positive ammonium ion, which is itself based on a positive nitrogen ion. A normal nitrogen atom has five valence electrons and must share three of these to reach the four pairs needed to complete an electronic shell. If it shares those electrons with three hydrogen atoms, it forms an ammonia molecule. But if it's missing an electron, the nitrogen atom must share four electrons to complete its shell and can actually bind to four hydrogen atoms. In that case, it forms a positive ammonium ion.

In quaternary ammonium compounds, a positive nitrogen ion forms covalent bonds with four other atoms. However, these atoms aren't necessarily hydrogen atoms. In fabric softeners, the central nitrogen ion binds to four hydrocarbon chains. Two of these chains are short, only one carbon atom long, while the other two chains may contain as many as 18 carbon atoms. These long chains are hydrophobic and have the same oily character as most lubricants.

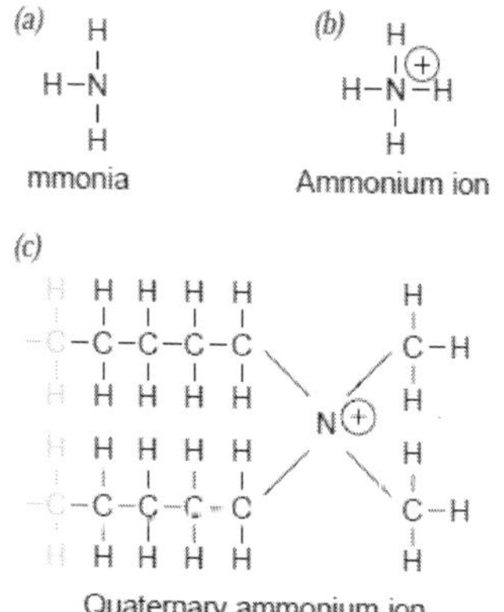

Fig. 17.2.12 - (*a*) An ammonia molecule is three hydrogen atoms bound to a nitrogen atom. (*b*) An ammonium ion is four hydrogen atoms bound to a positively charged nitrogen ion. (*c*) The quaternary ammonium ion used in fabric softeners is formed by replacing the four hydrogen atoms with hydrocarbon chains.

This oily character is what gives these compounds their fabric softening ability. When you apply the softener to wet fabric, its positively charged surfactant ions are drawn toward the negatively charged fibers and stick to them strongly. While anionic surfactants are repelled by wet fabric and help to clean it, cationic surfactants are attracted to wet fabric and help to soften it.

The surfactant molecules stick to the fabric with their long hydrophobic chains pointing outward. These molecules decorate every fiber in every thread of the clothing, giving them all an oily coating. The hydrocarbon chains lubricate the fabric so that each fiber slides easily within a thread and each thread slides easily within the fabric. This lubrication enhances the flexibility of the fabric and makes it feel softer and more flexible.

Fabric softeners also make fabric surfaces slightly hydrophobic, so that they dry more easily in the spin dry cycle of a washing machine. In this cycle, the clothes travel rapidly around in a circle, always accelerating toward the center of the circle and experiencing huge inward forces from the washer's metal drum. Water's inertia causes it to lag behind the accelerating clothes and it leaves the drum through perforations. By making the fabric slightly hydrophobic, the fabric softener helps the clothes to shed water as they spin, so that they don't have to spend as much time in a hot drier later on.

Fabric softeners also raise the nap on cotton terry towels. Cotton fibers are normally hydrophilic and cling tightly to water droplets. As water droplets dry up, they shrink and pull the cotton fibers toward one another. By the time an untreated towel is dry, its fibers have been crushed together by these forces and it has little nap. But a towel that has been coated by quaternary ammonium compounds is hydrophobic enough that the water droplets can't pull its fibers together as they dry. The nap remains loose and thick, giving the towel a fluffy appearance and feel. Unfortunately, this same hydrophobic coating slightly reduces the towel's absorbency—a real problem for cotton diapers. To keep it under control, don't use too much fabric softener.

Despite their hydrophobic chains, quaternary ammonium compounds actually attract a few water molecules to the surface of the fabric. They are hygroscopic, meaning that they attract water molecules directly out of the air. Since water conducts electricity very weakly, fabric that has been treated with fabric softeners is very slightly conducting. This conductivity reduces the accumulation of static electricity on the fabric and eliminates static cling.

In a drier, untreated clothes rub against one another and sliding friction transfers electric charge from one region of fabric to another. Large charge imbalances are created and the clothes leave the dry clinging to one another with electrostatic forces. However, treated clothes are lubricated in the drier and experience weaker frictional forces. They transfer less electric charge as they tumble and the small charge imbalances that are created quickly dissipate through the moisture attracted by the fabric softener.

Quaternary ammonium compounds are also used in conditioners and shampoos to soften hair and reduce static electricity problems—they will coat and lubricate just about anything. They are actually bactericidal because they coat bacteria and smother them. These compounds also deactivate some of the enzymes in bacteria and upset their metabolisms. Some antiseptic throat lozenges and mouth washes use quaternary ammonium compounds to kill germs.

Unfortunately, the positive charges of cationic quaternary ammonium compounds make them relatively incompatible with the negative charges of anionic detergents. When they're present together in the water, these two types of ions attract one another and may clump together. This clumping is avoided by keeping the two types of surfactants separate, which is why softeners are usually added during the rinse cycle, in the drier, or in a separate conditioner when washing your hair. However, some detergent and shampoo formulators have successfully combined cationic softeners and anionic detergents.

DETERGENT ADDITIVES

Formulated detergents contain a number of important components that work together to clean clothes. We've already examined the anionic and nonionic detergents (surfactants), the builders (water softeners), the bleaches, and the brighteners. But there are also foam stabilizers, corrosion inhibitors, soil redeposition inhibitors, and processing agents.

Foam stabilizers are there to control bubble formation. These chemicals can either enhance or suppress foaming. Believe it or not, foam is unrelated to a detergent's ability to clean clothes. The same goes for shampoos and dishwashing detergents. However, the amount of foam a detergent produces may influence its use. If the detergent foams excessively, you may think the detergent is more powerful than it is and cut back on the amount you use. As a result, you may not use enough to clean your clothes properly. If the detergent doesn't foam much, you may think that it isn't working and buy another brand. So the detergent and shampoo manufactures carefully control the foaminess of their products.

Air bubbles don't last long in pure water because water's surface tension causes them to tear. The final layers of water molecules on the bubble's outer and inner surfaces pull together so strongly that any tiny defect immediately initiates a rip that lets the air out of the bubble. By reducing water's surface tension, soaps and detergents remove its tendency to rip and stabilize air bubbles.

But how long each air bubble lasts depends on many features of the mixture and not on its ability to clean things. Some surfactant molecules make particularly stable and long lasting bubbles while other molecules deliberately introduce defects that pop the bubbles. Methyl silicone polymers ("methicones") are particularly effective at weakening bubbles so that they tear and collapse. These polymers are common in antifoam additives and are even included in some antiacid tablets.

Foam boosters are common in detergents and shampoos that are used by hand, where foam is regarded as a sign of effectiveness. Antifoaming agents are often used in washing and dishwashing machine detergents where you don't see the foam anyway and foam interferes with the machine's operation.

Corrosion inhibitors are important in detergent because the ions in detergent would otherwise quickly rust the steel in a washing machine. Rusting is an electrochemical reaction of the type explored in the supplement on batteries. In normal rusting, the iron in steel is attacked by negatively charged hydroxyl ions. However other negatively charged ions, including detergent ions, can also attack iron and rust it. So detergents include corrosion inhibitors. These compounds are usually sodium silicates—water soluble glasses that are discussed in Section 17.2. They form thin glassy coatings on the washer parts and inhibit rusting.

Soil redeposition inhibitors enhance the negative charge of wet fabric fibers. Some fabrics, particularly synthetic ones, don't acquire a strong negative charge in water. They need this electrostatic charge to keep the negatively charged detergent micelles from redepositing their soils on the fabric. So detergents include carboxymethyl cellulose, which attaches itself to the fibers and adds to their negative charge.

Finally, processing agents simply give the detergents the right structures in their boxes or bottles. Sodium sulfate helps to bulk up powdered detergent and make it pour easily. Sodium xylene sulfonate helps to keep all of the components of very concentrated liquid detergents in solution.

DRY CLEANING

Washing clothes in water isn't always a good idea. Fibers such as cotton, wool, silk, and rayon, are very hydrophilic and soak up water molecules like sponges. These fibers form hydrogen bonds with water molecules at various sites on their molecules and accumulate large quantities of water. This water takes up space and causes the fibers to swell. Cotton, wool, and silk fibers increase by about 1% in length and about 15% in thickness. Rayon expands even more, by 3% in length and about 25% in thickness. This swelling distorts the fabric and changes its structure. When the fabric eventually dries, it may have shrunk or wrinkled.

To avoid damage caused by this cycle of expansion and contraction, you can send your clothes to be dry-cleaned. Dry cleaning takes place in a nonpolar solvent. Since this solvent doesn't form hydrogen bonds, it's only weakly attracted to the fibers by van der Waals forces and doesn't cause them to swell. The clothes don't lose their shapes. The solvents used in dry cleaning have evolved over the years since petroleum oils were first found to remove stains. Early dry cleaning was done with gasoline, resulting in many dramatic fires. In 1928, a less flammable solvent became available. The Stoddard solvent, named for the president of the National Institute of Dry cleaning, W. J. Stoddard, is less volatile than gasoline because it contains larger hydrocarbon molecules. It's obtained by distilling crude oil and its vapor will not ignite in air at temperatures below 38 °C.

Nonetheless, Stoddard solvent is still dangerous during hot air drying so nonflammable nonpolar solvents have largely replaced it. The most common solvent in dry cleaning is now perchloroethylene. Its molecule consists of a pair of carbon molecules connected by a double bond and each attached to two chlorine atoms. The chlorine atoms bind so strongly to the carbon atoms that the molecule doesn't react with oxygen and forms a nonflammable liquid.

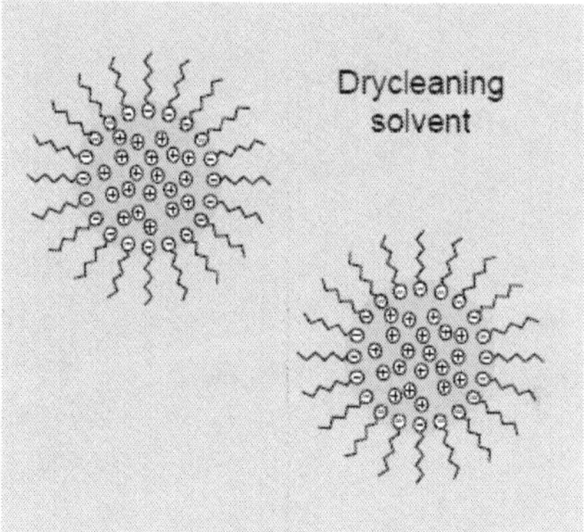

Fig. 17.2.13 - Detergents form inside-out micelles in dry cleaning solvent. The polar hydrophilic ends of the molecules project inward, toward a tiny drop of water. The nonpolar hydrophobic ends project outward into the solvent.

When you put clothes in either Stoddard solvent or perchloroethylene, the oily soils dissolve. These nonpolar solvents attract the oily molecules with van der Waals forces and carry them away. Chlorinated solvents clean better than hydrocarbons because they bind more strongly to oily soils. Chlorine atoms are more polarizable than hydrogen atoms and produce stronger van der Waals forces, which is why perchloroethylene doesn't boil until it is heated to 121 °C.

However, these nonpolar solvents are unable to dissolve salts and other polar soils. They are also poor at removing insoluble soils such as dust. To help in removing these other soils, dry cleaning solvents include detergents and a little water. The detergents form inside-out micelles in the nonpolar solvents, arranged with their nonpolar ends on the outside and their polar ends on the inside. Each micelle surrounds a tiny droplet of water. Just as in water cleaning, detergents help to carry away substances that aren't soluble in the principal cleaning liquid. The water in the dry cleaning mixture is carefully adjusted so that the clothes neither gain nor lose moisture during the cleaning process. In air, water molecules are continually leaving and returning to the clothing and an equilibrium is reached. At this equilibrium, the water molecules still move back and forth but the moisture in the clothing doesn't change significantly. The actual moisture level in the fabric then depends only on the relative humidity of the air, which is typically about 70% in a dry cleaning shop.

The same leaving and returning process takes place in the dry cleaning solvent. Water molecules move back and forth between the fabric and the solvent and establish an equilibrium. Like air, the dry cleaning solvent has a relative humidity and a dry cleaner tries to maintain this relative humidity at the same value as the air in the shop. That way, the fabrics don't accumulate too many water molecules and swell, nor do they lose too many water molecules and dry out. But the polar soils leave the fabrics, become trapped in the detergent micelles, and never return.

With the help of detergents, nonpolar dry cleaning solvents carry away nonpolar, polar, and insoluble soils from clothes without affecting the structure of the cloth. The dry cleaner then removes the solvent from the clothes by spinning them and drying them in hot air. Because solvents are expensive and environmentally damaging, dry cleaners collect the solvents for reused. They do this by filtering and distilling the liquid solvents and by condensing the gaseous solvent molecules onto chilled surfaces. When this type of solvent recycling is done effectively, a dry cleaner can operate for a long time on the same supply of solvent.

Bibliography

Shaloo Sharma : *Modern Methods of Teaching Home Science* , Sarup, 2002.

Shaloo Sharma: *Modern Methods of Teaching Home Science*, Sarup, 2002.

V. Lakshmi Kumari: *Techniques of Teaching Home Science*, Sonali Pub, 2006.

Renu Malviya: *Advanced Dictionary of Home Science (English to Hindi)*, Arise Pub, 2006.

Jainendra Kumar: *Encyclopaedia of Teaching of Home Science (3 Vols-Set)* : Jha, Anmol, 2001.

Shaloo Sharma: *Modern Methods of Teaching Home Science*, Sarup, 2002.

P. Nazni: *Multiple Choice Questions in Home Science for Competitive Examinations*, Daya, 2014.

Priya Bhargav and Tara Chand: *Principles of Home Science* , Commonwealth, 2005.

Nibedita Dash: *Teaching of Home Science* , Dominant, 2004.

Priya Bhargav: *Teaching of Home Science* , Commonwealth, 2004.

Mujibul Hasan Siddiqui: *Teaching of Home Science* , APH, 2007.

Meenu Grover: *Teaching of Home Science*, Saurabh Publishing House, 2012.

V. Lakshmi Kumari: *Techniques of Teaching Home Science*, Sonali Pub, 2006.

Jaishree S. Mehta: *Text Book of Home Science*, Aavishkar Publishers, 2011.

J. S. Mehta: *Textbook of Home Science*, Pointer, 2011.

Serene Shekhar and Santosh Ahlawat: *Textbook of Home Science Extension Education*, Daya, 2013.

Maimun Nisha: *Wings of Home Science* , Kalpaz, 2006.

A.A.N. Raju: *Facets of Library and Information Science*, Ess Ess Publications, Delhi, 2012.

Ajit Singh: *Siwatch Encyclopedic Dictionary of Library and Information Science, Vols. I to III*, Shree Publishers, Delhi, 2010.

Amjad Ali: *Ane's Encyclopedic Dictionary of Library and Information Science*, Ane Books India, Delhi, 2006.

B S Aggarwal: *An Introduction to Library and Information Science*, ABD Publication, Delhi, 2005.

B. Rajasree and P. Aravinda: *Glossary of Library and Information Science*, Anmol Publication, Delhi, 2010.

Ravikanth Sangwan: *Encyclopaedia of Library and Information Science*, Anmol Publication, Delhi, 2006.

Shiv Ram Verma: *Foundations of Library and Information Science*, Shree Publication, Delhi, 2005.

Shri Umesha, Mahesh Mudhol and K.M. Khan: *A Handbook On* Distance Education with Special Reference to Library and *Information Science in India*, Ess Ess Publications, Delhi, 2004.

T. Nasirudheen: *A Comprehensive Course in Library and Information Science*, Ess Ess Publications, Delhi, 2012.

T. Saravanan: *Library and Information Science : UGC, JRF-SLETNET*, APH Publication, Delhi, 2008.

Tariq Ashraf and Sanjay Kumar Jha: *Handbook of UGC Net for Library and Information Science*, Bookwell, 2008.

V.G. Choukhande: *Information Needs and Information Seeking Behaviour : Library and Information Science Research*, Shivneri Publication, Delhi, 2008.

Vaishali Khaparde: *Advancement in Library and Information Science*, Ess Ess Publications, Delhi, 2012.

Vrushali Dandavate, Ajay Khatri and Pradip Umdale: *Application of Six Sigma in Library and Information Science*, Ess Ess Publications, Delhi, 2013.

Y.L. Chopra and Mamta Chopra: *Challenges Before Library and Information Science in New Millennium*, Ess Ess Publication, Delhi, 2001.

Purushotham Tiwari: *Dictionary of Library and Information Science*, A.P.H. Publication, Delhi, 2011.

R P Bajpai: *Current Trends in Library and Information Science*, Shree Publication, Delhi, 2007.

R.G. Prasher: *Library and Information Science : Parameters and Perspectives : Essays in Honour of P.B. Mangla (2 Vols - set)*, Concept Publication, Delhi, 1997.

Index